PIL-99

D0281060

Local management of schools

Local management of schools

Analysis and practice

Rosalind Levačić

Open University Press
Buckingham • Philadelphia

Open University Press
Celtic Court
22 Ballmoor
Buckingham
MK18 1XW

and
1900 Frost Road, Suite 101
Bristol, PA 19007, USA

First Published 1995

Copyright © Rosalind Levačić

All rights reserved. Except for the quotation of short passages for the purpose
of criticism and review, no part of this publication may be reproduced, stored
in a retrieval system, or transmitted, in any form or by any means, electronic,
mechanical, photocopying, recording or otherwise, without the prior written
permission of the publisher or a licence from the Copyright Licensing Agency
Limited. Details of such licences (for reprographic reproduction) may be
obtained from the Copyright Licensing Agency Ltd of 90 Tottenham Court
Road, London, W1P 9HE.

A catalogue record of this book is available from the Brtish Library

ISBN 0 335 19375 7 (pb)   0 335 19376 5 (hb)

Library of Congress Cataloging-in-Publication Data
Levačić, Rosalind.
    Local management of schools : analysis and practice / Rosalind
Levačić.
        p. cm.
    Includes bibliographical references and index.
    ISBN 0–335–19375–7 (pb). — ISBN 0–335–19376–5 (hb)
    1. School management and organization—Great Britain. 2. Schools—
Decentralization—Great Britain. I. Title.
LB2901.L48   1995
371.2′00941—dc20   95–5855
                                                                        CIP

Typeset by Graphicraft Typesetters Ltd, Hong Kong
Printed in Great Britain by St Edmundsbury Press Ltd,
Bury St Edmunds, Suffolk

To Alex, Sasha and Anna

Contents

Preface

This book has taken seven years to gestate. It was in 1987 that I decided to find out more about the economics and financing of schools. As luck would have it, the government shortly afterwards brought out the Education Reform Bill. Local management of schools suddenly made school managers and students of school management interested in the defining problem of economics – the allocation of resources. In 1990, I was fortunate to be awarded a grant by the Economics and Social Research Council to study the implementation of local management. I had originally intended to complete this book two years ago but other work intervened, in particular a very interesting project with Sheffield City Council on the resourcing of Sheffield's schools, in which I was able to study further resource allocation patterns in schools and work on a needs-based funding formula. In the end, I think the book is better for its long gestation period, because it has given me time to work out a theoretical framework for analysing local management which draws on economics and organizational theory. In the meantime, other studies of local management have been published, which provide very useful evidence with which to compare, and mostly corroborate, my evidence drawn from a small sample of schools which is inevitable in case-study research.

I have tried to use the theoretical framework to undertake an assessment of local management, mainly against the criteria of efficiency and effectiveness, which are official aims of the policy. I have also made a more limited assessment of local management against equity and considered some evidence in relation to responsiveness and choice. I have aimed to set out and explain what we probably know about the effects of local management as it relates to resource management in schools and to indicate areas where we know very little. In particular, there is a lack of strong theoretical arguments and empirical evidence on how delegated budgeting improves the quality of teaching and learning as claimed by the government. One is on stronger ground in claiming that local management is more cost-efficient than the previous system, which can be labelled bureaucratic administration. This, in a nutshell, summarizes the book.

There are a number of people I would like to thank who, in various ways, have helped me considerably in writing the book. In particular, Eamon Marren contributed significantly to Chapters 5–7, which report the fieldwork he mainly undertook as research assistant on the 'Impact of Formula Funding on Schools' (IFFS) study, funded by the ESRC (Grant no. R000232234). Julian du Cassé helped with the statistical analysis of data from the IFFS study. I have also drawn on research undertaken with Jason Hardman and Derek Glover, and a joint article on economic cooperation with Philip Woods. Tim Simkins provided me with valuable comments on Chapters 1–7 and saved me from a number of errors, omissions and confusions. I would also like to thank Ron Glatter for his support in enabling me to change academic direction and Sindy York for secretarial support. I received considerable help from David Hill in my initial attempts to research local financial management in Cambridgeshire. I am also grateful to the officers of 'Barsetshire' for their cooperation in providing access for the IFFS study and assisting us in data collection, and to the headteachers, governors and staff at the case-study schools who all gave generously of their time. I hope I have not misinterpreted what they said and allowed us to observe, and accept full responsibility for any errors of fact or judgement. Finally, I would like to thank my son for his help with the computing, and my daughter and husband for putting up with neglect without complaint.

Rosalind Levačić

Abbreviations

ASB	Aggregated schools budget
CTCs	City technology colleges
DES	Department of Education and Science (until 1992)
DFE	Department for Education (from 1992)
FAS	Funding Agency for Schools
GM	Grant-maintained (school)
GSB	General schools budget
HMI	Her Majesty's Inspectorate
LEA	Local education authority
LMS	Local management of schools
OFSTED	Office for Standards in Education
PSB	Potential schools budget
SSA	Standard spending assessment

Decentralized school management: The UK experience in an international context

Introduction

It is a truth universally acknowledged that a single school in possession of its own decision-making must provide better quality education than a school run by a centralized bureaucracy. The seeming universality of this deceptively simple aphorism is reflected in its endorsement by many governments and their agencies, including the Organization for Economic and Cultural Development (OECD 1987), the Australian Karmel Report (Australian Schools Commission 1973), the New Zealand Picot Report (Picot 1988), the English 1988 Education Reform Act and its supporting circulars, and in a series of national reports in the USA (e.g. Carnegie Task Force 1986; NGA 1986). The US teaching professions' statement in a joint report, that they 'remain committed to the principle that substantial decision-making authority at the school site is the essential prerequisite for quality education' (quoted by Caldwell 1993), is echoed by the declaration of the English Department for Education,[1] that 'the introduction of needs-based formula funding and the delegation of financial and managerial responsibilities to governing bodies are key elements in the Government's overall policy to improve the quality of teaching and learning' (DES 1988). Many commentators have noted that despite differences in political and social context, there are striking parallels in contemporary educational reforms adopted by English-speaking countries, in particular Australia, New Zealand, the UK and the USA, which combine both decentralization of management decision-making to schools and a tendency to stronger centralization of control over specifying and monitoring educational standards (Lowe Boyd 1992: 511). Recent developments in these directions in continental

Europe seem less marked. While some countries, such as France and the Netherlands, have had publicly funded private schools for a number of decades, extensive school autonomy over resource management is a less pronounced feature (Louis and van Velzen 1990/91; Fowler 1990). In the Netherlands, there has been some development of delegated financial management since 1981 (Hill *et al.* 1990). Spain, the Netherlands and Finland were singled out by the OECD (1992) as having the highest proportion of decisions taken at school level (between 45 and 56 per cent). Eastern Europe has experienced rapid decentralization and the emergence of private schooling but, as Halasz (1993) points out, 'in contrast to what has happened in the West decentralization and school autonomy in Eastern Europe did not appear as a planned response to systemic problems', but as an unplanned consequence of the collapse of communism.

The trend towards decentralized school management in many countries has been paralleled in other public services by a similar development of 'quasi-markets', the term now widely used for a form of public sector organization characterized by the separation of purchaser from provider in order to make costs transparent and to stimulate competition (Le Grand and Bartlett 1993). Therefore, a study of the development of decentralized management and quasi-markets in education is of much wider interest than the education sector itself.

There is considerable agreement over the political and economic factors stimulating these structural changes in the public services, though the interpretation given to these explanations differs markedly according to ideological perspective. The major economic factor driving educational reform is concern about the inability of the country's workforce and management to be internationally competitive. The consequent diagnosis is that the education system must be reformed to turn out a more productive workforce. A further factor is that taxpayers' reluctance to pay more and the potential disincentive effects of high taxation on productive effort, conflict with the demands of public service users and welfare benefits recipients for improvements. If unresolved politically, this conflict manifests itself in inflation and worsening economic performance. A key to resolving the conflict is to make public service agencies more efficient and to shift costs to the private sector. A third factor has been disenchantment with the performance of the public sector, which has in part been fostered by 'public choice' and 'free-market' economists. At a more popular level, this has also been prompted by the increasing unwillingness of ordinary people to accept the authority of experts. Related to this is the fourth major development – the movement for greater participation of the general populace in the decisions which affect their daily lives in relation to the local environment and the services they consume.

Different ideological perspectives interpret these developments differently. From a neo-marxist or critical perspective (Smyth 1993), these developments are a further manifestation of the evolution of capitalist states

in response to inherent contradictions. In this case, the contradiction between the need to maintain legitimacy by providing restricted public services while denying responsibility for school resourcing decisions, and
sustaining capitalist production by cutting back the demands of public
welfare provision on company profits and private sector surplus consumption and using state schools to mould a productive labour force for capitalist employers. For pluralists, these developments reflect the interaction
of different interests, with some, such as the parental interest, becoming
stronger through political action. For those favouring right-wing or neo-
liberal theories, quasi-markets are developed as a superior alternative to
inefficient public sector bureaucracy.

The various policy changes which have brought about both increased
decentralization and centralization in education are entwined with a number
of distinct political aspirations. One is the drive towards greater efficiency
and improved performance through a technicist rational approach to
management. Another strand derives from the humanist school of management, which asserts the importance of worker participation in decision-
making as the key to improved performance. The third element is greater
participation by service users. This last thrust has two quite different and
potentially conflicting manifestations – either as 'choice' or 'voice' to apply
Hirschman's (1970) distinction. Choice implies greater powers for the individual to exercise preference in a quasi-market setting, whereas voice
requires democratic participation through the election of representative
groups who exercise control or influence over service providers. These
diverse strands explain why the phenomenon which this book is about
manifests itself in a variety of forms in the many educational locations
where it has taken place, and why it is impossible to give a single name for
it which will convey the same meaning to every audience.

Defining school-based management

Probably the most widely used term for decentralized school management
is 'school-based management', a term particularly in vogue in North America
at present. It is also known as site-based management (particularly in the
USA in the recent past), delegated or devolved management, school autonomy or, in Britain (excluding Scotland), 'local management of schools'.
David (1989), in a review of the US literature, defined school-based management as autonomy plus participatory decision-making. Her definition,
which is similar to that provided by Cheng (1993), consists of:

1 increasing school autonomy through some combination of site budgetary control and relief from constraining rules and regulations; and
2 sharing the authority to make decisions with teachers, and sometimes with parents, students and other community members.

(David 1989: 46)

The underlying assumptions upon which school-based management is deduced to improve schools' performance are subsidiarity (i.e. decisions are best taken at the lowest level where they apply) and ownership (i.e. policies are most effectively implemented when those whose work the policies aim to affect have ownership of the decisions).

Caldwell (1990: 303–304) offers a definition which emphasizes decentralized resource allocation within centrally defined parameters rather than participatory decision-making.

> School-site or school-based management . . . are all approaches to the management of public schools or systemic private schools wherein there is significant and consistent decentralization to the school level of authority to make decisions related to the allocation of resources, with resources defined broadly to include knowledge, technology, power, material, people, time and money . . . The school remains accountable to a central authority for the manner in which resources are allocated.

The above two definitions illustrate well the different forms which school-based management can take. Caldwell's definition comes closer to the characteristics of local management of schools in the UK than David's, which reflects greater emphasis in the US literature on teacher empowerment through shifting more decision-making to the school level. In order to appreciate the different forms which school-based management can take, a classificatory framework for its constituent elements is set out in Table 1.1. The three key elements are:

- the stakeholders to whom decision-making power and responsibility are decentralized;
- the management domains over which decentralized power can be exercised, the main ones being resources including finance, staff and the curriculum;
- the form of regulation which controls what the local decision-makers have discretion over and how they are held to account for their decisions and actions.

In different instances of school-based management these three factors can take different forms and these forms can be permutated in different ways.

Defining local management of schools

In this book, 'local management of schools' is used to refer to the form of school-based management which has been mandated by legislation in England, Wales and Northern Ireland. Scotland, which has its own legislation, had a milder form, significantly called 'devolved school management', introduced several years later (SOED 1992a). Although the landmark in restructuring the school system in the UK was the 1988 Education Reform Act, it was preceded by earlier legislation which paved its way and has

Table 1.1 Constituent elements of school-based management

Stakeholders to whom decision-making is decentralized	Management domain for school-based decision-making	Regulation

Headteachers (principals)
 	
Teachers
 	
Parents
  Voice via school councils or governing bodies;
  choice of school
 	
Local community via school council
 	
Business links and sponsorship
	Budget
	
	Physical resources
	
	Staffing
	
	Student recruitment
	
	Curriculum
		Use of resources:
		financial audit;
		teacher qualifications, pay and conditions;
		employment laws;
		class size;
		building standards
		
		Product specification:
		national curriculum;
		national tests and other performance indicators;
		inspection of educational standards and quality;
		
		Market conditions:
		exit and entry (school closure and new schools);
		admission of students;
		publication of information about school performance

since been extended further. The piecemeal evolution of Conservative education policy since 1979 creates a strong impression of policy-making on the hoof. I will here give an account of the combination of decentralizing and centralizing changes to the UK school system reached by the mid-1990s. It is important to bear in mind when comparing the restructuring of schools in the UK with similar trends abroad, that UK schools have always had considerable discretion. Prior to the 1988 Education Act, schools chose what to teach, constrained by external school leaving examinations, and headteachers already had considerable discretion in selecting staff. Thus there was in the post-war period a relatively high degree of headteacher autonomy over management and teacher autonomy over the curriculum in the UK, compared with the typically centralized North American school district which determined staffing and curriculum, leaving the school principal as a buildings administrator. It was from this form of centralization that one of the best known examples of school-based management, Edmonton Public Schools, broke away in the early 1980s (Brown 1990; Levačić 1992b). This example is discussed further in Chapter 8.

Diversity and choice

A major thrust of central government policy has been to 'break the provider monopoly' of state education held by local government education authorities (LEAs), which have administered state schools since 1902. In the 1970s, most LEAs changed from a selective system of secondary state schooling to a comprehensive one, in which all children – apart from the 7 per cent who are privately educated – attend their local school. Until the 1988 Act, LEAs were able to exert considerable influence over the allocation of pupils to school places. The attenuation of the selective system and the protection LEAs could offer to schools which might otherwise become unviable due to a lack of sufficient students, are considered by right-wingers to be major factors in the perceived lowering of educational standards. Under Conservative governments, new types of state school have been promoted. In inner cities, about fifteen city technology colleges (CTCs) have been opened, set up with private sector capital. The 1988 Education Act enabled parents to vote for their child's school to opt out of LEA control and become grant-maintained (GM). By late 1994, there were approximately 1100 GM schools in England and Wales; most were secondary schools, consituting about a quarter of all secondary schools. The 1993 Education Act acknowledged the problem faced by the Department for Education (DFE) in administering a large number of GM schools by setting up a quango known as the Funding Agency for Schools (FAS), which was to allocate funds to GM schools and share responsibility for the provision of schooling with LEAs. The DFE has been active in promoting GM status by favourable funding, management support services and by making opting out an easier procedure. However, opting out has only occurred to any significant degree in England, and has not yet reached the number aspired to by the DFE. Schools have largely opted out to avoid LEA reorganization plans, because of opposition to LEA policies or to reap financial benefits (Bush *et al.* 1993). Many parents and teachers oppose opting-out on ideological grounds, seeing it as a threat to the principle of comprehensive education, since GM schools administer their own admissions policy and can be covertly selective, if not already overtly so. In order to stimulate further opting out and to offset the failure of business to fund CTCs on a large scale, the government has introduced a further scheme of technology schools who are provided with additional sponsored business funding for developing a more technology-biased curriculum.

Parental choice of school was increased by the 1988 Act, which specified that a child cannot be refused admission to a state school which has spare places. A school has reached full capacity when its intake number is equal to the number of pupils specified as its 'standard number',[2] which can only be changed on approval of the Secretary of State for Education. A school can voluntarily admit more than its standard number of pupils or can be forced to do so if parents make successful appeals to an appeals panel. 'More-open enrolment' has stopped the practice whereby LEAs protected schools with falling rolls by holding down the admission of pupils to more popular schools. The actual choice parents can exercise is highly dependent on local conditions; in particular, the availability of alternative schools and the existence of surplus places. The main admissions criteria of comprehensive schools are proximity of residence or stated order of preference and sibling connection.[3]

Parental voice in the running of schools has been gradually strengthened over the years since the 1980 Education Act reinvigorated school governing bodies, which had been largely passive and symbolic creatures of the LEA. The Taylor Report (1977) recommended that the composition of governing bodies should reflect parental, teacher and community interests as well as those of the LEA, and that they should play a meaningful role in the running of schools. The 1980 Education Act laid down that elected parents and teachers must serve on the governing body. The 1986 Education Act increased the number of parent-governors depending on the size of the school and, by providing for co-opted governors, ensured that LEAs could not pack a governing body with councillors. Local education authorities were also required to give the governors a sum of money for their school to spend on books, materials and equipment. The 1988 Education Act considerably strengthened the powers of the governing body by making it formally responsible for the management of delegated school budgets and greatly extending its responsibilities for staffing. The governing bodies of GM schools and CTCs are trusts with responsibility for the schools' assets and are employers of the schools' staffs. A particular feature of school-based management in the UK (excluding Scotland), in contrast to other English-speaking countries except New Zealand, is the decentralization of decision-making power to a school council. In Canada (Brown 1990), the USA and Australia, school councils are advisory. This difference in both the UK and New Zealand reflects central government's greater constitutional powers over education and its desire to remove or emasculate regional government units as an intervening layer between it and schools.

As well as increasing the parental voice on governing bodies, the British Government has been keen to extend the influence of business on schools in various ways, including co-opting business people onto governing bodies and business sponsorship of school activities. Absent from the UK version of school-based management is the emphasis on class teacher empowerment present in US discourse and schemes. As will be shown in later chapters, the empowerment of the governing body in UK legislation has become in effect the empowerment of headteachers, who have considerable discretion as to how their managerial practice involves other teachers.

An overview of local management of schools in the UK

Local management of schools (LMS) refers to the set of measures by which LEA control of schools was diminished and the autonomy of schools enhanced, and which were set in train by the 1988 Education Reform Act. Among other measures, the Act required LEAs to delegate to each of its schools a budget to cover almost all its running expenses. Full implementation of local management was completed by April 1993 in all of England and Wales, except inner London, where it was completed by April 1995. School governing bodies became responsible for managing budgets as they saw fit for the purposes of their schools. It is up to governing bodies to decide how many teaching and ancillary staff to employ and they are responsible for appointing, disciplining and dismissing staff, although LEAs remain the employers of staff in LEA-maintained schools. Local education authorities can no longer appoint headteachers, although directors of education can advise governors on this.

The Act and subsequent LMS circulars (DES 1988, 1991a; DFE 1994) laid down strict guidelines on how LEAs should determine the budgets they allocate to their schools. The total money delegated by a LEA to its mainstream schools is called the 'aggregated schools budget' (ASB). This must be at least 85 per cent of the 'potential schools budget' (PSB), which is the total the LEA spends on schools, called the 'general schools budget' (GSB), minus certain items which the LEA cannot or need not delegate to schools. The items which must be centrally retained are capital expenditure and debt charges, central government and European Community grants, premature retirement and dismissal costs, and educational psychology and welfare services.[4] Initially, LEAs could retain more money centrally for services which they provided directly, such as outdoor education and advisory, personnel, legal and financial services. But since the implementation of LMS in 1990, LEAs have progressively been forced to delegate a higher percentage of the PSB, creating an internal market between themselves and schools which buy services from their LEA or from private providers.

A key element of local management is the allocation of school budgets by means of a formula which must reflect 'the objective needs' of each school. By 'objective needs' the DFE meant that the formula must be based on specified rules, which prevent individual education officers using discretion to fund some schools more generously than others. At least 80 per cent of the ASB must be allocated according to the number and ages of a schools' pupils, though up to 5 per cent of this may be allocated by a quantified index of pupils' special educational needs. As well as an index of special educational needs, other 'objective factors' by which the remaining 20 per cent can be allocated mainly relate to the school's physical size and nature (such as a split site), which determine operating costs. This means that economies of scale can be allowed for at the LEA's discretion, by giving small schools additional funding (Bullock and Thomas 1992). Although the DFE's tightly prescribed formula ensured that even the most reluctant LEAs were forced to delegate decision-making over almost all aspects of resource management, there has still been enough flexibility for LEAs to use the formula as a means of implementing LEA policies with respect to such issues as support for pupils with special needs or experiencing social disadvantage and the viability of small schools (Thomas 1990, 1991; Thomas and Levačić 1991; The LMS Initiative 1992). A major impact of age-weighted pupil funding has been to throw the spotlight on the differential between primary and secondary funding, which has been a long-standing and universal feature of school financing. The transparency of this differential has stimulated public debate on the issue, reflected in a Parliamentary inquiry which recommended increased primary funding (House of Commons 1994).

The connection between age-weighted pupil funding and more open enrolment is the linchpin of the new quasi-market created by formula funding, as this links parental preference for a school directly with its ability to maintain its finances and staffing. A strongly market-oriented feature of the funding formula is that schools are funded according to the average salary cost of staff in the LEA and not according to the actual salaries of the staff they employ. So two schools with the same number of teachers could have different staff costs. One school might have older staff at the top of the pay scale and who have safeguarded additional salary points due to occupying a post which has been removed in the course of school reorganization, while another has younger staff with no safeguarded salaries. Despite the professional outcry at this average-in-actual-out salary funding rule, the DFE has persisted with it, except in the case of schools with nine or fewer staff for which the LEA may devise a formula which funds the school according to the difference between the school's actual salaries and the LEA's average salary costs. Schools were also given a four-year transitional adjustment period during which the budget gains of schools 'winning' under the new formula arrangements were raided in order to support the budgets of those schools which were losing out. As a further concession, LEAs were allowed to centrally fund the safeguarded element of teachers' salaries. All ideas for creating a notional central pool of teachers into which all schools would pay the average teacher salary for each teacher they employed were rejected by the government. The DFE has insisted that schools must operate according to market principles, whereby the benefits and costs of a decision impinge on the same decision-making unit. Thus school managers are induced to consider the relationship between the cost of a teacher and his or her performance; a system whereby those who benefit from an action do not feel the full costs create greater pressures for expenditure increases. The average-in-actual-out salary funding rule is thus favoured by the government as a cost-restraining device.

The government's insistence on the average-in-actual-out salary rule is but part of a general move to change the system of teacher payment from a bureaucratic one, whereby pay is related to seniority and post in a nationally uniform hierarchy, to one based far more on individual performance and local circumstances. Within a set range on the pay scale, headteachers' and deputies' pay is now decided by governing bodies. Through a series of annual adjustments, the national pay scale for teachers has been changed to limit pay by seniority and to encourage additional payments for good performance.

Local management of schools seems to be unique among school-based management schemes in the extent to which it links the school's success in attracting pupils with teachers' job security. In New Zealand, where principals were placed on contracts with Boards of Trustees, who have many of the responsibilities of UK school governors, teacher salaries were still retained centrally in the early 1990s. In Edmonton, where teachers are dismissed from schools unable to afford them out of their budgets, they are retained on the district payroll and must have first consideration for employment at schools taking on new teachers (Levačić 1992b).[5] This was the form of teacher deployment practised in UK education authorities prior to the implementation of local management.

Local management has had profound effects on LEAs because of the large proportion of the PSB which must be delegated. Many delegated in excess of the required percentage in order to remove a financial incentive for schools to opt out. Consequently, many of the services that were centrally provided have either been cut or turned into business units, selling services to schools. The 1993 Education Act further constrained LEAs by specifying that they could not sell services to schools other than their own beyond a 2 per cent trading margin. This limitation is to encourage the development of private sector businesses supplying educational services and to prevent local governments straying too far into business ventures, thus risking local taxpayers' money. Local education authority personnel have experienced considerable upheaval and taken early retirement, moved into different jobs or have been forced to become more entrepreneurial in selling their services to schools.

The implementation of complex formulae for allocating school budgets and the introduction of computerized financial accounting systems for schools, linking their accounts with those of the LEA, has required an immense amount of effort and adjustment. It has nevertheless been achieved without undue breakdown and disruption and has now become quite well embedded. However, the funding of GM schools remains in a state of disequilibrium. The 1988 Act provided for GM schools to be funded on a par with LEA schools. A GM school would have applied to it the same formula as the one used by its previous LEA but would receive an additional amount to compensate for central LEA services which it did not receive. In addition, GM schools get additional funds for capital works, meeting the initial costs of GM status and staff development.

It proved difficult, given the complexity of LEA funding formulae, to apply them on exactly the same basis to GM schools or to ascertain for each LEA the appropriate allocation for central services. Consequently, the 1993 Education Act sought to remove GM schools from the influence of the LEA funding formula by introducing a common funding formula for GM schools, which in 1994 was tested in five LEAs. However, the common funding formula is not to be a national formula: the amount a GM school gets will continue to depend on the level of education spending in its former LEA. A national funding formula is unacceptable to the current government because per pupil funding in different LEAs varies to a quite considerable extent. To introduce a national formula for GM schools would mean either losses and gains for schools, with some GM schools getting less per pupil than LEA schools, or a rise in spending to bring all GM schools in line with the most generously funded. Both are unpalatable to the government. Hence the amount per pupil received by a GM school must correspond to the amount received by the LEA schools, by being tied to the amount of central government block grant, called the standard spending assessment (SSA),[6] which each LEA receives for education, as well as to any additional LEA supplement. Standard spending assessments have tended to be unstable from year to year, and this is reflected in school budgets if these are tied directly to the SSA rather than being moderated by local government decisions as at present. However, government policies to restrain local government spending in recent years have brought LEAs' education spending more in line with their SSAs and made for instability in school budgets in LEAs experiencing financial difficulties. The government has boxed itself into an increasingly complex funding mess with respect to GM schools, by insisting that GM schools must not be funded worse than LEA schools, must not experience a cut in funding as a consequence of going grant-maintained, and that spending increases must be constrained. It has thus been impossible to achieve the government's stated aim of a simple and transparent funding formula which lay people can understand. While the House of Commons Committee on Education has called for a national funding formula for school education, in which the government would announce an age-weighted pupil cash allocation to which LEAs could then add (Thornton 1994), the consequent transparency of the government's role in determining educational spending is unlikely to appeal to it. The current state of complexity and continual change in funding rules looks likely to persist. Given that central funding quangos for higher education and further education have now been established, a similar role for the FAS, with all secondary schools forced to become grant-maintained, would resolve the current instability in a way fully consistent with the centralizing tendencies of the Conservative government.

Given the extent of delegation of budgets and staffing to LEA schools, differences in the management implications for locally managed (LEA schools) and GM schools are only those of degree. The governing bodies of GM schools are employers in their own right, rather than exercising the bulk of employer functions. Grant-maintained schools own their own assets in trust and are therefore responsible for managing them. They are therefore responsible for commissioning new capital works and overseeing their completion and must undertake their own structural repairs. So far, the DFE has directly funded GM school insurance, whereas LEAs often shoulder the cost of the risk themselves, rather than pay escalating insurance premiums. Grant-maintained schools are thus responsible for managing all their resources rather than the 90–98 per cent delegated by LEAs. One major difference is that a GM school is its own admissions authority, whereas the LEA acts in this capacity for its own schools. While GM schools specify their character on incorporation and cannot change it without application to the DFE, the 1993 Act enables them to select up to 10 per cent of their pupils according to some specific aptitude such as music, art, science or sport, and they can select by interview. Grant-maintained schools can more readily change the age group for which they cater and many have successfully applied to the DFE to open sixth-forms or recruit younger pupils.

Despite this difference of degree between LEA and GM schools, both DFE officials and government activists assert that grant-maintained status of itself, because schools are free of 'local authority bureaucracy', provides better quality education. Nevertheless, from a more dispassionate viewpoint, the differences remain those of degree, so that issues relating to school-based management apply equally well to GM as to LEA schools. This stance is assumed in the rest of the book, so that unless a specific difference between the two types of school is highlighted, local management refers to the more autonomous management arrangements now instituted in all English and Welsh state schools and to those in Northern Ireland, though there the education authorities (Education and Library Boards) have retained control over more resources, such as those for in-service training and curriculum development.

Regulation

Both bureaucratically administered school systems and quasi-market systems, of the type instituted in the UK, require forms of regulation to control them. Thus the movement from one system to another is accompanied by a change in regulatory regime. I have classified the regulations affecting schools into three types: those concerned with setting the structure of the market within which schools may compete; those concerned with specifying the output produced by schools; and those concerned with specifying standards for the inputs into schooling. These three categories are shown in the right-hand column of Table 1.1. Education reforms in the UK have changed the market structure, created new regulations for the outputs of schooling, and by and large attempted to deregulate with respect to inputs.

Taking these in turn, the promotion of competition through more open enrolment and some limited encouragement of new entry by the formation of new types of school has already been outlined. Exit (i.e. school amalgamation and closure) remains a difficult and long-winded political process, by which LEAs and the FAS have to consult extensively and obtain DFE permission for their proposals. Concern about the waste of resources associated with surplus school places has been repeatedly voiced in official circles since the mid-1970s, when the school population began to decline. Government policies continue to reveal the conflict between cost-efficiency which requires the elimination of surplus places and the exercise of consumer choice which requires them. On the one hand the 1993 Education Act gave the new FAS and the secretary of state powers to rationalize school places, while on the other GM schools are permitted to open small sixth-forms and new CTCs are sited in areas with surplus places.

There has also been an intensification of regulations designed to give parents more information about schools in order to enhance their ability to choose between schools. In 1980, schools were required to publish their examination results. From 1992, the government began the national publication of examination results, and other performance indicators, such as attendance, are being added. The intention is still to implement the 1988 Act's provision that national curriculum test results for individual schools should be published. Schools have been required to publish more information in their prospectus and their governors' annual report to parents, to hold an annual meeting with parents and to publish inspection reports.

There has been considerable growth in regulations specifying the products of schooling. A particularly crucial element in the new centralizing regulations in England, Wales and Northern Ireland was the introduction in the 1988 Education Act of a national curriculum for children aged 5–16 in all state schools. The desire of central government to determine national standards for learning is a common element in reform movements, even in countries such as the USA and Australia where the constitution limits central government activity in this sphere. The main exception is in those European countries which have relatively recently abandoned fascist or communist dictatorships. The 1988 Act also specified national testing to be undertaken at the ages of 7, 11 and 14 to supplement the existing General Certificate of Secondary Education (GCSE) taken at age 16 and post-16 Advanced level examinations and vocational qualifications. The national curriculum has had a major impact on teachers' work. The curriculum and the national tests are in the process of being modified in response to manifest problems in erecting an over-ambitious and over-complex system. Consequently, teachers have been exposed to a continual barrage of change, to which there has a been a wide range of reactions. The specification of a national curriculum as a codified entitlement for all children has been generally welcomed and has improved practice and expectations, for example with the extension of science and modern languages to all mainstream pupils up to the age of 16. Other aspects, such as testing and the prescriptive nature of contentious parts of the curriculum, in particular English and History, and its over-ambitious scope have met with far more criticism. The government has responded by reducing the quantity of subject matter in the national curriculum, reducing the number of subjects tested and the length of the tests, and leaving scope for more flexibility, especially in the last years of compulsory schooling. While the focus of this book is on school-based management and not on curriculum issues, the national curriculum provides a set of standards against which a school's management are to be judged.

The 1988 Act decentralized considerable decision-making powers to schools, but was weak in specifying the system by which schools would be held accountable for their new responsibilities. As discussed in Chapter 8, standard models of decentralized management in organizations, including firms, specify that the concomitant to central management delegating decision-making to line managers is their monitoring of the latter's performance in achieving organizational goals. In the wake of the 1988 Act, it seemed as if LEAs were to be relied upon to monitor schools, though their past record in terms of inspection was regarded as suspect, at least by non-educational bodies like the Audit Commission (1989b). The 1992 Education (Schools) Act made good this omission by creating the Office for Standards in Education (OFSTED), a body independent of the DFE but headed by Her Majesty's Chief Inspector for Schools appointed by the secretary of state. Her Majesty's Inspectors, who had been within the DFE, were reduced in number and relocated to OFSTED. Inspections were privatized and carried out by teams of inspectors who tender to OFSTED for undertaking specified school inspection contracts for a fee. Some inspectors are self-employed, but many are teams of local authority inspectors. Money to cover the cost of OFSTED inspections was deducted from local government grants. Local education authorities were severely restricted in their ability to initiate inspections of their own schools.[7] The legislation specifies that each school is to be inspected every four years. The number of inspection days depends on school size. The Office for Standards in Education has published its criteria for evaluating schools (OFSTED 1993a, 1993b) and clearly specifies the content and structure of the inspection report. Parents are consulted as part of the inspection process, and the findings are discussed with governors as well as with the senior management team. A full report is published and must be made available by the school at a cost to all those requesting a copy. A summary of the report must be sent to parents, local employers and the press. Governors are required to prepare an action plan in response to the report within forty working days of receiving it and to keep parents informed of progress in implementing the action plan. There is a further provision that schools which are judged to be failing their pupils are declared at risk. If special measures instituted by the LEA do not turn the school round after a year, the 1993 Act provides for the failing school to be taken over by an *ad hoc* body called an education association which puts in new management. Such a school becomes grant-maintained when restored to health. A new development for schools inspection criteria is that as well as assessing educational standards achieved, the quality of learning and the ethos of the school, inspectors are also required to assess the efficiency of the school and reach an overall judgement on value for money. The quality of management exercised both by senior staff, middle managers and governors is also commented upon.

The efficiency of the school and more conventional financial auditing of school accounts is the one area where regulations concerning resource inputs have been increased by the current policy thrust. Regulation of inputs is typically associated with bureaucratic administrative structures and is used to limit the operation of market forces. Regulations concerning teacher qualifications, standardized pay and conditions, employment laws, building standards and class size, are all examples of regulations which serve to constrain local decision-making. Collective bargaining conflicts with the local flexibility which is the hallmark of local management, as noted by David (1989), Provenzo (1989) in relation to Dade County, Florida, Levačić (1992b) with respect to Edmonton, and Blackmore (1990) with reference to Victoria, Australia. In the UK (excluding Scotland), LEA-wide pupil–teacher ratios or maximum class sizes no longer determine school staffing: these are left to school level decisions. While national pay and service conditions still apply to LEA and GM schools, there is more discretion for governors to operate their own pay policy. Alternative routes to teaching than the traditional qualified teacher status are being experimented with. Compulsory competitive tendering legislation has diminished the influence of local government manual unions on rates of pay and productivity. These are all features of the deregulation of the markets supplying inputs to schools which are an important aspect of the market-driven form of school-based management developing in the UK.

Local management in the UK in its international context

Relative to school-based management elsewhere, that in England and Wales is notable for being radical in extent and comprehensive in geographic coverage, and for being driven by the desire to instil corporate management practices in schools. Scotland, by contrast, has experienced a milder and less controversial version of the English reforms. While more open enrolment was introduced in 1981, a national curriculum is operated by consensus rather then imposition, there is greater teacher control of testing, and devolved school management was introduced in 1994. Management responsibilities are delegated to headteachers rather than to school boards,[8] which have a mainly advisory role. Education authorities have much more discretion in devising their funding formula, which means that the average-in-actual-out salary rule has not been imposed. Grant-maintained schools are rare in Scotland. The Scottish Office Education Department (SOED) was always more successful than the equivalent ministries in England and Wales in influencing schools and education authorities through a policy network, and so did not experience the frustration felt by the DFE in the 1970s at its inability to influence the other two education partners. The SOED also differs from the DFE in working in partnership with education authorities and university departments of education to produce in-service training programmes and fund research on school improvement.

Significant restructuring towards school-based management in the USA is still restricted to a limited number of states and districts (Koppich and Guthrie 1993). Examples, such as that in Dade County, place much greater emphasis on shared decision-making with teachers and have required teacher union agreements and often work with volunteer schools. Given the focus on teacher empowerment, teacher unions in the USA have supported school-based management, whereas the classteacher unions have been mainly critical in the UK. However, Lowe Boyd (1992) considers the USA to be heading in a similar direction to Britain, an assessment supported by examples such as Kentucky, where the state is bypassing school districts (which supply 10 per cent of the funding), setting up school councils and funding schools according to pupil recruitment (Duckenfield 1990; Hodges 1990). School-based management schemes are now widespread in Australian states. Two earlier pioneers were Victoria and Tasmania. The former delegated decision-making to newly created school councils on which teachers and teacher unions had much more influence than they do in the UK (Chapman 1990), while the state government retained control of the curriculum and of school organization. Tasmania has given considerable power to principals. In none of the Australian states has so much power been delegated to school councils as to governing bodies in England and Wales. In Canada, despite the publicity given to Edmonton Public Schools, and the few examples of school-based management studied by Brown (1990), it is little practised (Lawton 1993), and again decision-making is delegated to the principal rather than to school councils, which remain advisory.

So while there is a general international trend to decentralization of management decisions to the school level, accompanied by some centralization of curriculum and accountability processes, there are some quite significant differences in how the elements set out in Table 1.1 are configured. In studying the effects of the implementation of school-based management in any one country, it is important to assess the relative contribution of the different elements of the specific version of school-based management being studied, so that those effects which seem similar across national boundaries can be distinguished from those which are attributable to the unique features of a particular form of school-based management.

Examining the case for local management

Introduction

Despite national differences in school-based management schemes, their advocates give very similar reasons for recommending them. The aim of this chapter is to provide an overview of the general arguments for and against local management and from these to distil four major criteria against which it can be assessed. The chapter therefore moves from an opening discussion of official arguments for local management to derive a set of criteria to be used in assessing local management. Explanations of the anticipated effects of local management are then reviewed. This chapter therefore moves from the more descriptive and general material of Chapter 1 towards the analytical framework used in the book and developed further in subsequent chapters.

The claims of political advocates

Ultimately, the advocates of school-based management claim that it is required in order to improve the quality and standards of education provided by schools. Kenneth Baker, the Secretary of State for Education, introduced the first reading of the 1988 Education Act by proclaiming:

This Bill will create a new framework, which will raise standards, extend choice and produce a better educated Britain . . .

If we are to implement the principle of the 1944 Act that children should 'be educated in accordance with the wishes of their parents' we must give consumers of education a central part in decision making. That means freeing schools and colleges to deliver the standards that parents and employers want. It means encouraging the consumer to expect and demand that all educational bodies do the best job possible. In a word it means choice.

The purpose of the bill is to secure delegation and widen choice. We want to see more decision making in the hands of individual schools and colleges. When governing bodies and heads control their own budgets, decisions will be taken at a local level. Schools and colleges will be free to make their own decisions on spending priorities and to develop in their own way.

(reported in *Hansard*, 1 December 1987)

This claim has been reiterated in subsequent official documents: 'pupil-led funding and delegated management . . . increase schools' control over resources and thereby improve the standards of education which they provide' (DES 1991a, para. 2). And the Scottish Office Education Department (SOED) made similar claims, emphasizing decision-making:

The Government believes firmly that devolving financial and managerial responsibility to school level will improve the quality of decision-making by giving schools greater flexibility and choice in deciding on their priorities and detailed arrangements in response to the needs of pupils and the aspirations of parents. Improving the quality of decision making is a key part of the government's overall aim of raising standards of learning and teaching in schools.

(SOED 1992a, para. 7)

The key managerial principle upon which school-based management rests was proclaimed in Australia over twenty years ago: 'responsibility will be most effectively discharged where the people entrusted with making decisions are also the people responsible for carrying them out, with an obligation to justify them and in a position to profit from their experience' (Australian Schools Commission 1973: 10). And it was still being reiterated in official exhortations over a decade later: 'the efficiency and effectiveness of the system can be improved only if schools have sufficient control over the quality of education they provide' (Ministry of Education of Western Australia 1987: 5).

In New Zealand, the radical decentralization of the schooling system was strongly motivated by the desire for greater responsiveness:

The Picot taskforce . . . members came to believe that the devolution of decision-making power, resources and accountability was an effective means of altering the balance of power between providers and the clients. Further, they assumed that this would lead to greater institutional, and hence system, responsiveness.

(MacPherson 1993: 73)

In Edmonton, Canada, the inefficiency of resource use, lack of teacher empowerment and the inability of the district to control quality in schools, endemic in a highly bureaucratic system, were cited as the main reasons for developing school-based management (Levačić 1992b). Smilanich (1988: 1) stated: 'With the increased opportunity for decision at school level provided in a climate of trust, more of the creative talents of teachers and potential of teachers could be released'.

Key criteria for assessing local management of schools

The justifications for school-based management contained in political and managerial rhetoric boil down to the espousal of a few distinct objectives, which can be summarized as follows:

• increased efficiency in schools' use of resources;
• increased school effectiveness through improvements in the quality of teaching and learning;
• greater responsiveness to clients and more 'consumer' choice.

The criteria of efficiency and effectiveness, those mainstays of normative public sector management, are particularly prevalent in school-based management in the UK, Australia, New Zealand and Edmonton, Canada, but receive less prominence in current US emphasis on school improvement through teacher empowerment. A criterion which is notably absent from the above list is equity. It has been given little prominence by official advocates of local (or school-based) management. This is in contrast to commentators and critics of local management, who express concern about its impact on equity, fearing that children with special educational needs will have fewer resources allocated to them than under the previous system. Equity is therefore added to the criteria of efficiency, effectiveness, responsiveness and choice to provide an analytical framework for assessing the impact of local management which will be used in this book. Before proceeding to consider various explanations of how local management might impact on the key criteria, it is important to clarify their meaning.

Efficiency

The standard definition of efficiency is that it entails securing 'minimum inputs for any given quality and quantity of service provided'; or the equivalent 'maximum output for any given set of resource inputs' (Audit Commission 1984). However, this definition does not imply that resources are used in a socially optimal way, since to make such a judgement requires output to be valued. Any attempt to define one particular combination of goods and services as having more social value than some other combination inevitably rests on a value judgement about the distribution of income associated with each combination of goods. Efficiency in the sense used by the Audit Commission is therefore restricted to meaning that a given quantity of output is produced at the least possible cost; it does not imply anything about the social value to be attached to that output. I shall use the term 'cost-efficiency' to denote this definition of efficiency so as to distinguish it from other concepts of efficiency, such as 'social efficiency' or 'allocative efficiency' used by economists, which depend on assumptions about the value of output. Often the term 'production efficiency' is used for the same concept (Simkins 1994).[1]

Effectiveness

Effectiveness is a concept which embraces an assumption about the social value of output and is therefore distinct from cost-efficiency. The standard definition of effectiveness used in public sector accountancy and management is 'how well a programme or activity is achieving its established goals or other intended effects' (Audit Commission 1984). The separate definitions of effectiveness and efficiency mean that a programme can be effective but not efficient or efficient but not effective. A popular aphorism is that effectiveness is 'doing the right things', whereas efficiency is 'doing things right'. The specification of the goals or intended effects depends on a prior value judgement about desirable ends. Quite often public sector evaluators, such as the Audit Commission, do not question the goals or objectives of the programme or organization being evaluated, because these have been politically determined and should not therefore be questioned by public servants. The intended outcomes are therefore accepted and used as a reference point for comparisons with actual outcomes. In other circumstances, evaluators can and do specify their own desired outcomes or outputs with which to compare actual effects.

Effectiveness is a general public sector accountancy concept, but it also has related concepts specific to particular sectors, such as school effectiveness. Some definitions of school effectiveness are akin to the public sector accountancy concept in being focused on the goals of the school, such as examination results or national curriculum tests, after taking account of the effects of differences in pupils' prior attainment and social background. Other conceptions of school effectiveness relate to the quality of the education process itself, rather than to the measurable outputs of schooling. For example, the Office for Standards in Education (OFSTED 1993a,b) inspection criteria include both outputs (standards of attainment) and processes, in particular the quality of learning and the ethos of the school. Thus school effectiveness can be defined and assessed in a variety of ways, only some of which are directly analogous to the public sector accountancy definition of effectiveness.

A fundamental issue for the assessment of local management is its impact on the quality of teaching and learning and hence on school effectiveness.

This is, however, extremely difficult to assess. First, there is the problem of agreeing and defining school effectiveness and then measuring or assessing it. If the government defines what it means by educational standards and hence improvements in these standards, and if school-based management promotes the achievement of these standards, then it would be judged 'effective' in terms of the public sector accountancy definition of the concept. However, for those who disapprove of the forms of education defined by the government as indicating 'good quality' and 'acceptable standards', a policy of school-based management which promoted the government's objectives would not be effective in their terms. The second problem in assessing the impact of local management is making links between the changes initiated by its introduction and any consequent impacts on school effectiveness.

Value for money

Effectiveness and cost-efficiency are thus distinct concepts.[2] If an activity, programme or organization is both efficient and effective, then it can be said to provide 'value for money'. However, it is quite often the case that good measures of effectiveness in terms of actual outputs against intended outputs are not available, and hence value for money has to be judged more subjectively from the observation of processes. For this reason, Glynn (1987) defines value for money in terms of a department or programme in which 'those who strive to provide the service do the best they can with the resources that are available'. The value for money achieved by the school is now a criterion for which OFSTED inspectors are required to provide a summary judgement (OFSTED 1993a,b). Both OFSTED guidance and inspectors' practice suggest that this is mainly done by judgementally weighing examination results in relation to the social background of the pupils and the inspectors' ratings of the quality of teaching and learning against the school's unit cost (recurrent expenditure per pupil) (Levačić and Glover 1994b).

Equity

The concept of equity in most usages of the term relates to the fairness with which different people or different categories of people are treated in relation to the distribution of resources they receive. When the general definition is made more specific in order to apply it in policy implementation or policy analysis it inevitably becomes controversial, as it is subject to many different interpretations, some of which stem from personal interest and others from a more altruistic concern for others' welfare. Le Grand and Bartlett (1993: 19) attempt to resolve this problem by defining distributional equity in relation to need, recognizing that need is itself a problematic concept. They 'consider an equitable service to be one where use is determined primarily by need and not by irrelevant factors such as income, socio-economic status, gender or ethnic origin'. This definition is useful for assessing the equity implications of local management, since a major concern of critics is that in comparison with the previous administrative system, it is biased more towards allocating resources to pupils according to their social background than according to their educational need.

Choice, responsiveness and diversity

Efficiency and equity are fundamental evaluative criteria which are traditionally used in normative (welfare) economics. Effectiveness is easily added in order to use a concept of efficiency which is not dependent on value judgements about output. The other policy aims for local management – greater parental choice of school, greater responsiveness of schools to their clients' wishes and greater diversity – are focused more on the processes and structures through which customers and providers interact than on educational inputs and outputs.

Greater choice can mean either more providers between which the customer can effectively select or a greater range of services between which the customer can choose. Diversity, in government pronouncements, refers both to a greater range of school types (e.g. grant-maintained schools and city technology colleges) and to a greater diversity of curricular provision in response to parental preferences, albeit within the confines of the national curriculum. Thus choice and diversity are closely related; however, diversity is a property of the product and the providers, whereas choice relates to the options open to individual consumers. Therefore, there could be greater diversity accompanied by unchanged or even reduced choice for some consumers. One would expect school responsiveness, defined by Scott (1989: 17) as 'the capacity to be open to outside influences and new ideas', to promote diversity in curricular provision and school ethos if such diversity reflects a range of customer preferences.

Greater choice is advocated both as a means for improving educational standards and as an end in itself. Advocates believe greater parental choice of school will promote school responsiveness, which in turn will encourage greater diversity in provision in response to differing parental preferences. Choice of school is also valued in its own right as a manifestation of the liberty of the individual, which is restricted by state administrative allocation of children to schools on the basis of where they live. In education, as in other spheres, incompatible objectives and ideological clashes stem from the conflict between the liberty of the individual and the consequences of that liberty for others, usually represented as a conflict between the interests of the individual and some difficult to define collective interest. This is well-trodden ground which I will not go over, as my main concern here is to raise the issue of the contribution of school-based management to choice, diversity and responsiveness. Local management has brought into schools the need to balance and resolve tensions between individual and collective interests, whereas schools are more insulated from these issues when administered as part of a hierarchical state bureaucracy (Glatter 1994). Thus in making decisions about resource acquisition and resource use, school managers must mediate between the interests of individuals and groups within the school, the collective school interest and the interests of the wider society. The key questions relate both to process ('How do these tensions affect internal decision-making?') and to outcomes ('How are parental choice of school, the diversity of provision within school and between schools affected by the creation of a quasi-market?'). These are complex and difficult questions to answer empirically, and I can promise only some limited answers in the later chapters.

The overall effectiveness of local management

In assessing the overall effectiveness of a policy, one can attempt to assess it either in relation to the objectives set out by the policy-makers, or against other objectives, defined by representatives of different interests or values than those of the policy-makers. In the case of local management, as indicated at the beginning of this chapter, official intentions for the policy have been expressed quite clearly and can be summarized in terms of a few broad criteria. Thus from the government's perspective, the effectiveness of local management depends on its improving the efficiency of resource use in schools, promoting educational effectiveness of schools, and increasing choice, diversity and school responsiveness. Critics of local management fall into two groups. One group accepts the aims of the government and argues that these aims will not be achieved by the policies adopted, with the stated intention of achieving the aims; the second group attacks the policy for having effects other than those the policy-makers explicitly intended and often do so from an ideological perspective in conflict with the values which inform the policy being critiqued (e.g. Smyth 1993).

My main intent in this book is to assess local management against the stated intentions for it by government, but to widen the assessment by including equity considerations. Local management will therefore be assessed in relation to its effects on cost-efficiency, school effectiveness and equity, and the process factors of choice, responsiveness and diversity treated as a catchall criterion.[3]

Mechanisms by which local management might promote efficiency and effectiveness

Having now set out the criteria against which local management is to be assessed, I turn to examine theories that attempt to explain how these changes to the incentive and organizational structures within which schools are managed might lead to the effects desired by government or might have other consequences.

Local management contains two distinct strands: delegated budgeting and greater parental choice of school. In principle, these are separate – one could have delegated school budgets without more open enrolment. It is important to distinguish the two aspects of local management, because they have potentially different roles in affecting the key criteria of efficiency, effectiveness, choice and responsiveness, and equity. Open enrolment promotes competition, whereas delegated budgets give greater managerial flexibility. The former is intended as a stimulus to improved organizational performance, whereas the latter provides the means for improving performance, by giving schools control over their decision-making with respect to resource acquisition and utilization constrained within a framework of government-specified outcomes set out in the national curriculum and its assessment. The 1988 Education Act deliberately coupled the two strands by making school budgets largely and immediately dependent on pupil numbers. Thus any analysis of the mechanisms by which local management is likely to impact on the key criteria will necessarily include the interaction of delegated budgets and more open enrolment.

Market competition

The hypothesis that increased competition between schools will improve efficiency and raise educational standards is a direct application of the market model from the private sector. The expectation that the market mechanism is more efficient and effective in satisfying consumer preferences than bureaucratic administration is derived from economic theory and empirical observation of market goods sectors. The theoretical deduction of the superior performance of the market as an allocative mechanism is dependent on a number of key assumptions, the first of which relates to the structure of the market: there needs to be sufficient alternative and independent suppliers for each supplier to keep its prices (and hence costs) as low as possible, while still attracting customers with the quality of its goods and services. A competitive market structure is essential for ensuring that firms act in the interests of customers, because they are driven to do so in the pursuit of profit. In contrast, economic theory predicts that a monopolized industry or one with a few colluding firms has little incentive to improve efficiency, innovate or lower prices. In the case of schools, the market structure depends on the number of alternative schools for which a family can actually exercise choice. This is dependent on the cost of transport between home and local schools and on the availability of surplus places in alternative schools. This will depend in part on geographical location and family income.

The competitive dynamic in a market needs to be sustained by ease of entry to the market by new firms and the exit of unsuccessful firms. In practice, the process of exit for schools remains slow and complex, with local education authorities (LEAs) required to engage in lengthy, expensive consultation procedures. Their proposals may then get rejected by the Secretary of State after representations by those opposing closure. Schools threatened with closure, and aided by the Department for Education's (DFE's) desire to expand the grant-maintained (GM) sector, have been able to opt out or threaten to do so, thus making LEAs more reluctant than ever to rationalize school provision.[4] Until the Education Act (1993), there was – apart from city technology colleges (CTCs) – no avenue for the entry of new schools except via LEAs building schools in expanding areas. The provisions of the 1993 Act for new sources of entry to the state sector are as yet untried.

Given that state school places are rationed by administrative criteria and not by price, schools with desirable characteristics as perceived by parents and with insufficient places to meet demand are over-subscribed, since excess demand is not rationed by price as in a normal market. To have a market structure in which schools are in competition for pupils, rather than parents being in competition against each other for school places, there needs to be surplus places. However, the existence of surplus school places is not cost-efficient, because having fewer surplus places would lower unit costs.[5] Over the years, the DFE, the House of Commons Education Committee and the Audit Commission have all criticized LEAs for having too many surplus school places and thus having higher unit costs than if some schools were closed. Thus the objective of cost-efficiency which leads to the elimination of surplus places is incompatible with the objective of parental choice and with stimulating educational improvements through competition. This incompatibility continues to be reflected in government policies, some of which put pressure on LEAs to reduce surplus places while others, such as encouraging GM status and permitting new small sixth-forms, sustain and even increase the supply of surplus places.

As well as having a competitive structure, a well-functioning market requires consumers to have access to sufficiently good information to enable them to judge correctly the relative merits of goods sold by different firms. Consumer information is obtained in a number of ways: by examining goods prior to purchase, through the experience of consuming the good after purchase, or by learning about other consumers' opinions. Schooling is an 'experience' good, in that the information of what a school is like is best obtained through experience, which for parents is at second-hand. Thus parents have limited information when choosing a school. Recent education legislation has increased the amount of information available to parents, particularly in relation to examination results, which must be published in school prospectuses and are made nationally available as a 'league table' together with attendance figures. However, because these are 'raw' data which take no account of students' prior attainment and social background, they are misleading indicators of schools' relative effectiveness. Such league tables may lead parents to prefer schools with apparently good exam results, but which are in fact not so effective once student ability is taken into account. A fuller picture of a school is provided in its OFSTED inspection report: summaries must be distributed to all parents and the full report is available for anyone to purchase.

For all its deficiencies of structure and information, the school quasi-market has become more competitive through more open enrolment in the context of surplus places in many areas, and parents now have more information, particularly if they choose to seek it out. The processes by which market competition is expected by its advocates to improve school efficiency and effectiveness are two-fold. One is Darwinian selection. Given sufficient surplus places and new entry, schools which are inefficient or ineffective will, like firms in a competitive market, be unable to survive and will close. Consequently, the average level of school costs will fall and that of educational standards rise. However, given the local unpopularity of school closure and the lengthy procedures involved, together with the absence so far of any significant new entry, Darwinian selection could only have a minor impact on the system as a whole. One must therefore attribute any significant causal connection between competition and higher educational standards, if it exists, to the stimulating effects of competition on improvement within existing schools. It must be assumed that headteachers, governors and school staff are anxious to avoid the undesirable consequences of poor performance in terms of falling rolls and budget cuts and therefore endeavour to operate efficiently and raise educational standards in order to recruit students and remain solvent.

Linking local management to school effectiveness

The two strands of local management – competition and budget delegation – are brought together when it is argued that competition stimulates internal changes in schools which result in improved efficiency and effectiveness. School-based decision-making provides the means by which school managements can respond effectively to the competitive pressures of the external environment. The managerial justification for school-based decision-making relies upon the same rationale as that for decentralization of decision-making in other organizations in both the public and private sectors. This is the subsidiarity argument, which states that decisions are best taken at that level in the organization where the most knowledge relevant to the decision is located and where the actions of the organization's members have most effect. Centralized systems are inefficient because they are inflexible and provide uniform solutions which fail to take account of local differences. Furthermore, system-level collective bargaining over pay and conditions is an important factor limiting flexibility and this needs to be weakened if local managers are to have meaningful decision-making powers.

It is further argued that by making the costs of each school more transparent through formula funding, and giving the governing body the responsibility for managing the budget, accountability for the use of public money is sharpened.

A typical statement of the rational model of management it is assumed schools will adopt is to be found in the consultants' report by Coopers and Lybrand (1988), which exerted considerable influence in the implementation of local management:

> The underlying philosophy of financial delegation to schools stems from the application of the principles of good management. Good management requires the identification of management units for which objectives can be set and resources allocated: the unit is then required to manage itself within those resources in a way which seeks to achieve the objectives; the unit is monitored and the unit is held to account for its performance and for its use of funds. These concepts are just as applicable in the public sector as they are in the private sector.
>
> . . . there can be major gains from delegation. It will increase the accountability of schools for providing value for money: it will give schools the flexibility to respond directly and promptly to the needs of the school and its pupils in a way which will increase effectiveness and quality of the services provided. Schools will have more incentive to seek efficiency and economy in their use of their resources since they will be able to apply the benefits of their good management to further improvements in their services.
>
> (Coopers and Lybrand 1988: 1.5 and 1.8)

This perspective on the relationship between efficiency and effectiveness is elaborated and given some empirical support in some of the academic literature (Caldwell and Spinks 1988; Brown 1990). In the academic – as opposed to the purely managerial – literature, the concept of effectiveness is translated into 'school effectiveness', thus linking school-based management with the findings of school effectiveness research. For example, Caldwell and Spinks (1988: 8), relying heavily on a survey article by Purkey and Smith (1983), maintain that 'the case for self-management is being argued on the basis of findings from studies of school effectiveness'. This article lists school-site management as giving schools 'considerable autonomy in determining the exact means by which they address the problem of increasing academic performance', together with another twelve characteristics of effective schools. Of these characteristics, school-wide staff development, parental involvement, collaborative planning, a sense of community and clear goals, and constant monitoring of pupil progress, could be promoted by school-based management but are not dependent on it. When attempting to translate such findings to the UK school system, one must bear in mind that it was never as centralized as the typical North American school district from which many of these research findings emanate. It should also be noted that Purkey and Smith single out as crucial district support in guiding and helping schools, a factor which in England and Wales has been deliberately weakened or annihilated by central government. Brown (1990: 83) also singles out certain features of effective schools which could be promoted by school-based management. These are leadership from the principal, school planning, support for school decisions and closer monitoring of school activity. Thus school-based or local management is linked to school effectiveness by positing that the former stimulates and facilitates processes which are associated with the latter.

Countervailing factors

Many of the counterarguments concerning the ability of local management to create more effective schools are made from within the same theoretical perspective.[6] An important critique is that financial management in practice gives schools very little additional flexibility, because the bulk of the budget is already fixed by staffing commitments and unavoidable operating expenses. Consequently, a lot of senior management time is devoted to financial management tasks which would be carried out more efficiently by the LEA because of economies of scale. This argument becomes more compelling the smaller the school, since budget flexibility increases and the unit cost of financial management decreases as the school gets larger. In the UK (apart from Scotland), even the smallest fifty-pupil village school is now locally managed. One line of argument is that local management has diverted the time of headteachers away from instructional leadership, which effective schools research has found to be important. Instead, headteachers take on the role of general managers, concerned with acquiring and managing resources and operating as the key link between the school and outside agencies. Drawing on a single case study, Bowe and Ball (1992) argue that managerial effectiveness is compromised because the tasks of local management, and the values it engenders in senior management staff, creates a gulf between them and classroom teachers. In a similar vein, Halsey (1993) infers from an application of organization theory to local management that it will drive schools away from being task- and support-oriented collegial cultures to becoming bureaucratically controlled and role-dominated organizations. He further argues, without empirical evidence, that conflicts in values between teachers and parents make the achievement of an integrated culture of shared values in schools less likely.

This critique of the deleterious effects of local management on school cultures is taken further by disciples of Habermas, who depict some idealized 'life-world' experienced by communities who are not organized along economic rational principles, but 'resolve their problems communally by means of collective will formation' (Laughlin et al. 1992; Watkins 1993: 148). Apparently, these communities' 'life-worlds', if 'colonized' by 'economic-instrumental rationality', suffer 'loss of meaning, anomie, alienation' and other damage done to the capacities needed for 'human emancipation'. Watkins, treating schools as having been such life-worlds in the days of centralized bureaucracy, depicts school-based management as redirecting schools to respond to the demands of 'technical instrumentality'. Along with other 'critical theorists', he interprets self-management as a device whereby the state attempts to maintain its legitimacy by off-loading onto schools its problem of reconciling demands for welfare expenditure and the need to maintain the rate of return on capital. Unless one can accept the whole set of assumptions upon which this critique is based, it is difficult to find it plausible. It depicts an idealized but non-existent social condition, in which decisions are communally reached, but fails to specify what these superior collective choice mechanisms might be or how they would address the universal problem of economics – that is, the scarcity of resources.

Similar but practical critiques of local management are made without all the trappings of critical theory. The argument that local management is just a government device for placing the responsibility for education expenditure cuts on school governors is a common one (see, e.g. South 1987). However, it is difficult to sustain the argument that the prime purpose of local management was to cut education spending and that without it expenditure cuts would not have taken place. The Coopers and Lybrand Report (1988) published by the DFE made clear that local management would not save money: its intention is to use more efficiently what money is made available to education. The current system, whereby local government determines the final education budget – admittedly highly constrained by the standard spending assessment (SSA) allocated to it – still enables central government to deny responsibility. If anything, more widespread knowledge of school financial matters among governors, and their closer contacts with education professionals due to local management, have increased the size and voice of the lobby for additional spending on schools (e.g. House of Commons Committee on Education Committee 1994).

Clearly, the possibility of financial cuts with their direct impact on school budgets and staffing has caused concern, especially with respect to smaller schools. A given fluctuation in pupil numbers leads to greater budget instability the smaller the budget. The fewer staff the school employs, the less likely it is that in the event of a reduction in the budget, the necessary reduction in staffing can come about through natural wastage. The average-in-actual-out budget rule and the inability of LEAs to redeploy staff to other schools (except through mutual agreement) has considerably decreased teacher job security. Critics of the average-in-actual-out rule argue that it forces schools, especially the least well off financially, to hire the cheapest rather than the best person for a post. The pupil-driven funding formula, and the requirement that schools do not run budget deficits, force governors and headteachers to practise low-risk staffing strategies, either by keeping staffing tight or creating a dual labour force of permanent staff supplemented by staff on temporary contracts. While this is cost-saving, it may lessen the quality and motivation of certain staff and militate against collegiality (Halsey 1993). Against this it can be argued that a policy whereby schools do not have to weigh the cost of staff against the likely benefits of employing them, and where teachers are kept on despite falling rolls, is not cost-effective. Teachers who are imposed on a school as a result of redeployment are less likely to fit the requirements of the post and therefore perform less well than teachers whom the head and governors select. Whether or not the guarantee of job security regardless of personal or organizational performance enhances or diminishes motivation and productivity depends on personal characteristics and attitudes. The highly centralized staffing practices of some North American school districts, under which principals have no say in staff selection, has featured as a factor which militates against school effectiveness (Purkey and Smith 1983). However, English headteachers have always had a considerable influence on staff selection, except in authorities with falling rolls where schools were forced to appoint teachers from within the authority. This practice is now unenforceable and schools have abandoned it.

The issue of whether local management enhances efficiency in the use of resources can be separated from that of its role in securing more effective schools. Improving the efficiency of resource use can occur without the more fundamental and deeper-seated changes to the organization which school improvement requires. Since the impact of local management on the efficiency of resource use and on the processes associated with school effectiveness are the major issues with which this book is concerned, they are examined further in later chapters.

The equity implications of local management

As already noted, equity, though a major criterion for evaluating public policy, has featured very little in official intentions for local management. Equity, however, is probably the focus of the most strident criticism of local management. The usual charge is that it will lower the welfare of the most socially disadvantaged and damage the collective welfare of society by increasing social divisions. These arguments are directed in particular at the competitive element of local management and are intended to demolish the case for increased choice and diversity as libertarian values (Ball 1993). However, there are also less well-publicized arguments that local management promotes equity. Part of the difference in such viewpoints is explained by two quite different conceptions of equity – procedural and distributional.

Procedural equity

Procedural equity, which refers to the consistent application of agreed rules, is a dominant criterion for social decision rules advocated by libertarian or constitutional economists who regard the market process as procedurally just. The key figure in this school of thought is Nobel laureate James Buchanan (Buchanan 1986). In this view, the market is procedurally just because it operates on a set of agreed rules governing the exchange of property rights. Even if all individuals entered a process of market trading with the same value of property rights to start with, they would, as the result of a process of market exchanges, end up with unequal distributions of wealth because of differences in luck, judgement and skill in undertaking market transactions. The allocative procedure of the market is seen as procedurally equitable, though the distributional outcomes are unequal.

The formula-funding aspect of local management is therefore seen as procedurally equitable in comparison with former methods of allocating resources to schools which depended to some extent on LEA officer discretion and hence on headteachers' ability to exploit their networks for the benefit of their individual schools. This procedural justification for formula funding was clearly stated in LMS circular 7/88: 'it [the formula] should be based on an assessment of schools' objective needs, rather than on historic patterns of expenditure in order to ensure that resources are allocated equitably' (DES 1988: 22).

In approving LEAs' local management schemes, the DFE adhered to the objective needs principle which they interpreted as meaning that formulae must be based on quantitative indicators of schools' need for resources and not on officer judgement. This was shown in a study by Thomas and Levačić (1991) of amendments to local education authority LMS schemes required by the DFE and the conditions it attached to interim approval of schemes for the first few years. The requirement to construct a formula based on 'objective' data only, when previous systems of allocation had contained an element of local discretion, meant that many LEAs found it difficult to construct a formula which replicated exactly their previous pattern of resource allocation to schools (Levell 1989; The LMS Initiative 1992).

Schools similarly should be concerned to ensure that their decision-making processes for allocating resources are procedurally equitable. Simkins and Lancaster (1988) include this as one of a number of criteria which a school resource allocation process should satisfy. Budget decision-making needs to be an open procedure in which all interested parties have access to the criteria employed to make decisions and to the final decisions reached. It is difficult to demonstrate that small groups taking decisions in secret which are not communicated to the rest of the school community are being procedurally just. With so much more of the school budget under local control, one would expect procedural equity considerations to require much more openness and codified deliberation over resource allocation decisions, with a movement away from the 'benevolent despotism' of the headteacher allocating resources through secret bilateral negotiations with individual budget holders (Knight 1993).

Distributional equity

Distributional equity is the form of equity which most people associate with the concept of social justice. It refers to the distribution of income and wealth and the means to obtaining these. This distribution is the outcome of social processes, including the market process. Distributional equity is a particularly important concept for education, since educational attainment is unevenly distributed and is closely associated with the distribution of income and wealth. As suggested by Le Grand and Bartlett (1993), an appropriate distributional equity criterion for assessing the impact of a quasi-market is the extent to which it distributes resources according to need rather than to other factors such as income and social status.

There are two principles of distributional equity – horizontal and vertical. *Horizontal equity* is the principle that every individual in like circumstances should receive the same treatment. *Vertical equity* is the principle that individuals who have different needs should be treated in ways which compensate for these differences. The formula-funding rules contain both principles of equity. Horizontal equity underpins the stipulation that each pupil in the same year group should be allocated the same sum of money in all the LEA's schools and that at least 75 per cent[7] of schools' budgets should be allocated on an age-weighted pupil basis. The fact that cash allocations per pupil vary considerably between LEAs, even taking into account differences in costs, shows that the principle of horizontal equity is sacrificed to the principle of local political discretion – though the stringent central government control over local government expenditure undermines the latter principle. A further breach of the horizontal equity principle is differential funding in favour of pupils in GM schools and CTCs. As noted in Chapter 1, the current system of funding schools of different types and in different LEAs is in a mess, while the rational solution of a national funding formula remains politically unattractive.

The vertical equity principle is reflected in the funding formula in two ways (DFE 1994). First, by the expectation that the formula will allocate additional money to schools according to the number and/or proportion of pupils who have non-statemented special needs. As studies by Thomas (1990, 1991) and Lee (1992) show, most LEAs use free school meals in their special needs index and have between them applied a wide variety of other measures of social disadvantage and special educational need, including in some cases indicators of high ability. The proportion of the aggregated schools budget (ASB) allocated for special needs also shows marked variation, as Fig. 2.1 illustrates.

The second vertical equity factor in the funding formula is allowances to schools with additional costs because of their small size or specific factors like split sites or staff on protected salaries.[8] This goes some way to ensuring that pupils are not disadvantaged by attending schools which, because of their structure, have a higher than average percentage of fixed costs in

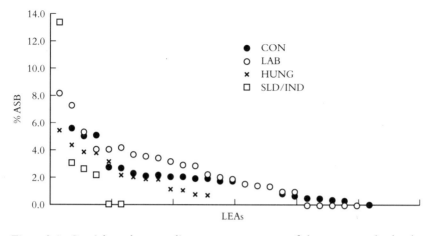

Figure 2.1 Special needs expenditure as a percentage of the aggregated schools budget 1990–91.
Source: Levačić, R. (1992a).

their total costs. If such schools did not receive an additional allocation of money, they would have less money per pupil than others to spend on direct educational activities.

Predicted effects of local management on distributional equity

Discussion about the distributional equity implications of local management is directed at two levels – the school system and the school itself. A typical criticism of the market mechanism for producing unequal distributional outcomes was expressed by the Campaign for the Advancement of State Education.

> The proposals for open enrolment, financial delegation and opting out are intended to provide the means by which a minority of schools can be allocated sufficient resources to deliver the national curriculum at the expense of all the others. The change in the admissions procedures to open enrolment is designed both to give the appearance of extending parental choice by increasing the number of children admitted to 'popular schools' and to concentrate resources in larger, more 'economic' units. The corollary is that other perfectly good schools will be allowed to deteriorate due to loss of revenue and resources in an increasingly underfinanced situation. To protect the Government from the charge that schools are suffering financial distress, all will be expected to raise additional funds from both parents and business interests. This will result in ever widening differences between the quality

of education possible in those schools with high-income parents and those in poorer circumstances.

(quoted in Haviland 1988: 5–6)

It is often claimed that inner-city schools in disadvantaged areas will be most badly affected if LEAs are unable to force pupils to attend these schools and to provide them with special discretionary support. OFSTED inspection reports indicate that most of the poorly performing schools, some of which are GM schools or CTCs, are located in inner-city areas (OFSTED/Audit Commission 1993). LEA policies in the past did not ensure that such schools either improved or ceased to operate. More open enrolment has enabled some parents to place their children in schools which they consider to be better than the catchment area alternative. The impact of local management on social equity and the standards of education provided in socially disadvantaged areas cannot be judged only in terms of the effects on those schools which in the short term face falling rolls and budgets. The much more difficult assessment is the overall effect on the education of students from a range of social backgrounds. It must be borne in mind that a policy which forces parents to use their local school will not disadvantage the wealthy, as they can buy either private education or a house in the catchment area of a school perceived to offer good education.

There are conflicting views concerning the distributional equity implications of schools determining the allocation of their resources between different pupils and groups. Advocates of school-based management (in particular Caldwell, 1993, citing earlier work by Garms *et al.* 1978) argue that it promotes equity by enabling the school to tailor its resources to meet the individual learning needs of students, in contrast to the uniformity of centralized systems. In order to use flexible learning methods, the decision of which particular mix of resources best suits the learning needs of individuals has to be made at the school level.

It is more common for educationists to worry that local management will induce schools to allocate proportionately fewer resources to the socially and educationally disadvantaged. In part, this is deduced to be the result of the removal of centralized resourcing for pupils with special educational needs. Prior to local management, resources for special needs were usually allocated by the LEA in the form of named staff with a specific remit. Under local management, it is up to schools how they allocate their budgets to serve the needs of pupils with non-statemented special needs. The amount a school spends may be more or less than the amount allocated for special needs by the formula. There is some concern regarding the lack of accountability of schools for this allocation, which the 1993 Education Act seeks to strengthen by requiring governors to develop, implement and monitor a special needs policy and to report this to parents. The OFSTED inspection also reports on special needs provision and equal opportunities.

However, it is not easy to assess how a school distributes its resources

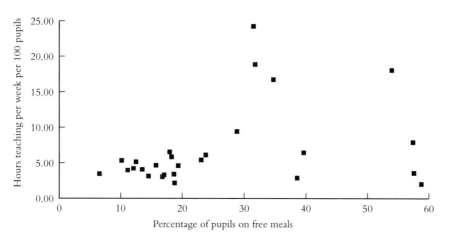

Special needs teaching: hours per week per 100 year 7–11 pupils by secondary school

Figure 2.2   Differences in schools' allocation of teaching hours per week for special educational needs.
Source: Jesson and Levačić (1992).

to pupils with special needs. When special needs pupils and other pupils are taught together, it is difficult to determine what share of the resources is used to support the special needs pupils. While additional staff support in the classroom or withdrawal of pupils from classes can be identified as resources allocated to special needs, resources spent on running smaller classes in order to provide additional support for special needs pupils are less easy to identify. The variability of school practice in relation to allocating additional resources to special needs is well illustrated by data gathered from a survey of Sheffield secondary schools (Jesson and Levačić 1992). The Sheffield funding formula gave schools additional money for both the number and percentage of pupils entitled to free school meals. Consequently, the additional amount received per pupil varied from £17 to £350 a pupil. However, as Fig. 2.2 shows, the schools which allocated the most teacher hours per pupil for supporting special needs either in the classroom or by withdrawal were schools in the middle range of social deprivation. Schools with the highest concentrations of socially disadvantaged pupils spent their additional resources either on smaller classes or additional non-contact time for teachers. The evident lack of knowledge concerning which resource combinations are most effective in promoting educational achievement among pupils with special needs is a further example of the ambiguity surrounding linkages between educational inputs and outputs, which makes it difficult to hold schools accountable for the resources they are given for special needs support.

In many instances, the way schools allocate their resources can have distributional consequences of which schools are unaware or have only a vague impression. Information technology expenditure may benefit boys more than girls, music tuition may be disproportionately skewed to middle-class children, while pastoral care resources may be disproportionately allocated to those pupils who are noticeably disruptive. Critics of pupil-driven formula-funding and competition for students are concerned that schools will discriminate against pupils whose behaviour or lack of achievement would adversely affect the popularity of the school. Thus distributional equity considerations pervade the values of the school, its aims and objectives, the educational activities it organizes and its interaction with the external environment.

The relationship between effectiveness and equity

While it is obvious that equity considerations influence how school effectiveness is defined and assessed, it may be less obvious that the efficiency criterion has distributional implications as well. The attractiveness of the efficiency criterion to economists, who make such extensive use of it, is that by definition an improvement in efficiency is a positive sum game: more is obtained with the same quantity of resources. In contrast, a redistribution of resources aimed at promoting equity takes from some to give to others and is thus a zero sum game, unless those who give up resources are altruistic. In principle, nobody should be worse off as the result of an efficiency gain, since the surplus generated must be sufficient to compensate anyone who has lost out by the changes which brought about the improvement in efficiency.[9] In practice, though, it is not usually possible to identify all losers or discover low-cost and generally agreed methods of compensating the losers. So while it is efficient for a school to find cheaper ways of maintaining its buildings, say by using a local handyman rather than the authority's direct labour organization (because union restrictions on the supply of labour have driven wages above the free market rate), the direct labour force is worse off once it can no longer earn the higher income its monopoly power had secured. Despite this caveat, I shall continue for the sake of clarity to limit the meaning of cost-efficiency, as is standard public sector accounting practice, to an assessment of the ouput/input ratio applicable to a specific good or service, ignoring any wider distributional implications, since these cannot be assessed without a much broader framework for modelling interactions between the school (in this case) and the economy.

Equity dimension to definitions of effectiveness

It is of course not possible to propose measures of educational effectiveness that are not based on some value judgement. For example, one could set the objective that a school should maximize the sum of all pupils' added value in exam results given their prior educational attainment. This might well mean that high-ability pupils gain more added value than low-ability pupils. Alternatively, a school could, in complete contrast, aim at five GCSE passes at grade C for the maximum possible number of students and achieve this by concentrating resources on the pupils of average and below-average ability. In the first example, equity is defined as equality of opportunity to be achieved by ensuring that each pupil receives an equal allocation of resources; in the second example, equity is equality of outcome and so justifies positive discrimination in favour of those with greater learning difficulties. Which definition one favours depends on one's values and conceptions of justice, and such preferences are not usually amenable to alteration through an appeal to empirical evidence.

Conclusion

School-delegated budgeting might at first glance seem a relatively narrow managerial issue, but seen as a constituent element of a fundamental re-structuring of the education system, which parallels similar developments in other public services, it raises many wide-ranging issues and deeply felt controversies based on differing values and ideologies. Having set out the wide range of issues which local management involves, in Chapters 4–7 I shall focus more narrowly on the management of resources within the school, attempting to assess this against the criteria of efficiency, effectiveness, equity and a fourth criterion which embraces the constellation of responsiveness, choice and diversity.

The locally managed school as an open system

Organizational analysis and local management

Common to the implementation of school-based management schemes across the world is the justifying claim that they will lead to school improvement, enhance school effectiveness and raise educational standards. Political rhetoric, certainly in the UK, has treated this as an obvious logical deduction which only needs asserting rather than explaining, as is clear from government circulars on local management. Given this lacuna in official thinking, this chapter applies organizational theory to schools to examine the possible links between increased school autonomy over resource allocation and the resultant effects on school outputs. By posing the issue in terms of linkages between resource inputs and educational outputs, the concepts of efficiency, productivity and effectiveness are re-examined.

An open systems model of school management

In a perceptive survey of educational management developments in the post-war period, Lowe Boyd (1992: 508) characterizes them as consisting of a 'movement from a closed-systems, process-oriented, and role-based approach to an open systems, outcome-oriented, goal-based approach'. The closed-systems, human-relations dominated approach focused on social psychological processes within the organization, assuming that if the processes were healthy, successful organizational outcomes would result. The major weakness with this approach was that it failed to specify the relationship between processes and outcomes or to focus on student learning. The impact of the school effectiveness research movement, which gathered momentum in the 1980s, was to turn the spotlight on the measurable learning achieved by students and its relationship with their personal and social characteristics as well as with the effects of the school they attend. Lowe Boyd also comments on the 'extraordinary influence of economic paradigms' on policy analysis, social policy and management, in contrast to its neglect in educational management.

There has been a distinct tendency for critics of the economic paradigm to associate it only with the discredited scientific management movement and to castigate it for being rigid, over-rational and narrowly technical and thus totally inapplicable to non-profit-making service organizations in which the quality of human relationships is of paramount importance. This critique, while valid when directed at attempts to apply mathematical models of optimal resource allocation to such organizations,[1] fails to address the key issue of how to design institutional arrangements in order to attain intended social purposes with the best use of scarce resources. The objective of using resources efficiently to provide effective education is the driving force of educational reform and restructuring movements since the 1980s. The problem for those involved in educational management is understanding how the concepts of efficiency and effectiveness can be applied fruitfully in educational institutions and integrated with more familiar concerns, particularly when there are competing definitions of what constitutes effective education.

A helpful conceptual tool for this undertaking is the open systems model. This depicts the organization as a complex living organism which interacts with its environment (Smircich 1983; Morgan 1986). Following Morgan, the organization as an organism is a metaphor for understanding organizational behaviour and is one of a number of such metaphors that can be used in this way. As an organism, the organization is seen as distinct and separate from its external environment but with permeable boundaries which are not necessarily clearly defined. The organization is dependent on its environment for resources, broadly defined to include support from its stakeholders. The organization is a purposeful entity that produces outputs which it exchanges with stakeholders in its external environment in return for resources and support. The model also focuses on how relationships between resource inputs and outputs are mediated by internal processes. Certain key elements, such as the technology of the organization's productive processes and the culture of its human relations, are singled out for study. These elements have important and interdependent effects on the processes which relate inputs to outputs and which connect the organization with its environment. A key process is feedback between the organization and its environment and within the system itself, so that the organization is responsive and adaptive, thus behaving like an organism.

The open systems model has been developed over the last fifty years and widely applied to many sectors, including education (Hoy and Miskel 1989).

In a recent example, Chrispeels (1993) uses the open systems model to structure her study of school effectiveness. By studying organizations through the metaphor of the organism, attention is focused on discovering which organizational characteristics are best suited to specific environments. Applied to local management, this focus poses the question of whether it is the organizational form best suited to the types of environment in which educational institutions are located and to the nature of the learning and teaching process. The open systems model also provides a unifying framework for synthesizing many strands within organizational theory and treating organizational design as a strategic issue of selecting structures and processes which are judged to best serve the purposes for which the organization has been set up (Butler 1991).

An open systems input–output model of the school enables one to trace out the possible linkages between increased flexibility in deploying resources and the intended desirable effects on school processes and outcomes. The model indicates, therefore, how local management might improve efficiency, responsiveness, effectiveness and impact on equity. It also assists in understanding why the necessary linkages between greater flexibility in resource allocation and the desired effects on educational outputs might not get established. Before examining the linkages in the model in detail, it is useful to consider the problem of lack of agreement on the aims of education and their relative importance and the difficulty of specifying the outputs and outcomes of schooling.

Educational outcomes and outputs

The aims of education refer to its broad purposes and usually include a productive labour force, transmission of knowledge and culture, socialization and enhanced ability to participate in democratic politics. The outcomes of formal and institutionalized education are the broad effects that it actually achieves on the individuals who have participated in the process. For schools, such outcomes would be students' knowledge, ability to appreciate and enjoy cultural activities, behave with social responsibility, participate in democratic politics and be productive members of the labour force. It is usual to distinguish the broad outcomes of schooling from its narrower and more specific outputs, some of which are measurable and some of which are not (e.g. Margolis 1991: 202; Scheerens 1992: 3). Outputs are the immediate effects of the school on its students, whereas outcomes are the longer-term effects both for the individuals who attended the school and the consequences of these effects for society in general. So examination results are a school output, and the students' income earning capacity in later life are outcomes. Examples of measurable school outputs are examination results and qualifications, rates of participation in higher and further education and training, and school leaver employment. Certain process variables are also used to measure school performance, such as attendance. Outputs which are much more difficult to measure are the effects of school on pupils' attitudes, beliefs and behaviour. Survey questionnaires are the usual method of measuring these aspects of students' moral and social development, such as the process indicators of school ethos developed by the Scottish Office Education Department (SOED 1992a,b) for use by schools for their self-evaluation. Qualitative judgements are also made, as in the Office for Standards in Education (OFSTED 1993b) inspection criteria. Such measures are at best rough indicators in which it is difficult if not impossible to distinguish the impact of the school as distinct from home, community and society.

Issues in the measurement of output

A major problem in using unadjusted indicators of school output is that they are measures of gross output – that is, the equivalent of measuring company performance by the monetary value of sales. In order to assess a school's net output or its value added to students, account has to be taken of students' social background and cognitive abilities, since these are the primary determinants of measured educational attainment. Statistical estimates of value-added measures of school effectiveness separate out the effect of the school on test and examination scores from the effects of social background and cognitive abilities or attainment prior to entering the school. Statistically unbiased estimates require data at the level of the pupils, not school averages (MacPherson 1992; Willms 1992). This requires considerable data and sophisticated multi-level modelling techniques (Goldstein 1987), which only a few local education authorities (LEAs) have so far employed (Hedger 1992; Jesson *et al.* 1992; Henderson 1993; Hill 1994).

Statistically estimated value-added examination indicators are a far cry from the raw descriptive statistics of school performance published nationally in England and Wales, which include examination results and attendance, and which are due under the 1988 Education Reform Act to be expanded to cover national curriculum test scores for primary as well as secondary schools. In the absence of resources for multi-level model estimates of value-added school performance indicators, the local authorities' National Consortium on Examination Results can provide a rough-and-ready adjustment of schools' average examination results for pupils' social background measured in terms of the percentage of pupils entitled to free school meals (Kelly 1993). Individual schools, especially secondary ones, often have the data and expertise to do their own value-added estimates, but these are incomplete without comparative data from other schools, such as that provided by the ALIS Project (Fitzgibbon 1992) for A-level examinations. In the absence of comparators, schools can set their own targets (Levačić 1994).

The problem that bedevils all attempts to relate inputs to the resulting outputs and outcomes of education is that they are multiple, many are intangible, and there is no agreement on their relative social value. Measuring school effectiveness in terms of quantifiable output indicators of educational attainment in relation to given student characteristics assumes that these measured attainments are important, even if it is recognized that there are other desirable outputs and outcomes which have not been or cannot be measured. Emphasizing measurable outputs is likely to bias schools towards concentrating on these at the expense of the less measurable, but making no attempt to measure output encourages schools to concentrate on short-term processes at the expense of longer-term attainment and fails to produce usable knowledge of the links between teaching organization and methods and consequent educational outputs.

Education as a private and public good

Although there is a reasonable degree of consensus in general terms concerning the aims or intended outcomes of education, this breaks down once the debate moves on to the appropriate balance between the different outcomes and specification in more detail of how they are delivered. A fundamental value conflict exists concerning the appropriate balance between the private and public good aspects of education and hence between the respective claims of private and collective choice. Private benefits are those enjoyed only by the individual, whereas public benefits are enjoyed by other members of society. A pure public good is one which yields benefits from which no-one in society can be excluded and which are jointly consumed by everyone – the amount consumed by one person does not diminish the amount left over for others.

The private benefits of education consist of the lifetime income stream the individual earns as a result of his or her education, as well as the consequent enjoyment of cultural and social activities. A skilled and educated workforce, which contributes more to the national income than the workers receive in after-tax personal income and spend on private consumption, is a public benefit of education. Further public benefits arise from having a socialized, law-abiding citizenry, who can participate in and contribute to a stable democratic political system. These social and political benefits are often associated with the degree of social cohesion and hence with a reduction in social inequality. A further public benefit sought from education is the transmission of culture and knowledge from one generation to another. Here the desire of minorities to preserve cultural differences may conflict with the promotion of social cohesion. The rival claims of curricula designed to promote vocational skills, personal development, citizenship and social equality are well rehearsed. The private and public benefits of school outputs which contribute to individuals' future income-earning capacity and cultural enjoyment may conflict with the claims of social distributional equality. Education is thus an extremely complex good, since at one and the same time it yields considerable private benefits and is partially a public good both in relation to national needs as well as to distinct local community needs. It is also a positional good, since one of the functions of an education system is to filter and select.

Economic theory justifies state intervention to provide public goods on the grounds that the theoretically optimal amount would not be provided by the market because of the free-rider problem – people will not pay for public goods since they cannot be excluded from consuming them. However, the production of public goods by the state involves coercion of the individual through such means as taxation and regulation. Both a national curriculum and state allocation of school places are justified by their advocates on the grounds that they produce public benefits compared with letting individual choice reign free. It can be argued that a national curriculum yields public benefits if it results in a more productive labour force and higher standards of cultural knowledge acquisition than leaving curriculum choice to parents and teachers. A further justification of government intervention in the curriculum is that parents and children are poorly informed about the processes, outputs and outcomes a given school will achieve for them unless these are prescribed and monitored by the government. There is also a public goods rationale for the administrative allocation of school places if it promotes social equality and cohesion. However, both a national curriculum and administrative allocation of school places deny individual choice. The tensions between collective and individual choice are played out both in the school's external environment and in its internal processes as it responds to those pressures. Local management places more responsibility for the resolution of those tensions within the school rather than resolving them in favour of collective choice, as does traditional state bureaucratic administration.

The school as an input–output system

The open systems model of the organization focuses on three key constituent elements (e.g. Butler 1991):

- the external environment;
- the production technology through which inputs are transformed into outputs;
- human relations, which encompasses a number of different perspectives on the organization, the main ones being organizational, cultural and political.

Figure 3.1 depicts such an input–output model in which the school transforms its resource inputs into educational outputs through a sequence of stages in the production process.

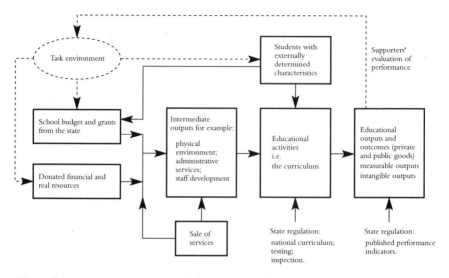

Figure 3.1   An input–output model of the school

The external environment

The external environment in which schools operate can be subdivided into the general environment which is influenced by the major technological, social, political and economic forces operating in society, and the specific environment made up of parents, the local community, local business, the local education authority, other educational institutions, and central government and its agencies. This immediate external environment is also referred to as the 'task environment' (Butler 1991), thus emphasizing that in order to survive the organization needs to pursue ends that satisfy sufficiently the needs of its stakeholders. The organization exchanges its outputs broadly defined for resources and support. Local management has been deliberately designed to increase schools' dependency on their task environment and thus the uncertainty attached to survival.

The school obtains resources in the form of students, finance and donations in kind in return for the educational services it provides. The success with which an organization obtains resources from its task environment depends on norms which its supporters – actual and potential – use to evaluate the organization's performance and the supporters' perceptions of the quality of the organization's performance relative to alternative suppliers. In the general model, organizations jostle with rival organizations to attract support and hence resources and face different degrees of uncertainty in their task environment. Local management is designed to enhance the importance of the school's own actions in securing support from its task environment by improving its performance as perceived by its supporters. As noted in Chapter 1, an important dimension of the external environment is the regulatory regime in which the school operates. In the case of schools, the government has tightened up the specification of the tasks expected of schools and promoted the dissemination of information outside the school about its performance in undertaking these tasks.

Students are a crucial input in that they are the 'raw material' which school processes are intended to transform. In the input–output model, the effectiveness of the school is judged in relation to the value it adds to students in the way of knowledge, skills, behaviours and attitudes. As the quality of these depends crucially on the students' social background and cognitive abilities, the importance of school effectiveness research has been to show that schools can still make a difference to students' educational attainment. How schools are managed and organized, therefore, affects the educational outcomes produced. One of the main criticisms of the UK Government's stress on raw examination results, school leaver destinations and attendance rates as measures of performance is that by themselves they are highly misleading indicators of school effectiveness. Emphasizing them in the context of competition between schools for resources may well encourage ostensibly non-selective schools to recruit students with characteristics positively associated with good performance in terms of raw statistics, a practice referred to as 'cream-skimming'.[2]

Transforming inputs into outputs: The production technology

Inputs acquired from the external task environment are transformed through schooling processes into outputs and outcomes which are exported back to the environment. The stages this transformation goes through are depicted in Fig. 3.1 as a flow of intermediate transformations preceding from left to right. Under a system of local management, the school initially obtains most of its resources as a lump sum budget, with additional specific or categorical grants earmarked for stated purposes. The school may also receive various donations from non-state supporters in the form of finance or real inputs, such as the time of volunteers, as well as a direct allocation of premises from the LEA. In terms of inputs, there are thus two major differences between a system of local management and the contrasting model of centralized administration. Under the latter, schools are allocated pupils whose characteristics they cannot influence; and they get all their resources in fixed amounts of real inputs. (Real inputs are distinguished from money as they are physical entities such as staff, books, equipment and buildings.) Actual systems may be located anywhere between the two extremes, with say limited delegated budgets for certain types of resource.

The flexibility of local management comes from tying the school into the market economy through the medium of money, which gives it the ability to decide for itself the mix of real resources it purchases. The school then uses the initial allocations of financial resources to purchase real resources in the form of staff, materials, energy, water and other services. This first intermediate transformation is planned and recorded through budgets. This is an important point, because the new unavoidable activity which local management introduced to schools is the financial function of preparing and monitoring budgets for the bulk of the expenditure on the school. As noted in Chapter 1, the emphasis in the UK's version of school-based management has been delegated budgeting rather than teacher empowerment.

The real resources acquired and financed through the budget are used in conjunction with other real resources, such as existing buildings, plant and equipment, to produce what can be called 'intermediate outputs' or 'operating services', which support teaching and learning indirectly. An appropriate physical environment has to be created and maintained in which learning can occur, administrative services must be provided to support learning, and investment must take place to maintain and develop the staff.

The next stage in the school productive process is utilization of the school's physical and human resources (i.e. the intermediate outputs) to produce educational activities. Unlike the operational services, this is the core technology of the school. The ways in which real resources are combined in order to produce educational activities, outputs and outcomes are subsumed under the term 'production technology'. The core technology embraces a wide range of issues, such as teaching method, class size and organization, the ratio of support staff in the classroom to qualified teachers, quality of teaching materials and the organization of the school day. As Knight (1989a, 1993) emphasizes, the most important choices the school makes concern the use of time by both staff and students. The organization of time, a resource which cannot be stored for future use, is the key to effective learning. School and teacher effectiveness studies have shown that the amount of student time on task achieved by teachers is a significant variable in explaining differential effectiveness. There is a wide range of alternative resource mixes which can be employed in producing a distinct educational activity, such as year 3 English. The problem is establishing criteria which would enable teachers (and inspectors) to judge the relative efficiency of the different ways of combining resources to produce educational activities. The cost of producing a specific activity, such as an English lesson, is not an adequate guide to cost-effectiveness, because the school's output is not the activities themselves, such as two periods of history a week for year 7, but the learning objectives thereby achieved. The educational activities are not the final outputs of the school: these are the improvements in students' knowledge, understanding, skills and attitudes achieved as a result of experiencing the educational activities.

The production technology of schools is highly conservative; its main activity, grouping children in classes with a single teacher for a specified period of time, has been the dominant production technique for centuries. Local management gives schools some additional flexibility in how they deploy resources and therefore change the core technology. Schools could use more support staff in classes with teachers, or more administrative staff to reduce the time teachers spend on clerical tasks. Alternatively, schools could develop flexible learning, with the associated need to acquire more learning materials and alter the arrangement of study space (Owen and Farrar 1994). How much flexibility the school has in determining these educational activities and the educational outputs at which they are directed is regulated by the state.

The input–output model is useful for analysing the potential effects of local management because it highlights the fact that local management only affects the school directly from two directions: at the very beginning of the input–output process by increasing schools' range of choice over inputs, and through school responsiveness to the external environment caused by linking the inflow of resources to how stakeholders respond to perceived school performance. An important and complex set of internal processes mediate between budget-setting and the production of educational output. These processes are not altered directly by local management, though they may be affected indirectly through changes in culture – an issue to be explored later.

In Fig. 3.1, three sets of sequenced decision processes are thus distinguished. The first is the translation of the financial resources via the budget into real resources and intermediate outputs. The second is the management of real resources so as to create and maintain the learning environment. The third is the deployment of resources to support teaching and learning. Delegated budgets impact on the first two processes: budgeting and real resource management. The latter can be subdivided into those concerned with the 'operational activities', such as the physical environment of the school and general administration, and those which are associated more directly with teaching, such as the acquisition of books, materials and equipment, and the recruitment, deployment and development of staff. Much of what concerns schools in operating delegated budgets does not impinge directly on improving learning unless the school makes a conscious effort to do this.

Efficiency, productivity and effectiveness

If local management can improve school efficiency and effectiveness, then it must do so via the processes that determine the way financial and real inputs are converted into educational activities and thus into school outputs. Using the input–output model of the school, it is now possible to re-examine and further clarify the concepts of efficiency and effectiveness in order to establish the ways in which local management might achieve its intended effects.

Efficiency and productivity are distinct but related concepts. Productivity is the relationship between the amount of output produced and the amount of inputs used. The average product of a single input or factor of production is simply the physical amount of output produced divided by the physical quantity of the input used. So, for example, the measure of the average product of teachers at a school in these terms would be the total value-added GCSE examination scores of all students divided by the full-time equivalent number of teachers. Productivity increases over time when the average product of the factor of production rises. The average product of one factor of production (e.g. labour) can usually be increased by raising the quantity of other factors of production (e.g. capital) with which the labour input works. Higher output per head of the labour force, and with this higher living standards, have been achieved over the centuries by increasing the quantity and quality of capital per unit of labour. Education, like some other service industries, has not been able as yet to raise teacher productivity significantly with the use of capital. The only exception is probably distance education. However, because of the difficulty of comparing educational standards over time, it is extremely difficult to ascertain whether productivity has improved. In the absence of easily available output measures in education, it is common practice, particularly of government agencies, to suppose that productivity has risen in education when the number of students per teacher increases. This is only an increase in productivity if the total educational output (e.g. total exam grade scores) per teacher time on the job rises.

The increase in the productivity of a single input may not mean an overall rise in productivity if it is due to a substantial increase in other inputs. Total factor productivity is a better measure of overall productivity, as it is the value of output divided by the value of all inputs used in production. The causes of increases in total factor productivity over time are improvements in technical knowledge, which is then embodied in more productive capital and production processes, and improvements in the organization of production.

I have elaborated the concept of productivity in order to distinguish productivity from efficiency. Efficiency is achieved when a given quantity of output is produced at minimum cost. Economists separate efficiency into two components, which I have shown using the standard diagram in the Appendix to this chapter. The first component is technical efficiency: this is the relationship between the volume of physical inputs used and the resulting quantity of output. If there are two inputs (e.g. capital and labour) needed to produce a particular good, and there are several production methods each using different quantities of the two inputs to produce a given quantity of output, then any method which uses the minimum quantity of one input for a given quantity of the other input is technically efficient. Technical efficiency thus exists if it is impossible to reduce the amount of one input and keep output constant without using more of some other type of input. If there are a number of different technically efficient methods of production, then it is possible to use less of one input and substitute it for more of the other input and still produce the same quantity of output. The production function is the name given to all the combinations of the different types of inputs which are technically efficient.

But which of all the technically efficient production methods are the cheapest to use depends on the relative price of the inputs. The cost-efficient production method is the one which produces a given quantity of output at least cost. (Alternatively, it is the production method which produces the most output for a given total monetary cost.) For example, a number of different combinations of learning materials per student and teacher time per student could produce the equivalent amount of learning. The cost-efficient method is the one which costs least given the price of learning materials and the salaries of teachers. If relative factor prices change, even though the available production methods remain unchanged, the cost-efficient combination of inputs will change. Efficiency is always judged relative to a standard. If production is cost-efficient, then it is not possible – with the current state of technical knowledge – to reduce the cost per unit produced by decreasing the amount of one input and replacing it with more of some other input. If an organization is inefficient, then it can reduce unit costs by cutting down on some of its inputs or by changing its method of production (i.e. using inputs in a different combination). For example, if a school reduces its expenditure on staff by running larger classes (with teachers each working the same number of hours but supported by more classroom assistants or more clerical back-up) without reducing students' learning, then it has become more cost-efficient. However, if the larger classes mean that teachers are working longer hours for the same pay because of the extra preparation and marking done at home, then teacher productivity per hour worked has fallen, even though output per pound spent on staff salaries has risen. In this example, the school may appear to have become more cost-effective when the costs taken into account are restricted to those which are financial, but this is not so when the actual quantity of resources used to produce the output is assessed.

Ultimately, the issue of efficiency cannot be separated from the distribution of costs and benefits, since making working practices more productive or more efficient often implies increasing work effort or changing working practices. The factors contributing to organizations not using the most efficient production techniques and quantities of input are all labelled under the term 'x-inefficiency' (Leibenstein 1966). These factors include employees slacking or using their time to pursue other objectives than the ones desired by the organization's owners or chief stakeholders (shareholders in the case of firms, and parents, taxpayers and politicians in the case of schools). Since making the organization more efficient by reducing slack or redirecting energies may diminish employees' job satisfaction, the pursuit of increased productivity and efficiency is not a value-free activity. Whether one approves of a particular efficiency drive or not depends on one's values and interests. There is a moral presumption that employees should endeavour to work efficiently and productively in return for the payment received, as well as a potentially conflicting moral judgement that employees should not be exploited.

Local management provides schools with incentives and opportunities to improve efficiency and productivity in a number of ways. An example of a technical source of efficiency is maintaining a given room temperature through substituting insulation for energy consumption. This is cost-efficient if the reduction in expenditure on heating over a number of years is greater than the cost of the insulation and alternative rate of interest which the money invested in insulation could have earned if invested in financial assets. Inefficiency due to slack can be eliminated by more careful monitoring in order, say, to stop heating an empty building. These are both examples of a more efficient use of resources in producing operating services. Moving further along the transformation process, schools can make choices between different input mixes to produce a given set of educational activities. For example, the history department could decide to shift spending from books to videos. However, the efficient combination of resources is not the one that produces the cheapest set of lessons, since this is an intermediate educational activity; it is the combination which produces the highest learning output for a given expenditure of money.

As well as finding the most efficient mix of resources for producing a given educational activity (e.g. national curriculum history to year 7), schools also have some choice over the mix of educational activities they produce. Different mixes may be more or less effective in achieving the ultimate educational objectives. For instance, it might be the case that an increase in the amount of time spent on English or on a course on problem-solving would improve test and examination results across a range of subjects. In this case, the output–input measure indicates improved efficiency through changing the mix of activities, rather than changing the mix of staff and materials used to produce a given set of activities.

If a change in the mix of activities leads to a demonstrable improvement in educational outputs without a parallel increase in the physical quantity of resources, then school productivity has unambiguously increased. If this increase in educational output involves no increase in total expenditure (i.e. total costs), then efficiency has also increased. In the earlier examples of more efficient ways of using resources to produce operating services, there is no improvement in total educational output unless the resources 'saved' through the more efficient production of operating services are used to improve educational activities, which in turn increase educational output. Assuming a given amount of expenditure, the school's total educational output could increase either by finding a more productive mix of activities or by producing more educational activities using resources saved from the more efficient management of operating services. A school could increase its operating services' efficiency, but not end up spending the money thus saved in ways which raised the total output of the school. In this case, overall educational productivity would not have increased. Alternatively, a school which responded to a budget cut by managing its operating services more efficiently and used the money saved in this way to sustain its previous level of educational output would be more efficient overall, more productive and provide better value for money, but it would not have increased its total educational output.

The problem facing teachers and school managers in making resource allocation decisions, especially those concerning the most efficient and productive mix of learning resources and educational activities, is the absence of a well-specified technical knowledge base which gives a 'blueprint' of efficient methods. Knowledge about what are efficient production methods in education has been particularly elusive. In the 1960s and 1970s – in the white heat of the new quantitative techniques – education economists sought to find empirical estimates of education production functions (i.e. efficient combinations of inputs), but largely failed. In a comprehensive survey of the literature, Hanushek (1986: 1162) concluded:

> The results are startlingly consistent in finding no strong evidence that teacher–student ratios, teacher education, or teacher experience have an expected positive effect on student achievement. According to the available evidence, one cannot be confident that hiring more educated teachers or having smaller classes will improve student performance . . .
>
> There appears to be no strong or systematic relationship between school expenditures and student performance.

However, Hanushek also pointed out that the evidence does show that individual schools and teachers have a significant impact on student performance, a finding supported by the effective schools literature, where much greater attention is paid to school processes than in education production function studies (Rutter *et al.* 1979; Purkey and Smith 1983; Mortimore *et al.* 1988; Reynolds 1992; Willms 1992). Writing from the classroom research perspective, Good (1989: 4–5) summarizes the state of knowledge about teaching:

> We know much more about the relation between teacher behaviour and student achievement than we did 20 years ago . . . It is important to realise that knowledge about classroom instruction is interactive and must be integrated with other knowledge to be useful (i.e. content knowledge, knowledge of students, etc.). Teaching success is not defined by a few broad variables but rather many aspects of instructional process and curriculum must be co-ordinated if classroom learning is to be productive.

The nature of schools' production technology is central to understanding how local management might affect schools' productivity and efficiency. If it is the case that the search for a clearly specified input–output relationship is doomed to failure because of the essentially ambiguous and subjective nature of the educative process as depicted by writers such as Weick (1976) and Greenfield and Ribbins (1993), then there are two lines of argument which can be pursued with respect to local management. One is that it will not impinge on these processes because they are not amenable to improvement through manipulating inputs in relation to specified outputs. The other is that the education production function is still meaningful as a relationship between inputs and resulting outputs, but that its exact form is highly specific to the local context. It is discovered by practitioners through personal experience and by the application of individual specific skills. The search for efficiency and effectiveness then depends on teachers' professional skill in making appropriate selections from a repertoire of possibilities. If knowledge about efficient and effective means–ends relationships has to be discovered by teachers in their specific contexts rather than be given to them by some generalizable technical blueprint, then local management may still work by providing greater stimulus to discover and apply professional knowledge about input–output relationships. Teachers can build up and disseminate their own knowledge of efficient means–end relationships through formal evaluation of their own practice. An example of this is Hughes' demonstration of the greater effectiveness of flexible learning over traditional methods for teaching GCSE geography (O'Connor 1993).

Human relations

The dependence of efficiency improvements and productivity increases on local and professional knowledge underlines the importance of the human relations domain of the open systems model. The external environment, technology and human relations elements interact. The technology of the productive process greatly influences human interactions, while certain technologies may be preferred for cultural reasons. For example, the dominant technology of schools whereby single teachers work on their own with a class of children breeds teacher isolation as the downside of professional autonomy. This technology is a major factor in creating the loose-coupling between different aspects of the school which Weick (1976) sees as the key characteristic of educational organizations, such as the often observed discrepancy between the policies headteachers espouse and what actually occurs in the classroom. The technology of secondary school teaching takes the form of specialist, separate departments, which means that a relatively large number of pupils are required for cost-efficiency. This breeds a different culture to the smaller primary school in which teachers are generalists and, until the impact of LMS and the national curriculum, management was usually undertaken almost entirely by the headteacher. Secondary schools are typically bureaucratically organized with a line management structure emanating from headteacher to deputy heads, and thence to heads of subject departments and pastoral units.

The open systems model and its variant, contingency theory, also focus on determinate interrelationships between the characteristics of the environment, the technology of the production process and the way human relations are conducted within the organization. The contingency approach to organizational structure maintains that the degree of complexity and uncertainty which characterize an organization's environment determine the kind of organizational structure required for effective performance. Organizational structure is defined by Butler (1991) as 'the enduring set of decision rules provided by an organization'. The structure:

> provides capacity for decision making by setting the degree of elasticity of decision rules: fuzzy structures lead to high decision making capacity; crisp structures lead to low decision making capacity; a fuzzy structure will provide a great deal of elasticity on variables such as who does what job, the extent to which operating procedures can be adapted to varying situations, who can get involved in decisions, who has influence, who reports to whom, how participants get rewarded, the amount of analysis done during decision making . . . crisp structures will provide a low degree of elasticity on the preceding variables.
>
> (Butler 1991: 12)

Thus bureaucratic structures are crisp and collegial ones fuzzy. It is now widely argued that bureaucratic management structures are unsuited to organizations which operate in changing and uncertain environments, since the organization needs to be responsive both in adapting itself and seeking to change elements in the environment in ways favourable to itself. We have seen that local management has led to a more demanding and uncertain environment for schools in order, it is claimed, to stimulate improved performance. The human relations element of the open systems model is the part where the major adjustments must be made, using the new flexibilities of internal resource management, if the intended improvements to efficiency, responsiveness and effectiveness are to occur.

The hypothesis that schools' organizational characteristics are the product of their institutional settings is the premise upon which Chubb and Moe (1990) construct their libertarian polemic in favour of school autonomy. State schools being 'institutions of direct democratic control discourage the emergence of coherent, sharply led, academically ambitious, professionally grounded, team-like organisations' (p. 141). Chubb and Moe measure school effectiveness as student progress in standardized tests in maths, science and English language over the two last years of high school. They also measure aspects of school organization from survey data of teachers and principals. These data are used to construct an index of ten indicators covering school goals, leadership, personnel, and management and teacher practices. Chubb and Moe report that after student ability, school organization factors are the most important determinants of student progress. The organizational factors associated with effective outcomes are: goal clarity; focus on academic skills and personal growth, rather than a focus on basic skills and good work habits; principals concerned with educational leadership, rather than career advancement; and principals encouraging the involvement of teachers in policy and planning. These factors are similar to those found to be associated with school effectiveness in other studies. Chubb and Moe conclude that 'low performance schools look less like professional teams and more like bureaucratic agencies' (p. 91). They report further tests to support the claim that effectively organized schools have more decision-making autonomy compared with ineffectively organized ones. An interesting finding is that economic resources, including teacher pay and pupil–teacher ratios, are less significant than the organizational variables. The point in summarizing the Chubb and Moe study is not to lend credence to the statistical results, since student ability explains 70 per cent of the test score compared with the 5 per cent contributed by the other variables. Rather, it is to provide examples of the organizational variables which are associated with school effectiveness in many studies but which in this one are linked explicitly to autonomous decision-making. A notable aspect of the Chubb and Moe study is that 'ineffectively organised' schools and 'low performing' schools tended to be situated in low-income urban areas. This leads to their conclusion that strong bureaucratic control by districts has been exerted in response to the problems associated with socially disadvantaged students. This suggests that relatively autonomous schools are more likely to arise in more favourable social settings, while schools in socially disadvantaged areas need more support from external agencies. This might imply that any positive impact of school-based management on school effectiveness depends on the social context of the school.

Research methodologies for detecting the effects of local management

The purpose of examining the different sequences in the school production process is to demonstrate the formidable problems in seeking to confirm or reject the hypotheses that local management will improve schools' efficiency, productivity and effectiveness. To test these hypotheses in the UK context using positivist methods, such as those employed by Chubb and Moe, requires data on measures of outputs and inputs over a number of years both before and after the introduction of local management. This involves making assumptions as to what constitutes an increase in school outputs. In addition, one would need to specify an explanatory model in which the effects of the introduction of the national curriculum on the mix of activities and resulting outputs could be separated out from the effects of the changes in decision-making brought about by local management. This is a very tall order. Nor is such a positivist research design, even if it could be executed, without its problems. A major drawback is its 'black box' treatment of the decision-making processes. As illustrated in the input–output model in Fig. 3.1, local management is primarily a change in the way schools receive their resources and can allocate them: it is a change in the first stage of the sequence of transformations that make up the school production process. Yet the impact on school output is detected, if at all, at the final stage of the production process. If local management of resources is to impact on school outputs, then budget-setting and resource management must be coupled to decisions about how school objectives are delivered by the educational activities undertaken and how these activities are resourced.

If educational organizations are loosely coupled systems (Weick 1976), then the linkage between budget management, educational activities and school outputs will be non-existent or weak. Decision-making in the context of ambiguity about organizational ends and means is, following Cohen and March (1974), characterized as 'garbage can'. Solutions and problems are not logically attached to each other through a process of rational decision-making, but become haphazardly linked according to the micro-political interactions of those who happen to be involved in a particular decision and are keen to promote solutions which benefit them. There is, therefore, a strong presumption that if local management is to improve efficiency and effectiveness, schools must operate rational decision-making processes. Rational decision-making requires the articulation of clear organizational goals and priorities, information on the costs and benefits of alternative means of attaining those goals, and the selection of the courses of action which best deliver the prioritized goals. In terms of Fig. 3.1, this requires that the planning process moves from right to left – that is, from output objectives to the educational activities which deliver these objectives, and to the allocation of resources which is most efficient in producing the planned activities. It is significant that criticisms of local management, particularly from a classroom teacher perspective, fail to see any linkage between budget management and what goes on in the classroom. The title of one such article from the 'critical theory' school (Broadbent et al. 1992) – 'It's a long way from teaching Susan to read' – captures well this apparent lack of coupling.

Whereas ambiguity and garbage-can decision-making – and, to some extent, loose coupling – are usually interpreted as undesirable features, fuzzy structures are regarded as effective for organizations characterized by complexity and uncertainty, including uncertainty about the production technology as well as about the task environment. However, an effective linkage between school outputs, educational activities and budget decision-making may well be difficult to detect from a superficial study of schools, since a fuzzy structure is more difficult for an outsider to understand and assess than a tightly specified bureaucratic structure operating rational decision-making with measured objectives and outputs. Assessing local management by focusing only on initial inputs and final outputs would miss the intermediate decision-making capacity, which must be affected by local management if it is to have the desired impact on efficiency and effectiveness. A naturalist methodology for assessing the impact of local management is therefore both feasible and provides insights into how local management affects schools' decision-making capacity (Levačić 1990b).

However, without added value measures of school output, no definitive conclusion can be reached of the impact on school effectiveness of local management or of different ways of internalizing it. This is why the concept of cost-efficiency is useful, because it enables one to make a judgement about efficiency despite being unable to measure output, though such a judgement does depend on the assumption that output has not declined as a result of local management. With the implementation of local management, there has been a new emphasis in official quarters (e.g. Audit Commission 1993; OFSTED 1993a, 1994) on the criteria of efficiency and effectiveness of resource use. In the absence of knowledge of input–output measures, the OFSTED criteria used for assessing efficiency and effectiveness of resource use are process indicators, in particular whether a rational decision-making process has been used by school managers.

Another problem in assessing the effects of local management is that these have to be separated from the effects of changes in the real value of schools' budgets that are due to changes in the LEA's education budget. In studying the impact of local management, one is concerned with the effects of a different way of allocating resources. The impact of different levels of the total school budget due to central and local government policies with respect to local government expenditure are distinct from the effects of local management as a different organizational design for the school system.

Conclusions

An open systems input–output model of the school shows that for local management to have an impact on the quality of education, it must impinge on the sequence of stages from the initial inflow of financial resources into the school to the intermediate production of educational activities and their consequent multiple outputs and outcomes. Given the absence of a well-specified and generalizable production function, teachers' and managers' judgements about how to allocate resources to promote school effectiveness are qualitative and highly dependent on the application of contextualized professional knowledge and values. This state of affairs, as well as the difficulty of gathering input–output data for schools, makes it extremely difficult to use input–output measures of school efficiency and effectiveness in assessing the impact of local management or the relative success of schools at exploiting its possibilities. Therefore, an assessment of local management needs to involve an examination of the processes by which schools manage their resources and the degree of linkage these processes achieve between budgeting, the curriculum and final outputs. Drawing on the research literature on the relationship between school effectiveness, organizational and cultural factors suggests a number of key questions which need to be addressed in order to assess the likely impact of local management on school effectiveness. These questions concern whether local management promotes:

- greater goal clarity concerning the educational purposes of the school;
- a more integrated school culture where these goals motivate most staff;
- more effective leadership;
- more collaborative decision-making;
- more highly motivated professionally oriented teams;
- a greater capacity to respond to the needs of external stakeholders;
- a greater capacity for organizational learning, in particular in relation to improving educational productivity.

Clearly, these questions are not separate but are closely interrelated. They are also complex questions which are not easy to answer. I raise them in order to make clear the issues which need to be addressed rather than to promise that I can answer them in the remaining chapters.

Contingency theory suggests that the complexity and uncertainty of schools' task environment and the ambiguity of their technology make fuzzy rather than crisp organizational structures more effective. However, fuzzy structures are more complex to observe and understand than crisp ones, which makes it all the more difficult to assess how organizational structures have adapted to local management and to what extent they contribute to the efficient and effective use of resources. Nevertheless, a fuzzy structure must still ensure that for local management to achieve the aims intended for it, the sequential stages of the production process must be linked so that decisions on how to utilize resources are closely informed by judgements on how different patterns of resource use would contribute to the school's aims and objectives.[3] This means that forms of rational decision-making are required whereby alternatives are considered and selected in accordance with how well they are judged to serve the school's aims and objectives. A notable development since the inception of local management has been the advocacy both by official bodies and by some educationalists of more rationally based approaches to decision-making, in particular school development planning. The implications of local management for normative models of financial and resource management are considered in the next chapter.

Appendix: Distinction between technical and price efficiency

The definitions of technical and price efficiency can be explained with respect to a single good, good A, which is assumed to be produced using just two factors of production, capital and labour.

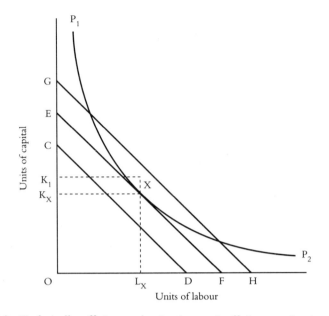

Figure 3.2 Technically efficient and price (or cost) efficient production

In Fig. 3.2, units of capital are measured along the vertical axis and units of labour along the horizontal axis. Good A can be produced using various combinations of labour and capital. The curve P_1P_2 shows the different combinations of units of capital and units of labour required to produce a given amount of good A, say 100 units. This curve is known as an iso-product curve, since output at 100 units of good A is the same all along it. Points to the left of curve P_1P_2 represent amounts of capital and labour which produce less than 100 units of good A, and points to the right represent larger quantities of labour and capital producing more than 100 units of good A. All points along curve P_1P_2 are technically efficient. Take any point on curve P_1P_2, such as point X; it is not possible to reduce the amount of labour and still produce 100 units of good A. One can only produce 100 units with less labour by using more capital and thus moving up P_1P_2 to the left. Similarly, it is impossible to use less capital to produce 100 units of A without using more labour. If a firm were using K_1 units of capital and L_X units of labour to produce 100 units of good A, then it would be technically inefficient. It could reduce its capital inputs to K_X and still produce 100 units of good A. Thus production is defined to be technically efficient when it is impossible to reduce the amount of one input used and keep the same level of production without increasing the amount used of some other input.

This definition of technical efficiency assumes a given level of technical knowledge. All the different combinations of labour and capital along the iso-product curve represent the current state of known technology. If technical knowledge changes and improves the productivity of capital or of labour, then this can be represented by the iso-product curve for each level of output shifting down to the left. As a result of improvements in technical knowledge, the same amount of output can be produced by fewer units of labour and capital.

A firm can therefore become technically efficient by finding out from existing technical knowledge what are the most productive input combinations to use. A firm is dynamically efficient if it improves the current state of technical knowledge and thus increases the productivity of its operations.

The third dimension of efficiency relates to the price or cost of inputs. The price-efficient method of production is a technically efficient method which also costs the least. In Fig. 3.2, the parallel straight lines CD, EF and GH show the different amounts of capital and labour which can be bought with different amounts of money for a given relative price of capital and labour. Line CD, for example, shows a constant total cost spent on different quantities of labour and capital. All the money could be spent on OC of capital and no labour, or OD labour and no capital, or all combinations of both labour and capital in between. Line EF shows a greater total cost than CD, hence more labour and capital can be purchased. The total cost along GH is greater still. The relative price of capital and labour determines the slope of the total cost line. Hence the three total cost lines all have the same relative price of labour and capital. In Fig. 3.2, the price-efficient method of production for 100 units of good A requires L_X units of labour and K_X units of capital. This combination is given by point X on the iso-product curve where it is tangent with the total cost line EF. Any total cost line below EF is technically infeasible (i.e. 100 units of A cannot be produced for this cost), whereas any total cost line to the right of EF, such as GH, means higher costs for 100 units of output. Thus point X on the iso-product curve gives the price-efficient combination of labour and capital – that is, K_X and L_X, respectively.

If the relative price of labour in terms of capital changed, then the slope of the total cost lines would change. For instance, if capital became cheaper relative to labour, then the slope of the total cost lines would become steeper. The point of tangency between the total cost line and the iso-product curve would then lie to the left of point X. Price- (or cost-) efficient production would require more capital and less labour: the input which becomes cheaper is substituted for the one which is now relatively more expensive.

Economic theory therefore distinguishes three sources of efficiency:

1 Selecting from a given state of technical knowledge input mixes which are technically efficient.
2 Choosing that combination of inputs which, for a given output, minimize total costs; or which maximize output for a given cost.

3 Innovation or improving technical knowledge so that new and more productive production methods become available or new products are created which satisfy consumer wants better.

The first and third sources are improvements in productivity. In relation to the local management of schools, technical efficiency involves finding more efficient resource mixes to produce given educational activities, innovation relates to finding new resource mixes or new educational activities which increase the productivity of the schooling process, while price efficiency concerns finding cheaper combinations or mixes of inputs.

Normative models for local management

Introduction

An official leitmotif of local management is the promotion of rational management processes and techniques. These, as we saw in Chapter 3, can be deduced from an input–output model of the organization, to be necessary for securing an efficient and effective allocation of resources. The inception of local management in the UK was accompanied by several official reports and training manuals advocating rational management processes (e.g. Coopers and Lybrand 1988; The LMS Initiative 1988; DES 1991b), though the term 'rational model' is not itself used in such literature. The drive towards instilling economic rationality in school management was given a substantial boost by enshrining it in legislation. The Education Act (Schools) 1992,[1] which set up the Office for Standards in Education (OFSTED), stipulated that inspectors must report on 'whether the financial resources made available to the school are managed efficiently'.

The official blueprint for local management was set out in an incisive and influential management consultancy report (Coopers and Lybrand 1988). The report emphasized that local management required a significant cultural change in schools, thus affecting their management functions and processes:

> The largest single change for schools will be in the attitude and culture reflecting a shift from an environment in which centrally determined programmes are administered locally to one in which the provision for education is locally managed. The differences between administration and management are considerable and necessitate a change in role for staff, head teachers and governors.
>
> (Coopers and Lybrand 1988: 34)

The model of good management practice contained in the Coopers and Lybrand report is essentially a rational one. It advocates a system for allocating resources which is directed at the explicit achievement of institutional objectives. This requires clarity in the specification of objectives, gathering and analysing information on alternative ways of attaining the objectives, evaluating the alternatives and selecting those actions judged most likely to maximize achievement of the objectives.

What is meant by rational decision-making?

The rational decision-making process is distinguished from other models of decision-making because it follows a sequence of three distinct but inter-related stages:

1 Agreeing and articulating organizational aims and objectives and determining priorities among the objectives.
2 Collecting, analysing and evaluating information on different courses of action. This involves learning from past actions by monitoring and evaluating them. This information together with other data, such as that from environmental scanning, is used to make conjectures about the future consequences of alternative courses of action.
3 Selection of the best set of actions which are judged to be most likely to maximize achievement of the objectives.

There is a long and well-honed debate in the management and economics literature, originating in Simon (1947), on whether the rational model of decision-making is far too idealized to be of any use in practice. Many of those who consider that organizations do not or cannot act rationally define rational behaviour in such a demanding way that it is clearly impracticable. The mathematical specification of rational behaviour in economic theory assumes that the organization can define its objectives in terms of a utility function. Organizational utility depends on the set of objectives, and the organization's preference ranking of the different objectives is specified as a mathematical formula. Organizational utility is then assumed to be maximized within the constraints facing the organization (e.g. its budget). Thus the organization chooses to pursue each of its various objectives to the degree which ensures utility maximization. A number of objections have been raised to the mathematical model of rational behaviour applied to organizations or communities. Within the education management literature, the most notable objections have been those of Greenfield (1989), who argues that it is impossible for an organization to have objectives because organizations do not exist outside the mental perceptions of the people who constitute them.[2]

My own view is that if the debate between rational and non-rational positions is to be at all meaningful, rather than a predetermined victory for the non-rationalists, then the definition of what constitutes rational decision-making in organizational contexts should be somewhat fuzzy and should not have to meet the requirements of mathematical specification in terms of a utility function. If this argument is accepted, then the issue of whether objectives are actually defined by an organization becomes a matter of judging the empirical evidence for this in specific organizational contexts. Evidence is then sought as to whether the organization's management have a common agreed set of aims and objectives and a common priority ranking for them and whether these are known and worked towards by the rest of the organization.

A fuzzy definition of rational decision-making encompasses Simon's concept of bounded rationality – that is, the limitations on decision-makers' intellectual capacities for processing information. Not all the possible relevant information has to be considered. Instead, all the second stage of the rational decision process requires is some consideration of alternative courses of action in terms of their likely impact on organizational objectives. Similarly, stage three of a practicable rational model does not require maximizing organizational utility. It is sufficient to have a ranking of some alternative courses of action in relation to their likely contribution to the organization's prioritized objectives. Rational decision-making requires selection of those actions which are judged more likely than the alternatives to lead to the achievement of the organization's goals. Such a fuzzy definition of rationality still leaves plenty of scope for disconfirmation of the hypothesis in actual organizational settings. I therefore take the current advocacy of rational management processes for schools to be concerned with the fuzzy variant. Judgements are made about whether it operates in any particular school context by aligning observations of actual practice against the criteria for rational decision-making set out above.

Rational decision-making for financial and resource management in schools

A standard rational approach to financial management is divided into four sequential stages. The first stage is the acquisition of resources. In schools, the main source of finance is the budget share or annual maintenance grant (for grant-maintained schools) determined by the total amount of budget the funding authority has to dispose of and by the funding formula which allocates that total among schools. As the open systems model emphasizes, the acquisition of budget is directly linked to pupil numbers and hence to the school's perceived performance as well as to the presence of rival providers. Local management has given schools the incentive to acquire further financial resources by selling services beyond the core of their required educational provision. They can rent out accommodation and equipment or earn marginal income from selling goods and services, such as software, training manuals, advisory services or by teaching adults.

The second stage of the financial management cycle is allocating resources and planning the budget. If this is to be done rationally, then it must follow the phases of goal definition, analysing alternative actions and selecting those best at delivering the goals and objectives. The work of preparing a budget is essentially one of planning. In a rational approach, the budget is the financial expression of institutional plans for relating resource inputs to the production of educational activities and the consequent achievement of school aims and objectives. A crucial constraint on budget planning is that schools are not allowed to budget for a deficit. Any planned expenditure for the next year in excess of current revenue must be financed out of accumulated reserves. The accounting packages used for setting up the budget do not permit a planned deficit, nor would a local education authority (LEA) approve it. This does not stop a school from covertly budgeting for a deficit by deliberately underestimating its expenditures, though proper LEA monitoring would prevent this.

The third stage of the budgetary cycle is implementation. This requires financial recording and reporting to provide information for monitoring the actual income and expenditure as the financial year unfolds against what was planned and expected in each month. These processes ensure that financial control is exercised, that spending occurs only on authorized items and that the budget keeps to plan. If this is not occurring, then deliberate changes are approved and made either to increase or reduce spending as necessary. One major flexibility of local management is the ability to vire (move) money between different budget heads. A key aspect of local management is that these financial control tasks were moved from the LEAs to schools. By and large these are administrative tasks (in the Coopers and Lybrand usage of the term) necessary to support management decision-making about how to use resources. The previous system of centralized accounting had obvious advantages of economies of scale and of ensuring financial probity and financial control. The offsetting disadvantage was inefficiency, in that central accountants had neither the local information nor the incentives to manage schools' resources cost-effectively.

The fourth stage of the financial management cycle is an evaluation of the implementation of budget plans to discover the extent to which the intended objectives were achieved, thus to providing improved information for the next round of budget decision-making.

Each financial year's budget goes through these sequences, though in a non-rational world the last one of evaluation could be omitted entirely. A school operating rational procedures would at any moment in time be engaged in a number of these stages of the budget life-cycle for budgets of different financial years. The phase of resource acquisition is continually being attended to as the school endeavours to satisfy its stakeholders. The school will always be in the implementation stage of the current financial year's budget. A rationally managed school will be planning next year's budget for a number of months before the start of the new financial year, and also outlining financial plans further ahead if it is engaged in longer-term planning. Part of this planning process will utilize information gathered from the evaluation of past and current plans and policies. In practice, the minimum a school needs to do is financial recording and reporting and the preparation of a budget for the start of the new financial year. The other processes of planning and evaluating budgets in relation to educational objectives are optional add-ons, which are adopted by rationally managed schools.

The efficiency of the school as a criterion for public accountability

The expectation that resource management should accord with the rational decision-making model is implicit in the OFSTED criteria for reporting on the 'efficiency of the school'. Four evaluative criteria are set out for this in the 'Framework for the Inspection of Schools' (OFSTED 1994: Part 4, pp. 19–20):

1 The standard of financial management and planning.
2 The efficiency and effectiveness with which staff, learning resources and accommodation are deployed to attain the school's aims and objectives and to match its priorities.
3 The effectiveness of financial control procedures.
4 Any steps taken by the school to evaluate its cost-effectiveness.

Each of these is further elaborated by the instruction that the inspection report should include:

Criterion 1: an evaluation of the strategic management of the resources available to the school; this should assess the role of the governing body and appropriate staff, the quality of planning, the extent to which budget-setting relates to the school's educational objectives and its priorities expressed through the school development plan.
Criterion 2: a judgement of the efficiency with which resources, i.e. money, staff, time, accommodation and resources for learning are used.
Criterion 3: an assessment of financial control, including the steps which the school has taken in response to the most recent auditor's report.
Criterion 4: reference to any measures the school takes to evaluate its cost-effectiveness.

Under the first criterion, inspectors seek to find evidence of formal processes of rational planning in which the budget is determined so as to explicitly deliver educational objectives. This expectation is further elaborated in a supporting paper on Financial Management in the *Handbook for the Inspection of Schools*. Here a direct link is drawn between the type of evidence sought and the definition of effective financial management occurring when 'governing bodies and head teachers plan their use of resources to maximum effect in accordance with national and local needs and priorities, making schools more responsive to parents, pupils, the local community and employers' (OFSTED 1993a: Part 5, p. 49).[3] A description of what constitutes effective practice for financial planning is given.

14 The majority of schools have a corporate school development plan. Ideally this is a plan covering at least three years, which is reviewed and updated at least once a year. Frequently such plans are based on a curriculum audit which is an analysis of the school's existing provision in relation to the school's aims and objectives and to local and national policies for education.

15 The introduction and implementation of the National Curriculum together with arrangements for assessment, examination and accreditation, should feature in development plans. An effective plan is based on a sound understanding of the quality and appropriateness of the school's existing provision and a clear view of what needs to be done in the future. Priorities for action should be established, together with a strategy which includes staffing and resource requirements, a time scale and clear goals and targets.

16 Implementation of a development strategy should be followed by a review and modification of the forward plan in the light of what has been achieved.

17 This planning process should be allied to budget planning. In the efficient school, the costs of major programmes and activities will be known. Priorities will be identified for development and for areas where savings can be made. The school carries out its developments in order of priority. If it receives additional funding it knows where to apply this to achieve the best results in accordance with predetermined priorities. If cuts are required, rational decisions may be taken accordingly.

18 Allocation of the budget should reflect both the existing programmes to which the school is committed and the priorities displayed in the school development plan. An efficient school will keep its programmes under review and will question whether they are cost-effective. Good financial management strives to make the best use of resources available. This is often difficult when the size of the budget is subject to a high degree of uncertainty and may be notified to the school very late. Schools may have indicative allocations to work on in advance of the final budget settlement. Efficient schools will also try to make accurate estimates of their future pupil intakes.

30 An efficient school will have given some thought to underpinning its development goals with quantitative indicators. Such indicators may relate to outcomes, processes or inputs. Inspectors should report on any procedures adopted by the school to measure gains in pupils' attainment (value added) or achievements in terms of input costs (value for money).

The framework for inspection also focuses on financial control procedures and on judging the quality of resource management through evidence of available resource inputs and their utilization. It is clearly difficult to determine the extent to which any deficiency in the availability of resources is due to inefficient decision-making as opposed to inadequate funding. This is done, to the extent that it is, by spotting discrepancies between different year groups and classes, where some are apparently more favourably resourced than others. Thus inspection reports tend to be critical of small subject groups, particularly in the sixth-form. Inspectors are also required to make an overall value-for-money judgement, whereby they attempt an aggregate judgemental evaluation of the educational outputs of the school in relation to its inputs:

In addition there should be a summative assessment of the value for money provided by the school; this should comment in particular where value for money is demonstrably good or poor in terms of the quality, standards, efficiency and effectiveness of the school in relation to the level of financial resources available to it.

(OFSTED 1993a: 20)

However, in the absence of adequate input–output measures for judging the efficiency and productivity of the school, the inspection framework is, understandably, left to emphasize evidence from processes, and interpreting evidence of rational decision-making processes as indicating efficiency. Two sets of processes are focused upon: those associated with the rational processes of the allocation and evaluation stages of the financial management cycle (OFSTED efficiency criteria 1 and 4 above), and those concerned with the traditional accounting concerns of financial probity, recording and reporting which are the subject of criteria 3. These criteria have been amplified in a number of official documents (OFSTED/Audit Commission 1993). I shall refer to criteria 1 and 4 as the efficiency and effectiveness criteria for allocation and criterion 3 as the financial probity and control criterion. As will be discussed in the next chapter, the research evidence shows quite conclusively that schools have adapted reasonably well to criterion 3 (financial control), but that the processes of rational decision-making required to satisfy criteria 1 and 4 are much less developed. Whether the processes listed under criteria 1 and 4 have to be operated in order to produce an efficient and effective allocation of resources (judged under criterion 2 and the overarching value-for-money judgement) is a fundamental question. The empirical evidence is not sufficient to attempt a satisfactory answer to the question, as we shall see in later chapters.

Management and development planning

In order to practise the rational approach to resource allocation and budgeting, schools need to connect decisions about the curriculum and its implications for staffing and other resources with decisions about the budget. The degree of integration required by the rational approach is new to schools. Schools can tack on the additional budgeting task – and the associated increase in the range of choices for staffing and physical resources – without fundamentally rethinking how decision-making processes and the information to support them need to be changed in order to ensure that budget-setting explicitly addresses educational aims and their related objectives. The responsibility given to governors for ensuring the effective management of the school means that the integration of educational activities and outputs with financial planning needs to be open and explicit if it is to be shared with governors. Integration between curriculum and finance, if it occurs intuitively and informally through the exercise of professional judgement by headteachers and senior staff, does not provide governors with the information they need in order to participate in making resource allocation decisions as opposed to just ratifying them.

School development planning

The proffered solution to improving the rationality of school management and promoting effectiveness in managing multiple and continuous changes is school development planning, alternatively called institutional planning. This was promoted early on in the implementation of local management by a Department of Education and Science (DES) funded project which resulted in published advice on school development planning being circulated to all schools (Hargreaves *et al.* 1989; DES 1991b). The particular emphasis of the school development planning movement is captured in Hargreaves and Hopkins' (1991: 3) definition of its purpose: 'to improve the quality of teaching and learning in a school through the successful management of innovation and change'. School development planning is promoted as the best way in which schools can cope effectively with the immense volume of change thrust upon them. The keys to effective coping are: (1) the empowerment of staff through participation in the process of developmental planning to secure commitment to the resulting decisions and to disperse responsibilities for managing the planned actions throughout the staff; and (2) a rational process of articulating school aims and objectives, auditing current practice against requirements and then determining a few priorities for development. When the process is complete, the development plan is finally written up as a booklet, which Hargreaves and Hopkins suggest should include:

- the aims of the school;
- a review of the previous year's plan;
- the proposed priorities and their time-scale;
- the justification of the priorities in the context of the school;
- how the plan draws together different aspects of planning;
- the methods of reporting outcomes;
- the resource implications.

However, this type of development plan does not provide a comprehensive set of educational objectives which can underpin the budget plan. This is hardly surprising, because this is not its main intent. While Hargreaves and Hopkins' model is commendably rational in setting out measurable outcomes of the plan (targets or success criteria) and specifying the resource implications, the proportion of the budget affected by development priorities, such as promoting home–school partnership or improving students' attendance,[4] is in fact quite small. Therefore, a school can have a very well implemented version of the Hargreaves–Hopkins model of development planning and yet fail to fulfil the OFSTED criteria of efficiency that the 'planning process should be allied to budget planning'.[5] The process of developmental planning can easily fail to be coupled with budget planning except to the extent that the budget contains a budget heading for development priorities, of the order of say £10,000 out of a budget of £3 million.

The basic reason for this lack of coupling between school development planning and financial planning is the distinction Hargreaves and Hopkins themselves make between maintenance and development. The maintenance tasks are those concerned with the day-to-day operation of the school, ensuring a smooth running organization which delivers a programme of teaching and learning largely unchanged from one year to the next. The bulk of the school's budget is spent on maintenance rather than on the year-by-year changes which are the consequence of development. Since an 'aim of the development plan is to move a new development into the school's maintenance activities' (Hargreaves and Hopkins 1991: 18), it is not surprising that it focuses on development priorities and does not involve formal rational planning for the totality of the school's maintenance, which is required for the rational approach to budgeting.

Management or corporate planning

Thus school development planning as advocated, and still more as implemented, is distinct from the concept of management planning, alternatively referred to as business or corporate planning – the latter term being

used by OFSTED (see quotation on p. 66). A management plan is comprehensive as it is concerned with the all the activities of the organization. It
is a concept derived directly from the business management literature,
whereas the origins of school development planning are more firmly rooted
within education. The original LMS circular 7/88 proclaimed an expectation,
not elaborated upon, that schools would engage in management planning:

> It will be for the governing body, together with the head teacher, to
> develop and carry out a *management plan* for their school within the
> general conditions and requirements of the LEA's scheme. In develop-
> ing such a plan, governing bodies will need to take account of the *full
> range of their responsibilities* for the management of schools, including
> those on curriculum and admissions set out in the Act.
>
> (DES 1988: 6, emphasis added)

The difference between school development planning and management
planning is well illustrated by contrasting Hargreaves and Hopkins' model
with that advocated in the training manual *Local Management in Schools: A
Practical Guide* produced by the LMS Initiative (a consortium of the Chartered Institute of Public Finance and Accountancy, the Local Government
Training Board and the Society of Education Officers). The latter sets out
a management plan as comprehending all maintenance aspects of the school
as well as development priorities, as is shown in the following extracts
(emphasis added):

Schools should identify their objectives *as a whole*. The areas to be
covered include:

- the desired aims and character of the school;
- curriculum development and priorities;
- extra curricular activities;
- performance targets (including numbers of pupils attracted and their
  activities).

The objectives will need to be set in the context of external factors . . .

The resulting objectives should be expressed in sufficient detail for
heads and staff, the governing body, the LEA and the public to be able
to know whether the school has been successful in moving towards
them . . .

Plans will be required for the activities designed to help achieve the
objectives. The process of planning consists of identifying all those
activities that would help achieve the objectives, adding up their cost
and realising that they cannot all be afforded. Planning really starts
with the need to determine priorities.

Plans should be derived from a base of thinking how the objectives can
best be achieved. Initial plans should specify:

- the actions to be carried out;
- their timing;
- the resources required (covering staff, equipment, materials and premises).

Plans should take account of any external constraints . . .

Many aspects of the plans are likely to stem from objectives associated with the curriculum. *Between them, however, the plans must span all the activities of the school . . .*

Many components will be concerned simply with maintaining existing activities, or improving them at the margin. The first call on available resources will be those activities to which the school is irrevocably committed . . .

It is essential that continuing activities are still recognised as part of the plan. In this way, all activities are justified each year and there is less chance of drifting into incrementalism – activities should not continue to be undertaken simply because they were done the previous year. This approach in its pure form is termed 'zero-based budgeting', a technique which requires the budget to be built up from scratch each year.

Planning cannot be considered in isolation from likely funding levels . . . The first task is then to decide approximately what can be afforded within the cash limit guideline. This will require a rough and ready idea of what activities cost, the best guidance for which is likely to be last year's expenditure on them. Outline plans should then be prepared. There may be an advantage in aiming for the aggregate cost of the first round of plans to exceed the guideline total by, say 5–10%; this device enables the school to take conscious decisions about priorities in refining its plans and reduces the risk of historical inertia.

(The LMS Initiative 1988: 4-1 to 4-4)

Thus the corporate school management plan is far more comprehensive and demanding in its information requirements than a school development plan of the Hargreaves–Hopkins model. However, it does explicitly relate the bulk of the school budget, which is for maintenance activities, to those activities and to the educational aims and objectives they serve. Such a process, because of the explicit documentation it generates, would enable governors to better appreciate and question the educational rationale underpinning the budget. However, such detailed planning is time-consuming and may for this reason, if for no other, remain confined to the senior management team and governors and thus not involve staff in the way envisaged in the Hargreaves–Hopkins model. This type of planning may be too bureaucratic and rigid for schools facing rapid and unexpected change, where the informal, emergent and oral style of strategic management would be more effective. Formalized and highly rational corporate planning in the private sector has been subject to considerable criticism, such as Minzberg's (1994) critique of strategic planning, and has fallen from favour.

Rational and non-rational approaches to budgeting

A rational approach to budgeting is thus set within a wider planning framework which attempts to link resource use to educational objectives and their associated activities. There are a number of distinct approaches to budgeting, which vary in their demand for information and extent of integration of budget planning with other management processes.

Programme budgeting

The rational approach to budget preparation involves evaluating costed alternative activities which are directed at fulfilling school objectives; the latter are carefully specified to be as measurable as possible and to relate clearly to qualitatively expressed overarching school aims. This type of budgeting is called objective budgeting (Levačić 1989) because it focuses on the costs of meeting the organization's objectives. These are translated into distinct programmes of activities which form the key units of analysis. Hence this form of budgeting is also known as *programme budgeting*. In schools the programmes are the major areas of study, such as the subject areas, and other separately identifiable activities, such as home–school links, records of achievement, administration or cleaning.

The programmes are costed by estimating the quantities of each type of input they require multiplied by the price or cost of each input type. A well-known example of programme budgeting at school level is the collaborative school management cycle of Caldwell and Spinks (1988; see also Beare *et al.* 1989). The financial planning outcome of this process is a total school budget derived from a matrix, with programmes represented in each row and each type of input recorded in columns. Table 4.1 gives an example of such a programme budgeting matrix. It shows a few sample programmes with hypothetical costs. The programmes are labelled in the extreme left-hand column and each is represented by a row across the matrix. Each input is recorded in a separate column. To keep the table small, only some programmes and inputs have been entered. The incompleteness of the table is indicated by blank rows and columns. The costs of a programme are derived from first specifying the number of physical units of each input required, then multiplying by the cost per unit of input. The total cost for each programme is the sum of the costs of all the input requirements and is entered in the far right-hand column. The total planned expenditure is the sum of all the individual programme costs, when all the school's activities have been accounted for in programmes. This will be the sum of all the entries in the far right-hand column. The collaborative school management cycle requires several iterations of the programme costings until the budget balances (i.e. the total planned expenditure can be afforded out of the school's income.) As recommended by the LMS Initiative, the initial excess of planned expenditure over available income forces a careful consideration of priorities. The total cost of each type of input used in all the programmes is arrived at by summing the amounts in each input column: these are entered in the bottom row. The sum of all the input costs (i.e. the costs appearing in the bottom 'total' row) will be the same as the sum of all the programme costs. Programme budgeting by being focused on programmes can more easily be coupled to the educational aims and objectives that the educational programmes are designed to deliver.

Subjective budgeting

In contrast, *subjective budgeting* focuses on the subjects of expenditure – that is, on the separate inputs which appear in each column heading of Table 4.1 – and does not consider programmes at all. In practice, school budgets are expressed in terms of the subjects of expenditure: teaching staff, non-teaching staff, books, materials and equipment, telephones, water, gas, electricity, etc. The accounting software used by schools is structured in terms of the subjects of expenditure not programmes, except in so far as departments can be budgeted for as separate cost centres, or certain budget heads like cleaning could be defined as programmes. The subjective structure of school financial accounts is driven by the requirement to pay and account for inputs and by the absence of income flows for programmes. For financial control purposes, the financial records need to be structured in terms of the planned, committed and actual payments for inputs.

In the commercial sector, there is a clear distinction between cost and works accounting for costing the product (or the educational activities in the school analogy); management accounting, which supports longer-term, forward-looking decision-making; and financial accounting, which is for financial control purposes. The objective budget matrix serves cost-accounting purposes by costing individual programmes, and supports organizational planning by providing management information on the relative costs of different programmes or different ways of delivering programmes so that these can be judged against their potential for achieving school objectives. Financial accounting information is supplied by the total expenditure in each input summed up in the bottom row of the matrix. School accounts are in practice structured according to subjects of expenditure, so as to give paramount importance to financial accounting and thus neglect the needs of cost and management accounting.

Zero-based budgeting

An alternative way of trying to ensure that the budget is allocated so as to deliver educational objectives, without necessarily using the elaborate

Table 4.1 A programme budgeting matrix

Programme	Inputs or subjects of expenditure							
	Teaching staff	Ancillary staff	INSET	Consultancy	Books and materials	Equipment	Other inputs	Total
Science	£130,000	£31,000	£500	£500	£2100	£1500	—	£180,000
Personal, social and health	£25,000	£2,000	£200	£0	£200	£0	—	£28,000
Other programmes	—	—	—	—	—	—	—	—
Administration	£80,500	£100,000	£0	£200	£2000	£2000	—	210,000
Other programmes	—	—	—	—	—	—	—	—
Total	1,350,000	250,000	2000	2000	70,000	10,000	—	2,100,000

structure of programme budgeting, is zero-based budgeting. This requires scrutinizing every area of expenditure by asking whether it is justified and what would be the impact of not having this expenditure at all or of cutting it by a given percentage. Each expenditure area is evaluated against the organization's or unit's prioritized objectives and ranked in order of importance (Hartley 1989). Those areas that can be afforded within the budget are funded. The advantages of zero-based budgeting are that it promotes change and the optimal utilization of resources. Its disadvantages are that it is time-consuming and potentially disturbing for staff who are made to feel insecure.

Incremental budgeting

Zero-based budgeting, as the National Association of Head Teachers (NAHT 1991) *Guide to School Management* notes, is not used much in schools. Incremental budgeting is considerably more popular, as it involves only making minor year-by-year adjustments to the budget. Last year's budget provides the basis for planning next year's budget, which is rolled forward with the same expenditure patterns as the previous year with an allowance for inflation. Only marginal changes are made, if either the projected total cannot be afforded or additional money is available. The attractions of incremental budgeting are that it requires far less information processing than zero-based or programme budgeting and is less likely to arouse micro-political activity as the *status quo* is not disturbed by groups and individuals being asked to justify their claim on resources. Its disadvantages are that the efficiency and effectiveness in resource use are not promoted by an unquestioning adherence to past patterns of resource allocation.

Schools are attracted to incremental budgeting because the bulk of the schools' maintenance tasks continue unchanged from year to year. Normally over 80 per cent of a school's budget is spent on staff, most of whom are on permanent full-time contracts. Much of the rest is spent on unavoidable operational activities. The existing maintenance requirements thus dominate the budget, leaving only 2–5 per cent available for new departures. From this perspective, it therefore doesn't seem worthwhile spending a lot of effort on costing programmes which will be continued anyway. In addition, new ways of thinking and new practices would have to be developed, whereas incremental budgeting is reasonably easy to adopt.

Traditional budgeting in schools

Traditional budgeting is incremental budgeting using a subjective budget structure. As already noted, school budgeting software structures the budget into subject headings because this is easier for monitoring and control purposes. In addition, incremental budgeting demands less information and less skill in managing potential internal conflict and insecurity than objective budgeting or zero-based budgeting.

A traditional approach to budgeting is incompatible with using the school development or management plan as a basis for the budget. It thus leads to a lack of coupling between the development plan and the budget. Another problem in linking the two is that the opportunity costs of the alternative courses of action which feature in school development planning are largely off-budget: they do not involve the school in additional expenditures of money which would not have otherwise occurred. Deploying staff (and student) time in one way rather than another incurs an opportunity cost,[6] but not a financial cost, unless supply cover has to be provided. Opportunity costs which are not also financial costs are not usually formally estimated as part of the evaluation of a course of action or recorded as an actual cost. Opportunity costs may well informally or intuitively enter into teachers' and managers' assessments of what is worthwhile doing and what is not, but the perceptions of most school managers[7] within the culture of calculation they are used to do not give rise to formal records of estimated opportunity cost.

Compromise approaches to rational budgeting

There is thus an apparent trade-off between the quality of the decision-making outcomes in terms of efficiency and effectiveness secured by the rational approach to resource allocation and its information and transaction costs. Much more information has to be gathered and analysed and more time spent reaching decisions than for incremental subjective budgeting, thus opening up opportunities for disagreement as the costs and benefits of different courses of action are made transparent. Normative texts on school financial management tend to advocate a compromise between the informational demands of fully rational objective budgeting and the much lower decision-making costs of incremental subjective budgeting.

For example, the NAHT (1991) *Guide to School Management* advocates school development planning in the context of budgeting, but only spares a page for zero-based budgeting. A similar but less radical approach to zero-based budgeting, called baseline budgeting, is recommended by the Audit Commission (Kennedy 1991). In the baseline approach, the school prepares the minimum cost budget on which it could survive. This should be done well before the actual budget revenue for the next financial year is notified. Expenditure priorities for the remaining money – the difference between the actual budget revenue (uncertain until announced) and baseline spending – are then determined via development or management planning processes. In this way, the school development plan and the budget plan are linked. When the budget is finally notified a few weeks before the start of the new financial year, the preparation of the final budget is simply a matter of funding priorities by moving down the ranked list until all the difference between the actual budget and the baseline budget has been allocated. A somewhat vague compromise was suggested by Knight (1989b) in LMS training materials, which he termed 'limited planning', in contrast to the full planning of programme budgeting. The budget is prepared using the historic budget and the school timetable supplemented by expenditure priorities drawn up through a management plan for areas where changes are needed. The most recent official pronouncement on good school budgeting practice from OFSTED, referred to above, clearly advocates a compromise rational approach but, given the novelty of school budgeting and the variety of actual practice, does not specify the precise elements of such an approach.

Participation in budget decision-making

As well as the extent to which a budgeting process is rational and thus explicitly constructed to address issues of efficiency and effectiveness, a further important issue is the range of stakeholders who participate in the process. The two main sets of interests – other than the headteacher and senior staff – who are likely to participate in the process are governors and staff. For LEA-maintained schools, the LEA has a role as generator of the budget, and as monitor of financial rectitude who, as a last resort, can withdraw a delegated budget from a school in cases of mismanagement. The major role for parents in budgeting, in so far as they have one other than as governors or in electing governors, is in supporting the school and fund-raising.

The governing body

As noted in Chapter 1, one of the distinctive features of the English and Welsh version of school-based management is the significant formal powers of the governing body,[8] whereas in Australia, Canada and the USA school councils are advisory. The official *Guide to the Law* for school governors states that 'the governing body has a general responsibility for managing the school effectively, acting within the framework set by legislation and the policies of the LEA. But it is not expected to take detailed decisions about the day-to-day running of the school – that is the function of the head' (DFE 1993: 15). One of the major responsibilities of the governing body is the management of the school budget:

> The principle of Local Management of Schools (LMS) is that governing bodies, working with the head, decide how to spend the overall budget to get the best for the needs of the school and its pupils. This includes deciding how many staff to employ.
> . . . The governing body is responsible for deciding how the budget

is spent for the purposes of the school, depending on any conditions in the LEA's approved scheme.

(DFE 1993: 35, 39)

The normative model of the school governing body promoted by the government is that of a board of directors accountable to the parents as 'shareholders'. The formal and legal powers of the governing body over finance and staffing, including the appointment of the headteacher, and the requirement to produce an annual report to parents on the past year's performance and hold an annual meeting for parents where the governors could be held accountable, are key elements in this model. The headteacher is the chief executive for policies determined by the governing body and is accountable to the governing body for their implementation. The rational approach to resource and financial management is fully consistent with the governors acting as a board of directors. Apart from the headteacher,[9] the governors are non-executive directors. However, their motivation has to be somewhat different to that of company non-executive directors: they get no remuneration and are less likely to benefit from business networking as a consequence of being governors. Governors who initiate commercial transactions with the school for personal financial gain are abusing their position.

We therefore have to look to political models of citizen participation to provide rationales for private individuals' motivation to be governors. A particularly apposite model is Hirschman's (1970) triad of exit, voice and loyalty as stimulants to organizational improvement. Consumers of an organization's output can express their dissatisfaction by exit, taking their custom elsewhere or by voice, which is communicating dissatisfaction and seeking improvements. A loyal participant will stay with the organization and if dissatisfied will use voice to secure improvements rather than exit. Hirschman argues that voice allied to loyalty is more effective than exit in improving the performance of the organization because exit drains it of resources. However, customer voice is only effective if managers and workers respond to it. Voice is stimulated by reducing the costs of exercising it. The opportunity to become governors and the formal powers of the role reduce the cost of voice to parents and community representatives by providing a formal structure within which to influence the school and by the pressures on teachers to attend to the views of the governing body. Hirschman elaborates his analysis by pointing out that only some customers – the alert ones – need to exercise voice and that organizational recuperation is particularly dependent on retaining the more quality-conscious customers. Thus the model of the governing body as a board of directors, rather than as supportive lay helpers, is more likely to attract people who are quality-conscious about education and more able to shop around for alternatives and who are more capable of exercising voice because they have experience of operating at managerial levels in other organizations.

However, this may be offset by the ability of quality-conscious parents to exit and choose another school rather than to work through the governing body.

A difficulty with the board of directors model of the governing body is that it is not fully specified. A considerable degree of ambiguity remains in the respective roles of the headteacher and the governing body. There is an extensive grey area between what is properly the role of the governing body in exercising its responsibilities for the effective management of the school, and the executive decisions of the headteacher exercised in the context of day-to-day management. The *de jure* powers of the governing body are not fully explicit and have to be set against the *de facto* powers of the headteacher who, in contrast to governors, works full-time, possesses professional expertise and controls information flows.

Teachers' participation

The UK version of school-based management, unlike that in the USA, has not been driven by the rhetoric of classroom teacher empowerment. However, the British educational management literature does reflect the advocacy of greater teacher involvement in management. The concept of leadership is made applicable to most posts by defining it to mean behaviours which facilitate cooperation among staff to work to achieve organizational objectives. There has also been considerable advocacy of collegial management, though much more in relation to curriculum issues than financial ones. As already noted, the school development planning movement strongly advocates teacher involvement in order to ensure commitment to decisions and hence successful implementation. While teacher involvement is recommended for instrumental reasons, its advocacy is also proselytized as an end in itself from value perspectives associated with dislike of hierarchical power structures (Bottery 1992).

According to the contingency perspective, participative decision-making is suited to some circumstances and not to others. Such an instrumentally normative model of participative decision-making in schools has been developed by Hoy and Tarter (1993) building on existing concepts, including those from earlier writers on organizations (Barnard 1938; Simon 1947). Their model applies to hierarchically structured organizations. They deduce that it is effective for subordinates to participate in decision-making when they have a personal interest in the outcome and expertise to offer in making the decision. If neither of these two conditions are present, then the decision is said to be inside the 'zone of acceptance', since subordinates do not seek to be involved and their participation will be ineffective. Ritualistic participation in such circumstances will irritate and demotivate subordinates who perceive that their time has been wasted to no good purpose. In the contrasting situation, subordinates have both an interest and expertise, so that the decision is outside the zone of acceptance. Participation is therefore called for and is effective. The acceptance zone is marginal if only one of either personal stake in the decision or expertise applies. Participation has to be handled carefully, since in the first case subordinates will be alienated by sham participation if their wishes are not responded to, or in the second case feel their time is being wasted by advising on a decision in which they have no interest. The third contingent variable in Hoy and Tarter's model is subordinates' commitment to organizational goals. If commitment exists and the decision is outside the zone of acceptance, then decision-making by consensus is appropriate. If there are conflicts over goals but subordinates possess expertise and have a personal stake in the decision, then their participation in decision-making requires the headteacher to negotiate a compromise or to educate teachers into understanding and accepting a decision based either on majority voting or the final arbitration of the head. A fourth variable, time, is mentioned by Hoy and Tasker but not given much consideration. It can easily be included, since the less time there is available for a decision, the less viable is participation.

Financial management is unlikely to be within the expertise of classroom teachers.[10] It is a relatively new aspect of educational practice, and overall responsibility for the budget rests with the head and governing body and thus training has been directed in the main at headteachers and specialist administrative staff. Because school budgets are in practice structured around the subjects of expenditure, only a few of the budget heads, such as books, materials and equipment and classroom support staff, are within the range of expertise normally expected of classroom teachers. Teachers clearly have a personal stake in the school's finances, since these affect job security, promotion prospects and conditions of work. Applying Hoy and Tarter's model implies that teachers should be involved in decisions about the budget heads for which they have expert knowledge and which will also involve a personal stake, since conditions of work are affected. However, decisions regarding the bulk of the school budget are in the marginal zone of acceptance – no expertise and some interest. The extent of the personal stake will vary, both with the state of the school's finances and the situation of the individual teacher. The personal stake will be greater when budget cuts have to be made, threatening redundancies or diminished working conditions. Doubts about teachers' commitment to common school aims and objectives will make headteachers reluctant to seek the participation of subordinates in budget decisions, since this is likely to exacerbate conflict.

A good practice model for local management

A recommended 'good practice' model for local management can thus be constructed from the various strands of official thinking and current educational management literature. In the good practice model, the school is managed along rational lines with the governing body taking a leading role in articulating aims and objectives. The governing body operates at the strategic management level by utilizing key management information provided by the headteacher. Utilizing this information, the governing body and senior managers engage in management planning, of which the budget is a crucial constituent element. The budget is determined in relation to the educational objectives thereby secured. Budget and other policies are monitored and evaluated by the governing body utilizing the management information provided by the headteacher. The headteacher ensures that staff are appropriately involved in decision-making, so enhancing the quality of the information obtained by tapping into staff expertise, fosters an integrative school culture and secures support for school aims, objectives and policies. This good practice vision utilizes three main models of decision-making in schools – the rational, the bureaucratic or hierarchical, and the collegial or collaborative – and aims to combine them in an appropriate mix. Rational decision-making processes are consistent with both hierarchically and collegially structured decision-making, though not a necessary feature of them. Organizational goals can be defined both by senior managers in a hierarchically run school and through consensus in a collegial setting. In both management structures, alternatives can be evaluated and the actions deemed best at promoting school objectives selected and implemented. The 'good practice' model for local management is inescapably hierarchical, since specific responsibilities for decision-making are placed upon governing bodies and headteachers. Official sources emphasize both the rational and hierarchical aspects of decision-making, with asides on staff involvement. For variants of the collegial model, emphasizing staff participation, one has to look to the educational management literature (e.g. Caldwell and Spinks 1988; Hargreaves and Hopkins 1991).

Alternative perspectives: Non-rational decision-making

There are a number of highly influential perspectives on organizational decision-making which are sidelined and largely ignored by the literature devoted to the 'good practice model' of local management. The two major perspectives neglected by the good practice model are the political and the ambiguity perspectives. In the political model, the main unit of analysis is competing interests groups within the organization who utilize various resources in their power to serve the interests of the group. Organizational goals cannot be agreed because of conflicts of interests. Resource allocation decisions are the outcome not of rational analysis but of the interplay of power, involving negotiation and bargaining. Thus the spending decisions represented in the budget are determined by the relative power and tactical strategems of the different interest groups. The leadership role is depicted either as the weaker one of negotiating viable coalitions between interests (Baldridge 1971), or the stronger role (Hoyle 1986; Ball 1987) in which headteachers engage in micropolitical manipulation in order to gain their ends. The critical perspective (e.g. Smyth 1993) noted in Chapter 2 can be treated as a variant of the political model, since it asserts that management hierarchies in schools and the external imperatives they serve function to ensure that schools service the reproductive requirements of the capitalist system. This perspective is concerned not so much with the internal political analysis of the school as with emphasizing the broader political and social context. From this perspective, the 'good practice model' is to be decried as a repressive tool of capitalism, which seeks legitimation through the rhetoric of decentralization and teacher empowerment. To find this perspective useful, one must subscribe to the political and economic analysis which underpins it.

A very direct critique of organizational rationality comes from those organizational theorists who, in various ways, emphasize the importance of ambiguity, particularly in certain sectors such as education where output is not easily measurable and is not sold on a market at a price. The rational model is undermined by ambiguity, since it is so heavily dependent on the availability of information about relationships between inputs and outputs – between means and ends. If ambiguity prevails, then it is not possible for organizations to have clear aims and objectives. Reliable information about the relationships between different quantities and combinations of inputs and resulting outputs cannot be obtained, and so the second and third stages of the rational decision-making process cannot be carried out. This state of affairs would explain why decision-making, particularly in the public sector, does not in fact follow the rational model, but is characterized by incrementalism and 'muddling through' (Lindblom 1959, 1979). The antithesis of rationality is the garbage-can model of Cohen and March (1974); in an ambiguous organizational environment, problems and potential solutions to other problems circulate, each promoted by particular interests. Organizational members participate with differing degrees of regularity and intensity in settings where decisions are made. How a particular solution becomes attached to a given problem depends on who is participating in decision-making in any particular moment in time, what is their interest in promoting a particular solution for adoption, and on the bargains and compromises struck between organizational members. Thus in the garbage-can model, there is no clear distinction between means and ends, no articulation of organizational goals, no evaluation of alternatives in relation to organizational goals and no selection of the best means.

Conclusion

A summary of the implications of political and ambiguity perspectives for organizational rationality is given in Table 4.2. Both perspectives, but especially the ambiguity perspective, undermine the pursuit of efficiency and effectiveness. Micropolitical and ambiguity models of management are

Table 4.2   A synopsis of critiques of rational decision-making

Requirements of rational approach	Problems: drawn from alternative perspectives
1 Organizational aims: Can be determined by senior management in a bureaucratic model or through collegial agreement	*Political*: conflict over aims and objectives *Ambiguity*: organizational aims and objectives not clear
2 Alternative ends–means relationships known and not disputed	*Political*: knowledge of means–ends relationships contested by different interests *Ambiguity*: information on means–ends relationships not known – either not sought or knowledge not obtainable
3 Best alternative in relation to organizational aims and objectives selected by analysing the evidence	*Political*: choice depends on power relations *Ambiguity*: 'garbage can' process by which solutions search for problems

primarily descriptive models. They are used as metaphors to interpret what actually happens in organizations. In contrast, rational and collegial models are largely normative or prescriptive. They are put forward as models of good practice to be emulated, rather than as a description of everyday reality in organizational life. Thus the political and ambiguity perspectives as descriptions of reality act as salutary inhibitors of managerial panaceas based on rationality. I have chosen to concentrate much more on the rational model of decision-making than on the micropolitical one because I am interested in assessing the extent to which local management has had the effects intended for it. The criteria of efficiency and effectiveness are as central to this assessment as they are to rational decision-making processes.

Having now set out the most relevant theoretical perspectives for understanding how local management might affect schools as organizations, the next chapters are concerned with examining the empirical evidence concerning how schools have responded. The analytical framework adopted is directed to addressing the question of the extent to which local management appears to be succeeding in achieving the aims intended for it and what might be its impact on equity – issues set out in Chapter 2. A substantial amount of the empirical evidence is drawn from a study of eleven schools, ranging from small primaries to secondary schools with sixth-forms in one LEA. Chapter 5 examines the impact on decision-making and so addresses the question of how schools adapt to the good practice model; Chapter 6 is concerned with the roles of different decision-makers involved in local management within the school; while Chapter 7 is concerned with the outcomes of the budget decision-making process and so attempts to assess the impact of local management on efficiency and effectiveness.

Decision-making in locally managed schools

Introduction

Chapters 5–7 examine some empirical evidence gathered to attempt an assessment of the impact of local management at school level. The criteria for assessing this impact are derived first from the intended aims of local management examined in Chapter 2. These are:

- greater cost-efficiency in the utilization of resources;
- promoting greater school effectiveness through improvements in the quality of teaching and learning;
- increased responsiveness to the preferences of parents and employers.

In addition, the equity implications of local management need to be addressed. These have in the main been unintentional consequences of the policy, since distributional equity has not featured as an official objective for local management in central government thinking.

The main source of the empirical evidence reported here is an ESRC-funded project on the Impact of Formula Funding on Schools (IFFS), which studied the implementation of local management in one education authority. Further evidence on the processes of resource management in schools is cited from a study by Levačić and Glover (1994b) on the assessment of schools' efficiency by OFSTED inspectors. It should be made clear at the outset that the two projects reported here focus mainly on the efficiency and effectiveness aspects of local management and were not designed to address the full complexity of the range of associated equity issues. Responsiveness was not a major focus of the IFFS study, as it is of the Parental and School Choice Interaction (PASCI) study also being carried out at the Open University (Glatter *et al.* 1993; Glatter and Woods 1994). In part, this is because the focus of the IFFS project on schools' resource management did not throw up much evidence on responsiveness; it did not emerge as an explicit and transparent factor in schools' financial decision-making.

The issues at school level, examined using evidence from the IFFS study, are divided into three main categories: processes (Chapter 5), roles (Chapter 6) and outcomes of decision-making (Chapter 7). Since the IFFS study was a relatively in-depth study of only eleven schools, the findings when reported are compared with those from other studies of the impact of local management. Two major reports on local management which will be cited most often in making comparisons are Bullock and Thomas (1994) and Maychell (1994). The former study, commissioned by the National Association of Head Teachers (NAHT), obtained questionnaire responses from 800 primary and secondary schools in 1991, 188 in 1992 and 169 in 1993. In addition, one-day visits were made to thirty-eight schools where semi-structured interviews were conducted. The latter study by the National Foundation for Educational Research in 1993–94 obtained evidence by questionnaire from 284 primary and 325 secondary schools maintained by LEAs and from seven detailed case-studies. There were also earlier surveys by HMI (1992a) and the Audit Commission (1993). Together these sources provide evidence on decision-making processes and the resource allocation decisions made.

The overarching question addressed in this chapter is the extent to which schools are developing the rational processes of resource management which are consistent with (though no guarantee of) efficiency and effectiveness as discussed in Chapters 3 and 4. As explained in Chapter 4, the OFSTED inspection framework set out by far the clearest elaboration yet of official expectations regarding 'good practice' resource management. Within this overarching issue there are a number of sub-themes: the linkage of school development planning and budgeting; the changed role of the headteacher; the allocation of budget manager and financial officer tasks; the role of the governing body as practised compared with the 'board of directors' model; and the extent of staff involvement in financial decision-making.

The context for studying schools' decision-making

The IFFS project was undertaken in 'Barsetshire', a large county LEA with around 250 primary schools and 50 non-selective secondary schools, including some middle-deemed-secondary schools. The LEA has a reputation for being well-run and open, with a 'hands-off' approach to its schools, described by one headteacher as 'values leadership'. The LEA has encouraged school self-evaluation within a cooperative and supportive culture. So far, opting for grant-maintained (GM) status has been minimal. Barsetshire provided a representative setting, being politically 'middle-of-the-road' and offering a wide range of schools for case-study work. The authority began to implement an approved local management of schools (LMS) scheme in 1990–91, having run a pilot scheme in 1989. In 1990–91, LMS was fully implemented in the entire secondary sector and in thirty primary schools. Thus both secondary and primary schools with full management delegation[1] could be studied.

One aspect of the IFFS study was a quantitative analysis of the LEA-wide impact of formula-funding (Levačić 1993a). The other major component reported here was a set of eleven individual school case studies of how schools had responded to local management, in particular its budgeting aspects. Case-study schools were selected in order to include in our sample a range of schools by size and age-group taught. It was also hypothesized that schools' responses to local management would be influenced by whether they lost or gained financially by the introduction of formula-funding. Five pairs of schools matched by type were selected, one a 'budget winner' the other a 'budget loser'. A school was designated a budget winner or loser according to whether it had gained or lost budget because of the introduction of formula-funding. A school's 'winner' or 'loser' status is given in Table 5.1 in the column headed '1989–90: % change in budget due to formula'. This shows the percentage difference between the actual budget received in 1989–90 under the old system of resource allocation and a simulation of what the new formula-funding mechanism would deliver given the 1989–90 number of pupils and LEA schools' budget. In the event, schools did better than this in 1990–91 because of an increase in the LEA's education budget. The LEA increased the 1990–91 primary sector budget by 5 per cent per capita in real terms and it was therefore difficult to find a medium to large-sized primary school with a fully delegated budget which had a reduced budget in 1990–91. As the initial selection of four primary schools included only one 'loser', another 'losing' school was then included. The eleven case-study schools are listed in Table 5.1 along with their main characteristics.

The schools were studied between 1991 and 1992 with a short follow-up in 1993. The main issues investigated were how budgetary decisions were made, who was involved in making them, how the associated tasks and processes were undertaken, and what resource decisions had been made. School members' own assessment of the advantages and disadvantages of local management were sought. The sources of evidence were school and LEA documents (budgets, minutes of meetings and supporting papers), observation of full governing body and finance committee meetings, and interviews with a range of staff and governors and four LEA officers. Further details of the research methods employed are given in the appendix to this chapter.

Table 5.1 Case-study schools: Pupil roll, budget changes and unit costs

School	Type	No. pupils, 1990–91	Pupil roll as % of places	Change in rolls, 1989–90 to 1990–91 (%)	1989–90: Change in budget due to formula (%)	Change in budget: 1990–91 compared with 1989–90 (%)	Unit cost per pupil, 1989–90 (in Nov. 1990 prices)	Unit cost per pupil, 1990–91 (in Nov. 1990 prices)
Harrimore (loser)	11–18	811	75	-6.0	-0.7	-2.6	1537	1593
Fenmore (loser)	11–16	750	82	-1.3	-2.6	-1.3	1533	1535
Peacehaven	11–16	874	92	3.9	1.1	7.9	1461	1516
All Saints	11–18	540	97	-7.7	3.0	0.5	1449	1578
Waterton	9–13	419	107	7.4	8.1	20.0	1078	1219
Graceland (loser: only by formula)	9–13	282	75	0.0	-12.3	4.9	1422	1534
Yellowstone	5–11	449	107	5.4	7.7	20.0	849	965
Pentland	5–11	249	75	-3.1	0.6	6.6	1046	1151
Horsefield (loser: only by formula)	5–11	345	77	2.1	-1.7	8.1	1187	1257
Fishlake	5–11	50	50	8.7	4.7	17.7	1329	1439
Candleford (loser: only by formula)	5–11	43	50	-2.3	-8.0	0.3	1493	1532

Allocating resources: Budget preparation and planning

Greater flexibility in the allocation of resources is the major potential source of the efficiency and effectiveness improvements sought from local management. At its most minimal, budget-setting requires the headteacher and governors to prepare a budget for the beginning of the new financial year which ensures that the school's expenditure does not exceed its income. At its most sophisticated, as discussed in Chapter 4, budget planning requires a well-orchestrated and lengthy cycle, with the active participation of staff and governors, whereby educational aims and objectives are translated into curriculum plans and thence into staffing and material requirements which are then costed out and budgeted for. Thus the budget is fully integrated into school corporate and development planning, which consists of a medium-term strategic plan and short-term action plans which are fully costed.

Clearly, schools are engaged in a long-term process of evolving their resource allocation procedures. There has been an initial learning process which was probably at its most rapid in the first two years of local management, followed by more gradual refinements. A second spur towards the development of the rational approach has been OFSTED inspection encompassing the 'efficiency of the school'. When the IFFS study commenced, the eleven schools were about to enter their second financial year with full delegation and so were observed at a rapid stage of learning. Re-interview in 1993 revealed no major changes in process, mainly refinements towards better integration of educational planning and budgeting, though in almost all the schools this was done informally rather than through an explicit documented process which links development planning and budgeting.

Prioritizing and planning

The eleven schools demonstrated, as do OFSTED inspection reports (Levačić and Glover 1994a,b), a wide cross-section of practice with respect to the development of the rational approach to budgeting. At its most minimal, the headteacher draws up a budget in February and March to finance existing patterns of staffing and premises costs, leaving some money over for materials and equipment. This is then ratified by the governing body. In setting its budget, only one school in our sample, Yellowstone, made explicit use of a school development plan, drawn up through a process of widespread consultation of staff, governors and parents. Six other schools had less well-documented development plans and associated school priorities which informed but did not feature explicitly in budget-setting. None of the schools practised pure incremental budgeting – that is, just replicating last year's budget with price increases. All schools had in mind educational priorities which informed budget-setting, derived from the exercise of professional judgement. There was no documented evidence of input–output relationships to show that addressing these priorities would improve school efficiency or effectiveness.

Schools which had lost out from formula-funding were forced to consider their educational priorities much more carefully, while some of the 'winning' schools spent money without such careful assessment. As the head of Fenmore, a budget 'loser', explained:

> The whole process of drawing up a budget means that we have to examine our priorities and to sift through, trim down and reorganize and replan. It is bound to concentrate our mind on the service we are offering, how we can improve it, how we can direct money to crack a certain problem, but the exasperating side of this is that we have had so much docked away that the service we offer is going to be threatened severely.

Teachers at Fenmore were aware of the constraints facing the school and on the whole accepted the budget decisions which had been made:

> The full budget has been presented to staff and they have had the opportunity to question such things as a reduction in INSET money . . . LMS has made us more aware of money and ensuring that the budget is properly spent.

In contrast, at Waterton, the biggest gainer in our sample, the headteacher stated:

> We did not have to come to any hard decisions and perhaps that makes us complacent, but perhaps we ought not to be as I foresee more cuts. We have not really evaluated the way we have carried it out. So far, problems have not arisen and one tends to be *laissez-faire*. LMS has made one consider the financial aspects but I do not think that it is any different than it was.

As a consequence of the extra money, more staff had been appointed, the head's salary raised, more spent on curriculum resources and the premises. However, staff did not perceive any whole school planning. One reported that:

> We are a winning school to quote the head but there has been no noticeable increase in resources, though there does seem to be more money around. I have no input into the School Development Plan but it is on ice in this period of transition.

Another teacher was aware that 'money had doubled, but I don't know why or if it is fair'. It may be significant that in this school, where there was little apparent change in decision-making processes, apart from the governors becoming more assertive, the headteacher took early retirement.

Headteachers derived their priorities from the general knowledge of the school and *ad hoc* discussions with staff; some also had more formal committee structures which encouraged this process. For example, the Peacehaven headteacher believed in 'organic planning' and not detailed documentation containing closed targets. Whole school priorities emerged from consultative committees and were continually communicated through informal discussions and negotiations. There was frequent reiteration of the principle that the curriculum must drive the budget:

> We make serving the needs of the curriculum our major priority. We forget about the budget for a while. Though I have found myself on occasions saying recently, 'If we can afford it'. By and large we have our curriculum discussions in their own context: 'What do we want to achieve?'; 'What are the implications of that in terms of staffing and non-contact time, group size, forms of entry, level of classroom assistants, all of which impinge directly on the quality of the curriculum?' ... We tend to have this debate as fully as possible. People are reasonable – they don't ask for the moon – so the debate tends to have its own restraint. Then we translate this into the budget and have a pecking order of things.

At Peacehaven, the policy priorities evolved from discussion in the Curriculum Planning Group and departmental clusters. The detailed resourcing was then determined by the senior management team and presented to the governors' LMS group. The full governing body was then presented with a fully worked-out budget to discuss and approve.

While there was considerable variation in the detailed practice of how priorities emerged and shaped the budget, a common core could be identified in all the schools. The priorities which informed budget-setting emerged from the strategic thinking of headteachers (and senior management teams in secondary schools). This involved discussions and negotiations with other staff, though the extent and nature of such consultation varied. In the two small primaries with two to three teachers, such communication was easy and a formalized process inappropriate. In general, the budget reflecting such priorities was drawn up by the headteacher in the primary schools, and by the senior budget manager and headteacher in the secondary schools. It was then presented to a governors' finance subcommittee, which tended to focus on the financial data and be less aware of the educational rationale underlying the figures. The full governing body, having delegated scrutiny of the budget to its finance committee, would ratify the budget plan after some questioning which varied in its extent and depth. The description of budget-setting by the headteacher at Fenmore three years into LMS is fairly typical of secondary school practice:

> Financial planning is done by the deputy in charge of the budget who draws up a budget plan in broad terms. This gives us ball park figures. He consults various areas of the school to ascertain their reactions to the amounts they are likely to get. We then look at that and agree a

set of priorities. When we get the budget share figure from County we turn the amorphous figures into a hard-nosed plan. We then go through the same process with the hard figures. It then goes to the governors' sub-committees (curriculum, staffing, pupils, parents and community), who put in recommendations to the finance committee made up of representatives from the other committees. This has worked very well so far as the recommendations have not been far apart, but it would have been very difficult if we had had to make redundancies. We then have a full staff meeting and go through the budget. People will say there is not enough for capitation and we give them some options for increasing that and not doing other things. We had quite a discussion on learning support.

The proposed budget is then scrutinized by the finance committee, which asks detailed questions, before being forwarded to a full governors' meeting for discussion and approval.

In middle and primary schools budget preparation was, with two exceptions, done solely by the headteacher, with differing degrees of support from the school finance officer. For example, the headteacher at Horsefield, in the absence of an interest in finance by the deputy, did the budget preparation:

I do not have an open staff meeting to discuss the budget, but I do discuss with senior staff elements of the budget such as special needs, the structure throughout the school, the balance of ancillary staff and non-contact time, as these are the bits of the budget we can play with and be flexible about . . . there is always the opportunity for staff to come and see me and raise a point . . . Someone somewhere must make the final decisions and that must be me.

In the early years of local management, school development planning was at an emergent stage and in most schools was not explicitly linked to budgeting in any formalized and transparent way. By 1993, development planning had become a more important feature of the annual management cycle, but the schools were still not fully integrating financial and educational planning in formal processes as laid out in the OFSTED model.

Similar conclusions have been reached from official studies of larger samples of schools. The Audit Commission (1993: 21), in a study of 100 locally managed schools, concluded that: 'Few schools see the process of setting the budget as a means of achieving educational objectives which they have set out in the school development plan'. OFSTED's annual report for 1992–93 reiterated the same point as a key issue:

. . . there have been widespread weaknesses when it comes to longer-term planning. Despite the increasing prominence given to producing School Development Plans, these do not always take the vital step of matching the process of drawing up budgets to educational priorities and ensuring that resources are harnessed to improved quality of teaching and learning.

(OFSTED 1993b: 6)

Development planning at Yellowstone School

Of all our sample, Yellowstone School, a large 'winning' primary situated in a medium-sized town in an area of socially mixed housing, had the best developed processes for integrating educational and financial planning and so is worth considering in greater detail. The 450-pupil school was operating at full capacity, unlike some other local primaries. The headteacher had begun development planning in 1985 after being seconded to a government-funded management course. He wryly noted that little interest in the plan had been shown by HMI during a full inspection in 1986. The original plan had been drawn up in response to the views of governors, parents and staff solicited through questionnaires. In order to emphasize that development planning is an on-going process, the plan is always referred to as a draft and is redone in full every three years. In 1993, the consultation process was observed in action. The staff, governors and LEA adviser spent an evening deciding which priorities should enter the reworked plan, drawing upon evaluative evidence gathered from a questionnaire to parents, staff and governors.

The headteacher embraced local management enthusiastically and had seized the opportunity to be a pilot school for the LEA's scheme in 1989, which was financially beneficial. He articulated clear links between the aims of the school and its resourcing policies:

> The aim of the school is quite clear – children spending the day together in learning, laughter and love . . . our priority is to achieve the first of these, the learning part, by resourcing the school with both human and material resources to the highest level possible and to offer the best learning environment possible. I feel, and I believe that all the governors share the view, that with formula-funding we are able to set our own objectives into operation under the wing of the school's aims and to see them through.

The school development plan summarizes the relationship between aims and resourcing objectives, which are placed in the separate categories of staff, premises and curriculum, each of which is overseen by a governors' sub-committee. This summary is shown in Table 5.2. The school was fortunate in the first years of LMS to have a growing budget and was not, unlike the budget 'losers', faced with the need to make any hard decisions as to what areas to freeze or cut back. By 1993, resourcing was getting tighter and choices had to be made between an extra full-time or part-time teacher and other areas of expenditure.

As each section of the plan was the responsibility of one of the

Table 5.2 Yellowstone School development plan

General principles underlying the objectives of our development plan
(i) The absolute need for the school community, especially governors and staff, to have a shared vision for the school and its children.
(ii) Monies will be devolved to individuals and teams for expenditure purposes, having agreed an overall budgetary strategy, with priorities.

Staff and development objectives
1 To achieve, within the limitations of the school's budget, the following priorities:
 (i) to improve pupil–teacher ratios, or at least maintain present average levels;
 (ii) to develop and improve levels of non-contact time;
 (iii) to maintain ancillary support, at least, in line with the County formula (i.e. 1 hour a week per 4 pupils) and to seek improvements;
 (iv) to follow the DFE 60 per cent upper limit for allowance posts.
2 To maintain and develop, in the light of the Evaluation exercise, the school's staff development policy, giving special attention to area and staff review meetings and mutual support of staff through cooperative partnerships, consultancy, age-group coordinators and mentors for inductees.

Premises objectives
1 To achieve the best use of the re-modelled building and new extension.
2 To develop the environment adjacent to the 'temporary' classrooms.
3 To develop closer links with the two schools sharing the site so as to secure a well-maintained and secure sight.
4 To maintain all parts of the buildings to the highest possible standards within budget constraints.

Curriculum development objectives
1 To prepare and agree policy documents for all core and foundation subject areas, which include aims, objectives, teaching approaches, resources and schemes of work, and be compatible with national curriculum requirements.
2 To further develop, agree and implement policy and procedures for assessment, profiling and recording.
3 To ensure continuity and progression through all age groups.
4 To communicate the above to parents.
5 To resource the curriculum needs of our school to the highest possible level, giving priority to:
 (i) developing central resources for science, music, PE/games, library, artefacts and teacher resources;
 (ii) ensuring good class-based resources, especially fiction books and equipment;
 (iii) achieving at least one Nimbus computer per class with appropriate software, plus an extra administrative computer.

sub-committees – curriculum, staffing and premises – it was referred to continually in decision-making. The fourth committee, finance, was responsible for drawing up the budget and did this by receiving bids from the other committees. The headteacher sat on all the committees and was thus the main integrator of all the information required for securing coherent planning. The finance officer, a member of the support staff and a governor, sat on all the committees as well, providing vital support to the headteacher. The chair of governors was a member of the premises and finance committees and the deputy head attended all committees regularly by invitation.

The curriculum committee met once a term to review and approve curriculum policies developed by teacher working parties. Certain areas of the curriculum were given priority in any one year, usually in response to national curriculum implementation. The development of a revised curriculum in science, say, was accompanied by a plan for its resourcing, in the case of science a central resource equipment centre. Thus science received a particularly large allocation of money in that year.

The headteacher described the budget planning process as follows:

> The broad budget planning is done by me, the chair of finance goes through it and then if necessary it will be redrafted, and that is what sees its way through to the other sub-committees, who are then working within what is possible and the best for the whole school rather than just a particular aspect. In the spring term, when budget-making takes place, each sub-committee reviews its own part of the school development plan and makes their proposals so that the budget is seeking to support and develop the SDP.

The budget-planning process at Yellowstone and its integration with school development planning is only one aspect, though an important one, of a well-integrated school culture, in which all staff were well aware of and supported the fundamental aims of the school. Staff participated in budget decision-making, but in a collaborative rather than a democratic school culture. The leadership of the headteacher and his primary influence on decisions were recognized and appreciated. The processes of resource management at Yellowstone had taken a good number of years to evolve and were still evolving. It is notable that they developed not because of the spur of local management, but through the initiative of the headteacher who seized on local management as a major opportunity to promote effective management and better resourcing. It is probably significant that the headteacher had been in post since the opening of the school in the mid-1970s and so had been able to build up a cohesive staff with shared values.

Problems and difficulties with planning

All the schools experienced common difficulties in planning, even those most successful at achieving the necessary degree of internal cohesion, involvement of stakeholders, and scheduling of tasks and processes over the annual planning cycle. The major complaint of all the schools concerned the uncertainties created by external agents. First was the uncertainty created by changes to the National Curriculum and second was that related to financing. While the LEA provided schools in January with an indicative budget share for the financial year starting in April, the schools still did not know their budget share for certain until February or even as late as mid-March. A major cause of this uncertainty was central government policies to restrain local government spending, in particular the threat to cap authorities which spent in excess of their Standard Spending Assessment (SSA).[2] Barsetshire, as an authority which had spent in excess of its education SSA, was being forced to cut back from 1992 onwards. A pattern became established whereby in the autumn the LEA would issue dire warnings of cuts to come, which in the event it managed to avoid imposing on school budgets to any great extent by means of cutting back on and delegating central services, such as special needs support and educational centres (e.g. farms and outdoor recreation), and by raiding reserves. Fiscal retrenchment was particularly worrying for small village primary schools, the future of which was being reviewed in 1991–92. Energy was expended mounting a successful campaign to prevent the County mounting a closure programme, as it was decided that the financial savings were not that great and not worth the political costs.

Even had the LEA's education budget been stable, there were other sources of budgetary uncertainty for schools. One was the problem of forecasting pupil numbers in each school for the coming September. The Barset formula originally weighted the January Form 7 DFE pupil count and the LEA's forecast of September rolls at 50 per cent each. However, this led to its having to claw back money from schools where actual enrolment was less than forecast and to vociferous complaints from schools with higher enrolments than forecast. In 1994, the LEA moved to funding entirely according to the January roll. This provided a cushion to schools with declining rolls, but made for tight resourcing in schools with expanding rolls, thus diminishing their incentive to expand rapidly. This change has increased budget stability and predictability but at the cost of tighter resourcing for schools with growing rolls.[3]

A further problem was a lack of adequate financial information. Delegated budgeting for local authority schools (as opposed to GM schools) did not involve schools managing their own money, since the school budget remained a book-keeping entry in the LEA's computers. The Education Department's central finances, in common with other departments, were run on a mainframe computer system referred to as LAFIS, while a new computerized school accounting system, SIMS, had been introduced into schools. Schools would only know what payments and receipts had been recorded in their account by receiving information from the LEA. Partly because of incompatibility between LAFIS and SIMS, there were delays in

schools receiving financial reports from the LEA. Schools found considerable discrepancies between the LEA's financial records and their own, often
due to miscoding of transactions. A particularly difficult delay for school
planning was the length of time taken to close the accounts at the end of
the financial year: schools did not know how much money they were
carrying forward into the next financial year and which could be used for
financing future spending until June. The problem of tardy and inaccurate
financial information was experienced by all eleven schools. Graceland's
complaints were typical:

> Every school has had reams of mistakes. Some are fundamental –
> people on the payroll who have left, paying someone else's gas bill. It
> is very difficult to say what your income is and therefore what your
> expenditure is going to be, so the whole decision process is mangled.

Some of these were teething problems due to having to get a complex
financial system operational in eighteen months, and others were eliminated by the introduction of school chequeing accounts where non-staff
budgets were paid into a school bank account so that schools were no
longer dependent on the LEA for these financial records. The financial
system's complexity grew with the introduction in 1993–94 of further
delegation of previously central services, such as financial and personnel
administration and advisory services:

> Financial recording continues to provide frustration . . . The LAFIS
> print-outs are out of date and we have to keep our own records. The
> closing down disk which leaves you with the carry-forward figures
> did not arrive until well into May.
>
> (Peacehaven headteacher)

The absence of accurate information about next year's budget until very
late in the financial year encourages schools to delay budget preparation.
However, this is not a necessary response, since the educational planning
for next year can be done in the autumn and winter so as to produce a
costed list of priorities. When the budget figure is finally available, it is
then just a matter of incorporating the priorities which can be afforded into
the budget plan. Yellowstone coped with the problem by preparing a 'standstill' budget for the start of the new financial year, since it was thought
important to have a budget to open the new financial year with. This was
basically the historic budget worked out by assuming an unchanged pattern
of resourcing (e.g. the same staffing). When the carry-forward figure was
available, the finance committee considered the bids made by the other
committees and made recommendations to the governing body so that a
revised budget was produced in July. It should be noted that Yellowstone
had not had to make this procedure work with a declining budget.

The lack of synchronization between the financial year and the academic
year is frequently cited as a complicating factor, since an annual school

development plan has to be financed out of two budgets, while one year's budget relates to two development plans. However, a considerable advantage of the lag of one term between the start of the financial and academic years is that the summer term gives schools time to adjust to budget changes, especially when these necessitate cutting staff. A school system with delegated budgeting which has synchronized the financial and academic years is that of Edmonton, Canada. In September, when schools finally know their pupil roll and hence budget, they may have to do some rapid adjustment to numbers of classes and teachers. Surplus teachers are rapidly discharged from the school payroll, and are redeployed by the school district, since schools with vacancies must give precedence to relocated district teachers (Levačić 1992b). Given the lateness of budgetary information and the inability of LEAs to deploy teachers, the lack of synchronization provides a much needed adjustment period.

Apart from external factors making planning more difficult, there are internal factors as well. First, there is the problem of finding sufficient time to involve staff and governors, so that they contribute to and support the resulting decisions. As the headteacher of Harrimore explained:

> We are having to deal with so much so quickly, especially in response to external events, that consultation is not what it was. Even though we are fairly participative – we have lots of working groups – often a working group doesn't have time to report back before a decision has to be made and staff feel short-circuited.

The internal process has to be designed so that all the relevant information is gathered and considered; this requires both the right network of consultation and the correct sequencing and timing of discussions. Fenmore's headteacher was aware of needing to improve this aspect of planning even after three years:

> We need to tie in all of the plan to the time-scale of the budget. This year a number of things which all add up to £10–12,000 have emerged since we set the budget but ought to have been in the budget . . . Had we planned better we would have had these things in front of us when we did the budget.

Despite various problems and differences in its stage of development in the schools, planning had been stimulated by local management and was regarded by 80 per cent of senior managers in the eleven schools as a beneficial outcome (Marren and Levačić 1994).

Resources for curriculum support

Prior to local management, schools had a fixed allocation for spending on what used to be known as 'capitation' (i.e. books, materials, stationery, furniture and equipment) and which OFSTED (1993b: Part 8, p. 27) now refers to as 'educational resources'. Local management has enabled schools to choose, within financial constraints, the amount spent. The experiences of the case-study schools indicate that local management tends to stimulate changes in internal procedures for allocating educational resources. In two of the secondaries and one primary, governors were taking an increasing interest in having this expenditure accounted for. Three of the secondary schools were relying less on a formula for allocating departmental resources and more on a bidding system by departments tied to departmental development plans and curriculum priorities. In this way, schools could target resources to particular curriculum areas as needs varied year by year. This was also a way of breaking down departmental isolationism and promoting a more integrated school culture in which departments become more responsive to whole school issues.

Peacehaven had spent a lot of time in the first two years, without apparent progress, on changing its departmental resource allocation procedures, having disbanded the previous resource committee of departmental heads for one containing people from the senior management team and governors. But by 1993, the headteacher reported that:

> We are now entirely on a bid basis and have gradually abandoned the formula. We have spent the last two years on departmental development plans and the quality has improved markedly. They are much more detailed and previous expenditure is looked at carefully. The underspends are questioned hard. So this whole process has become much more significant, constructive and accountable.

The primary and middle schools had moved to giving class teachers individually or in groups money to spend on curriculum resources. They also changed their curriculum priorities for funding from year to year, particularly to reflect the implementation of the national curriculum. Processes for planning that involved collaboration and coordination among staff were more strongly developed with respect to resourcing the curriculum than to other aspects of provision. This was seen by one of the small primary schools as a major advantage of local management: 'We have much more control over what we want to do and getting resources for our development plan and projects' (Fishlake finance officer).

Again the allocation procedures for curriculum support resources were particularly well developed at Yellowstone. The total amount of money to be allocated for curriculum support was worked out by the headteacher after a formal process of collective consultation with staff, rather than relying on *ad hoc* discussions with individual staff. Each area of the curriculum was the responsibility of a curriculum consultant. The process was explained by a teacher:

> We start off with the areas of responsibility like maths, English and science and they put in a bid. Obviously, it changes from year to year

because sometimes you need an expensive item which will last a long time. The bid is discussed at a staff meeting and agreed. The money left after resourcing particular parts of the curriculum is divided equally per class and allocated to each year group teacher partnership according to the number of classes.

The headteacher then prioritized the bids and put them to the curriculum committee together with a report on the school's financial situation. The committee had before it reports of the various curriculum working groups, which included the resourcing implications of the policies which had been agreed. Using this information, which the headteacher had already incorporated into his presentation to the committee, it approved the bids and made a recommendation to the finance committee to include these in the overall financial plan.

Linking resource use to its effects on learning

The Yellowstone example illustrates a highly developed process in which curriculum and financial planning are integrated. However, it is still focused on material resources to support the curriculum. Other key resourcing issues, such as the number and organization of classes and hence the number of teaching staff, the amount of non-contact time for teachers and the amount of classroom and administrative support staff to employ, were assessed with less formal deliberation. Their impact on the quality of learning was assessed by professional judgement alone. For example, it was thought to be better to keep class size down by means of mixed year groups (even in schools with two to three classes per year group) than to have bigger class sizes in some year groups but single year group classes. There was no formal research-based evaluation of this policy being undertaken – nor was there in any other school. The absence of such an evaluation and an associated knowledge base lies at the heart of the problem of tracing linkages between local management and improved learning. Important decisions about what resource mixes to use to produce educational output are taken in schools on the basis of professional judgements, the results of which are very difficult to assess in terms of resulting educational outputs.

All one can tentatively conclude from the evidence on the decision-making processes in these schools is that local management has given some stimulus to the development of the rational approach to the allocation of school resources. Schools were beginning to think more carefully about their educational aims and objectives and how best to achieve them with available resources. However, this approach is much better developed in some schools than others. It will probably take a considerable time for resource management to evolve from the rather basic form practised in some of the schools to the sophisticated official 'good practice' model.

In all the case-study schools, the greater flexibility brought about by local management and improvements to planning were generally welcomed by senior staff as the main benefits (Marren and Levačić 1994), even in those schools which had lost budget as a result of formula-funding. The head of Gracelands, a major loser in our sample, which had succeeded in raising its intake from seventy-five to ninety, judged that after three years of local management: 'Had the cuts been such that the money was cut in the same amount, we would have been worse off without the flexibility of LMS to allow us to do our own manipulating'. Whereas the head of Peacehaven School was able to be more positive: 'With the kind of quality of decision-making we are now able to do, I feel very positive about LMS'.

Budget monitoring

The benefits of improvements in planning processes by which goals are clarified, communicated and better served by the ability of schools to make their own resourcing decisions, incur costs in management and administrative time, not only to undertake the planning discussed so far in this chapter but also to perform the routine financial recording and reporting needed to support the implementation of the budget and to provide information to feed into future allocation decisions. Schools are required to 'establish sound internal financial controls to ensure the reliability and accuracy of financial transactions' (OFSTED/Audit Commission 1993) and the 'effectiveness of financial control procedures' is now a criterion by which OFSTED inspectors assess the efficiency of the school. The keeping of accurate and meaningful financial records is also essential in rendering accountability for the public funds entrusted to school managers. Monitoring the budget by comparing planned receipts and expenditures month by month with those which actually occur needs to be undertaken so that the budget manager can make adjustments to the budget as new events and information unfold. The value for money which schools are now expected to deliver requires careful assessment of alternative purchasing arrangements and management of bank balances as well as a rational approach to budget preparation.

Financial record-keeping and budget monitoring have been tasks which in practice have taken precedence over the development of a rational approach to budget planning. Headteachers have been fully aware that financial accounting is the major additional demand placed on schools by local management and LEA training reflected this. The task of disaggregating LEA's spending on schools and turning each school into a cost centre funded by formula was a considerable undertaking which, given the constraints of time and resources, was tackled reasonably well despite initial imperfections. The initial workload of local management for headteachers (or senior teachers to whom the task of budget manager was delegated) and their administrative staff involved learning how to operate the new financial systems. The problems of inaccurate and tardy financial reporting from the LEA, which Barset experienced in common with other LEAs, have already been noted. The implications of the financial accounting work load on the roles of headteachers and other involved staff are discussed in the next chapter.

Educational monitoring and evaluation were seen as separate from financial monitoring and evaluation. Barsetshire already had in place a system of four yearly school self-evaluations in which schools chose which key areas to assess and report to a panel of councillors. There were plans to incorporate this into an LEA review of school development plans, but as a 'hands-off' authority there was little pressure on schools to conform to any particular model of development planning, nor was this referred to in budget-setting. Teachers seemed largely unaware of the self-evaluation process and its findings remained within the professional circle of senior managers and LEA advisers. As the head of Waterton remarked: 'I assume educational monitoring is continuing but I never had a general inspection'. In contrast, Harrimore's governing body had taken an active interest in the self-evaluation report which pointed to the need to improve examination results. In general, the evaluative role of the LEA was unclear at this stage (Levačić 1993b) and not well linked to budgeting – a state of affairs transformed by the OFSTED inspection system which began in September 1993.

The efficacy of schools in financial and resource management

Chapter 4 noted that management accounting and cost accounting (which in schools relate to the allocation of resources and the costing of educational activities and outputs, respectively) are distinct from financial accounting for management control and accountability purposes. The latter is the dominant accounting mode in locally managed (and grant-maintained) schools. All financial documentation studied in the IFFS project was couched in terms of financial accounting and subjective budgets. Additional staff or the non-staff elements of curriculum developments might be costed separately, and alternative tenders for premises-related projects were considered, but we did not observe any estimates of the cost-effectiveness of an educational programme or development, such as that sought by OFSTED's efficiency of the school assessment.

The finding of the IFFS study that financial accounting is much better developed in schools than rational approaches to resource allocation, is corroborated by a content analysis of sixty-six OFSTED secondary school inspection reports in 1993, focusing on the efficiency of the school aspect of inspection (Levačić and Glover 1994a,b). The criteria OFSTED use for judging efficiency, as noted in Chapter 4, are very largely concerned with judging the processes of decision-making according to whether they reflect a rational approach to resource management. The inspectors' comments on the attributes of school management related to efficiency in the inspection framework were classified in our study as either 'supportive', 'refinements' or 'recommendations'. The first indicates practice regarded as satisfactory or better, the second refers to minor recommendations for otherwise satisfactory practice, and the third refers to suggestions for improvement where practice was found wanting.

This evidence indicated that schools had achieved the greatest success with respect to financial control, which was given supportive comment in fifty-seven of the sixty-six school inspection reports. However, schools still had some way to go in fully adopting the rational approach to resource management in all its aspects. There was evidence of school development plans with aims and objectives in forty-seven schools, a descriptive plan in twenty-five schools but only in eighteen reports was there favourable comment on a fully costed plan, whereas there were thirty-six recommendations for schools to cost their plans. Twenty-six reports contained recommendations for improvements in the development planning process and twenty-three sought a link between expenditure and defined school priorities. Considerable concern was expressed by the inspectors about failures to integrate departmental and school planning and to evaluate the alternative use of resources. Recommendations for engaging in longer-term strategic planning were made for eighteen schools, there was no comment on this for forty schools, while only eight were commended for their strategic planning. In only eight schools were all stages of rational planning fully developed to the extent that:

> The school development plan is very comprehensive and gives a very detailed picture of the school's priorities for development. Financial planning is becoming closely linked to the school's aims and priorities, with funding appropriately targeted. Governors are closely involved with the strategic management of resources and there are detailed policies for charging and pay. The school recognises the importance of value for money and carefully assesses the benefits of expenditure on staffing, premises and learning resources.

Responsiveness, choice and diversity

Responsiveness, choice and diversity are a further set of government policy objectives for local management. Responsiveness, defined as 'the capacity to be open to outside influences and new ideas' (Scott 1989: 17), is distinguished from accountability in that it is freely arrived at by the choice of the institution or individual and is not an imposed requirement. Local management is intended to give schools a greater incentive to be responsive to the preferences of parents (and pupils in so far as they influence parents' choice of school), employers and the local community, as well as giving schools the means to be responsive. The theory of market competition would predict that schools would adjust their educational provision in order to recruit more pupils. However, the motivation for a school management adopting policies to increase demand for the school's places is somewhat different between schools which are full and those which are not, and between non-selective LEA and GM schools, since the former cannot select whereas the latter can select 10 per cent by aptitude or covertly select by interview. A non-selective school which is full has little need to be responsive to its customers, except in so far as it needs to retain its local reputation and so maintain demand for its places.

One of the case-study schools, Peacehaven, was a good example of the reluctance of LEA non-selective schools to expand. The school had declined in numbers and had temporary accommodation removed from an otherwise attractive site. The governors had applied successfully for a reduction in its standard number of intake pupils from 224 to 192. As the school was over-subscribed, the governors were forced, much to their annoyance, to admit twenty-eight more pupils after successful parental appeals and thus create an extra form of entry. Because the forecast roll had been less, the school did not get extra money for these pupils until two terms after their entry. The school made every effort to resist growing larger and attracting pupils from a less popular school in a nearby town. In the period studied, only two of the authority's secondary schools were continuously over-subscribed. Data on first preference applications and appeals indicated some increase in parents' registering a choice of school other than in their catchment area. The number of appeals in two divisions had risen, while the proportion that was successful had declined (Hardman and Levačić 1994b).

Of the schools which were under-subscribed, there was no evidence of more than very minor efforts to respond to what might be perceived as image improvement or responsiveness to parental preference. The only such responses noted were more active steps to deal with truanting and poor behaviour by pupils. There was a great reluctance by the headteachers to compete for pupils. In three of the four areas studied, headteachers had agreed to actively discourage parents from choosing an 'out-of-catchment-area' school. Graceland, situated on a socially disadvantaged housing estate, felt it did well to recruit 80 per cent of its feeder school pupils. The school prided itself on already providing a good education and having good relationships with the community and parents. However, the headteacher thought it was very difficult to counter the desire of some parents to choose a school off the estate and perceived other schools as engaging in such recruitment in order to bolster their numbers. The financial incentive to expand rolls was also dampened by a 'discontinuous marginal cost function', which means that costs rise suddenly as pupil numbers increase when another class has to be created. This discontinuity makes it difficult to afford the extra staffing required by a larger roll. When the intake year at Graceland rose from seventy-five to ninety, the school thought it had to run four classes of twenty-two or twenty-three rather than three of thirty because of the educational needs of the pupils. Fishlake also responded to expansion by increasing staffing and thereby increasing the risk of a budget deficit.

Thus the motivations that underlie schools' policies towards student recruitment are considerably different from those of the standard firm in the market model, which is assumed to expand output in response to increased demand. The incentive of higher prices and hence profits is absent. It is therefore a limited response by over-subscribed schools to unsatisfied parental demand, which leaves some parents unable to choose their preferred school.

The incentive to be responsive is considerably greater for those schools with empty places and which would find financial and educational advantages in additional enrolment. However, there was no evidence among the case-study schools with surplus places that they were responding by means of greater diversity in provision. The schools responded to the pressures to market themselves, in so far as they did, by seeking to emphasize their existing characteristics; for example, as a denominational school, a village primary school, a community secondary school which sought to build links with parents through running a parents' room, or as a school with rural studies facilities. Headteachers defined for themselves what they considered to be of educational value and sought to promote it in low-key ways, rather than seeking to find out what parents wanted and respond to it. Only at Waterton, in the town where some competition was in evidence, was there a hint by some teachers of responding to middle-class parental preferences by organizing musical events and providing French at an earlier age.

That the lack of observed responsiveness to parents in the case-study schools is probably due to the absence of a competitive environment is supported by the findings of the PASCI study (Bagley et al. 1994; Woods et al. 1994). In two of the 'competitive arenas' studied, there was more competition between schools and greater perception by parents of choice of school than in the third rural area (Woods 1994). In a survey of 1922 parents, between 63 and 73 per cent in the two urban areas perceived themselves to have a real choice of school, compared with 56 per cent in the rural area. There was more evidence of some schools in the two more competitive areas being responsive to parents by making substantive changes in relation to such issues as homework, increased examination practice and more assertive discipline, than in the rural area. The researchers concluded that 'schools are keen to promote themselves, but much less likely to initiate ways of finding out how parents view the school and how it might accommodate their expressed wishes and concerns' (Woods et al. 1994: 11). It would appear that schools are more 'institution responsive' than 'consumer-responsive'. They respond to what 'competitor schools' are doing by putting pressure on their neighbours not to engage in rivalry and by cultivating relationships with their feeder schools. Among the eleven PASCI schools, the academically successful are confident that they are doing what parents want and can select some of their customers. Schools with surplus capacity and lower-ability pupils interact more with their local community and encourage more parental contact. However, they are much more inclined to seek to convince parents of professional values, for example with respect to promoting technology and anti-racism, than to be 'customer-led'. This suggests that the quasi-market is operating to give academically aspiring parents what they want and to persuade socially disadvantaged parents to value what educationalists think is good for their children.

Conclusion

This chapter has focused on the processes of decision-making with respect to resource management, with a particular emphasis on resource allocation. This is because the factors which research has indicated are positively associated with school effectiveness include goal clarity and a focus on learning achieved through school planning. Here the important factor is not the production of documented plans, but the integrative processes of reaching shared values among staff, agreeing common approaches to the curriculum which deliver continuity and progression for students, and ensuring that the physical and non-teaching staff resources are used to best effect to support learning. Local management is clearly not sufficient to guarantee that these processes are generated within schools. One cannot even be sure that it is a necessary condition for effective schooling. The most favourable verdict one can deliver is that local management stimulates these processes within schools where management is attuned to them, and that over time these processes are developing in an increasing number of schools. However, no rapid transformation of school cultures was observed and, as will be discussed in Chapter 6, classroom teachers did not appear to be significantly affected by local management so long as it did not threaten their job security. There is therefore little evidence from this sample of schools of local management stimulating any significant changes in the ways schools operate with respect to their core technology of teaching and learning.

However, there are other factors which could offset the benign effects of improvements in decision-making, in particular the time demands of local management on school staff which are considered in the next chapter. Further detractions are budget uncertainty, and loss of resources to those schools which suffer declining pupil rolls. None of the eleven schools in the IFFS study, even those which had lost out by formula-funding, fell into the latter category. The four schools which at the start of LMS faced the greatest budgetary difficulties had, by 1993, developed positive attitudes to

Table 5.3   Interviews undertaken for Impact of Formula Funding on Schools study

Role of interviewee	Number interviewed	Length of interview	Method of recording
Headteacher	11 in 1991–92; 8 in 1993	Two 1-hour interviews; 1 hour in 1993	Taped
Senior teacher in charge of finance (where appropriate)	9	1 hour	Taped
School finance officer	9	1 hour	Taped
Chair of governors or finance sub-committee	8	1 hour	Taped
Teaching staff	41	30 minutes	Taped or notes

local management; they had survived and had been forced to focus on their educational priorities to a greater extent than other schools, though they did not have the best developed rational resource management processes. Bullock and Thomas (1994), in a major study of the impact of local management, also conclude that it has stimulated improvements in school management, though with the caveat that this depends on the school's financial situation and headteacher's management style.

Appendix: Research methods for school case studies

1 *Semi-structured interviews*. These were conducted with four LEA officers with major responsibilities for LMS and seventy-eight people with school-related responsibilities. Details of the school interviews are set out in Table 5.3. Different interview schedules were used for each type of post-holder. Interviews were transcribed and sent to the interviewee for verification.
2 *Observation*. At each school, at least one full governors' meeting and one meeting of a sub-committee dealing with finance was observed. (The latter was not observed at Candleford.) In some schools, more than one meeting of each type or meetings of additional committees were observed. Notes were taken at all meetings and later transcribed. These

observations gathered evidence on how decisions were taken and what was decided.

3 *Documentary analysis.* At each school committee meeting, papers concerned with financial decision-making and related issues were studied in order to obtain information on how schools were responding to LMS. Local education authority committee papers and correspondence with schools were studied in order to understand the LEA's LMS scheme, and the issues arising in implementing it in the context of further government regulations and the threat of community charge-capping.

4 *Analysis of qualitative data.* The qualitative data were coded and sorted using Hyperqual, a text manager for the Macintosh computer. The codes were derived from the full set of research questions referred to above, and further development of research hypotheses on the postulated effects of LMS derived from the literature and modified by ideas arising during the research.

5 *Time-scale.* The data were collected between schools between January and December 1991. Additional case-study work was done at Yellowstone in 1992 and further interviews conducted in June and July 1993.

Key roles in local management

Introduction

Local management of schools (LMS) has brought about significant changes in the roles of key personnel in schools. The role most affected by these changes has been that of the headteacher. The expanded responsibilities of headteachers mean that other roles within school are immediately affected if they are to find the time to conduct their job effectively. In supporting headteachers, the tasks performed by deputy heads and administrative staff are of particular importance. Governing bodies, which now have overall responsibility for overseeing the management of the school, its finances, its staffing and the implementation of a mandated curriculum, have also seen a significant increase in their potential powers and thus changes in their ways of working. For headteachers, their relationship with the governing body is now of far greater importance and requires careful management.

This chapter examines how these various roles were adapted and conducted in the case-study schools in order to provide some evidence against which to assess the impact of local management on school leadership. This factor has been singled out in the research literature as a major contributor to school effectiveness,[1] and is therefore of particular salience for assessing the possible links between local management and improvements in educational outcomes. The issues discussed in this chapter are particularly relevant for addressing three of the questions posed in Chapter 3 – whether local management promotes more effective school leadership, more collaborative decision-making, and more highly motivated and professionally oriented teams.

The headteacher's role in locally managed schools

There is a reasonable degree of consistency in the research literature concerning the general characteristics displayed by an effective headteacher. Rutherford (1985) summarizes five main features:

* clear vision and goals;
* the ability to articulate and translate this vision for the school community;
* the provision of a supportive environment for teaching and learning;
* monitoring classroom and school practice;
* intervention to reinforce the positive features of teachers' and students' work and to take corrective action.

Beare *et al.* (1989), in *Creating an Excellent School*, specify that instructional leadership includes:

* ensuring that resources are acquired and allocated in a manner consistent with goals, needs, priorities and plans;
* supervising teachers and their development;
* supporting teachers through maintaining an orderly school community;
* quality control through monitoring and evaluation of teaching and learning;
* co-ordination;
* trouble shooting.

Both the above lists focus on internal school processes, no doubt reflecting the institutional contexts from which the reported knowledge emerged, and so do not give sufficient place to the headteacher as chief mediator between the school and its task environment. The repositioning of schools as semi-autonomous organizations in a regulated quasi-market is more fundamental to changing the role of the headteacher than just the addition of the task of financial administration. A school administered as part of a bureaucratic public sector hierarchy requires a different leadership to that of a self-managing school. The contrast between the two should not be exaggerated in the British context, as headteachers prior to local management had considerable discretion in managing their schools, though the degree of this varied across local education authorities (LEAs). Key differences between the leadership requirements of administered hierarchies and semi-autonomous schools are captured by Chapman (1990: 227), writing in the Australian context of Victoria:

> The principal is no longer able to see him/herself as the authority figure, supported and at times protected by system wide and centrally determined rules and regulations. Instead the principal must become a co-ordinator of a number of people representing different interest groups among the whole school community, who together will determine the direction the school will follow.

The main elements of the headteacher role in locally managed schools are closely related to the components of the open systems model of the school. These are:

- *Boundary management*: this is important for resource management, because it is central to the acquisition of resources.
- *Resource management*: this embraces budget management and the creation and maintenance of as good a learning environment as possible with the resources available. It encompasses the linkages between allocating financial and physical resources and the resulting educational outputs and outcomes.
- *Instructional leadership*: managing the technical core of the school, i.e. its processes of teaching and learning, and embraces both curriculum and human resource management.

Overarching all three domains of leadership is the distinction between maintenance activities and development. Maintenance activities are concerned with the coordination of the life of the school on a daily basis: class organization, production of schemes of work, recruitment of staff, recording and reporting pupils' work, preparing and monitoring the annual budget. All this can tick over smoothly and cost-effectively, but unless development work is being undertaken, progress, adaptation to new circumstances and further improvements in learning are unlikely to occur. The movement to local management, with its greater environmental uncertainty, has increased the importance of developmental activities, but at the same time made schools responsible for more of their maintenance (literally in the case of premises and grounds). For headteachers, the key personal question is the balance they choose between the various elements of the role. This will depend on their own interests and skills, those of other staff and governors, and on the characteristics of the school and its environment. How the different headteachers in the eleven schools responded to this balancing act is examined in the first part of this chapter.

Boundary management

In all the schools, the headteacher was by virtue of the post the chief link between the school and the outside world, and cultivated a network of contacts with other headteachers, with the LEA and with key members of the local community. One of the functions of this networking is to cooperate with others and thus to exert influence and pressure in order to modify the external environment in ways which benefit the school. Headteachers in Barset generally valued cooperation between schools and reiterated the need to avoid schools taking individual action which would harm the system as a whole.

The authority's funding formula was an important focus of headteacher lobbying, exercised in particular through the primary and secondary headteachers' local associations and through this and other consultative channels operated by the LEA. As a hung council, representations to councillors were also an effective tactic as the Education Committee voted over individual elements in the formula and budget. The primary school budget had been increased in 1990 in response to lobbying by primary headteachers, among whom the Yellowstone headteacher had been prominent. Another issue was, as the 11–16 schools saw it, underfunding of years 7 to 11 compared with sixth-forms, in an authority where some schools had small sixth-forms:

> All 11–16 schools in the Authority have come off poorly in comparison with 11–18 schools and upper schools. In two years we will have lost £38–40,000 compared with our historic budget. The main reason is because the Age Weighted Pupil Unit (AWPU) for Key Stage 3 pupils[2] is low. Sixth-forms get extra fixed costs for being sixth-forms and get generous weighting in the AWPU for post-16 pupils.
>
> (Fenmore headteacher)

Peacehaven complained similarly about the formula. In the second year, the LEA responded by removing the fixed cost weighting for sixth-forms.

The most crucial issue of all – survival – faced small village primary schools. As discussed in Chapter 7, the formula, with 75 per cent of funding allocated by pupil numbers, disadvantaged small schools, which have relatively high fixed costs compared with larger schools. In 1991, the council was debating a substantial cut to the lump sum amount given to primary schools, which would harm the smaller schools in particular. A review of primary school provision was also getting under way. This prompted a vigorous campaign by village communities to preserve village schools, at the forefront of which were headteachers and governors. The newly appointed head of Candleford was faced with this crisis:

> I had only just taken up my position when I heard of the threatened cuts to small school budgets. It was a question of rallying round and getting the right people to write letters. In the end it was not as bad as feared.

Headteachers in one town and its surrounding villages had collaborated to obtain business sponsorship for joint school events and information technology (IT) investment. Headteachers also collaborated in order to manage their pupil rolls, and there was considerable emphasis in interviews on not poaching other schools' pupils:

> Our school could take a lot more pupils as we have two extra rooms . . . There are four schools in this town . . . The heads work together. We have an agreed system of referring parents to the catchment area school first. It seems to work quite well.
>
> (Horsefield headteacher)

This kind of agreement seemed to operate in three of the localities, though not in one large town where Graceland and Waterton were located.

As well as securing resources and support through collaborative networks, some headteachers were more active than others in seizing upon opportunities to further the interests of the school. Thus the head of Yellowstone was keen to see the school become a pilot local management school and to benefit financially from this. The headteacher evidently seized upon opportunities large and small – on one visit, he was observed stacking away carpeting left behind by a bankrupt firm. It was generally remarked by staff and advisers how well resourced the school was, though it was not more generously funded than the rest. It had the advantage of new buildings and large numbers, but much of its high level of resourcing was attributed to the head: 'We are very well resourced, generally speaking, because the head is an excellent manager. Over the years we have with care managed to accumulate stock' (Yellowstone teacher).

Networking in the community in order to obtain voluntary donations of resources, usually in the form of people's time, or low-cost but high-quality services, such as repairs, was particularly prevalent in the two village primary schools and to some extent offset the disadvantage of high fixed costs in a regime of pupil-driven formula-funding. In a socially disadvantaged area, the Graceland head was able to play upon this fact in securing business sponsorship for a minibus.

The effect of local management in stimulating networking and micropolitical activity by headteachers is reported in an interview study of twenty secondary heads, which concluded that:

> Heads have more scope for devising aims and goals and for matching resource allocation to their stated objectives. Under LMS heads are even more strategically placed than before to take decisions, advise, recommend, manipulate, bargain and negotiate.
>
> (Evetts 1993: 55)

The change in orientation required of headteachers was well expressed by Fenmore's head:

> Initially, I was philosophically opposed to local management, as I saw my role as an uncomplicated pressure for delivering an education service and I had always seen it as other people's tasks to tell me how much money was available and how much of the service I wanted to provide I could or could not provide. I hoped I could be persuasive enough to wring more resources out of the Authority to do the job. Part of me still feels this is a more honest way of proceeding but one mellows with the practicalities of life and we are now using the new system to our best advantage.

By 1993, he thought that schools were in the best position to make choices regarding resource use. He now made the general case for more resources for education not to LEA officers but to local politicians.

Budget and resource management

The new tasks of budget management, encompassing financial reporting and budget-setting, are the most transparent and obvious of the changed role of the school and hence of the headteacher. Headteachers had the most influence on how these tasks were undertaken by determining both their own approach and that of others. This was also the finding in a set of case studies done for the Resourcing Sheffield Schools Project, which reported that 'the headteacher was central to the organisation and distribution of resources' (Burgess *et al.* 1992: 3).

In examining how headteachers conducted budget management, it is necessary to consider two key roles – that of budget manager and that of finance officer. The budget manager is a role undertaken by a member of the school's senior management team. The budget manager is responsible for drawing up the budget plan and steering it through the school's decision-making structure. The budget manager role is not that of decision-making *per se*, but of overseeing the decision-making process (Anthony and Herzlinger 1989). In secondary schools nowadays, the budget manager role is often a major component of the job description of a deputy head, but the budget manager does not by virtue of his or her position make key decisions except as part of the senior management team or other decision-making bodies. The finance officer services the budget manager by being responsible for the day-to-day operation of the financial control system. The finance officer works with computerized accounts packages, preparing financial reports and chasing up budget queries. The finance officer is normally a member of the non-teaching staff. In relation to physical resource management, schools have acquired responsibilities for managing their buildings and sites to a much greater extent, thus creating a third role – that of 'site manager'. Since this embraces taking decisions about premises expenditures and health and safety, it is a much expanded and more responsible role than that of the old-style school caretaker.

The budget manager role is of greatest significance, since it is pivotal to the allocation of resources at school level. How the Barset headteachers allocated the budget manager role and their degree of interest in financial management is indicated in Table 6.1. The variation in the extent of finance officer support is also indicated.

At Peacehaven and Fenmore, the headteachers maintained a central interest in financial management but delegated the role of budget manager to a deputy head. This enables headteachers to devote more time to boundary management and instructional leadership, and to their private lives. It also has the advantage of sharing responsibility and decision-making within the senior management team, whereas budget management by the headteacher might well be associated with the centralization of power. The Fenmore head gave his rationale:

> I delegated responsibility for LMS to the deputy to play on the strengths
> of the team as he wanted to do it. I thought being absorbed with

Table 6.1 Allocation of the role of budget manager in the case-study schools

Head's interest in financial management	Head acting as budget manager	Budget manager role delegated	Considerable finance officer support
Central interest	Pentland Yellowstone Horsefield Graceland Harrimore	Peacehaven Fenmore	Pentland Yellowstone Harrimore Peacehaven
Muted interest	Candleford All Saints	Fishlake Waterton	

finance would stop me being concerned with the other areas of the school, such as staffing and curriculum issues, which are still the core purpose of what the school is all about.

Peacehaven's headteacher gave a more detailed justification:

> I can never delegate ultimate responsibility. I wanted to delegate the day-to-day management and implementation of LMS which has two levels. There is the whole administrative paraphernalia – the financial/ clerical aspects undertaken by the finance clerk working to the bursar. In terms of the day-to-day management of LMS – monitoring and processing the different aspects of the income and expenditure. This I wanted to delegate. I wanted to have that summarized for me, trends observed or early warnings sounded. That by and large is the deputy's role. But anything that fundamentally affects the school and what it is here for are decisions that I would not delegate away but would be a strong participant in.

The Harrimore head retained the role of budget manager and initially used a retired deputy to act as finance officer, together with some internal clerical support: 'My responsibility for LMS is to carry the can at the end of the day, I guess, making decisions as best one can based on the information coming in'. The retired deputy finance officer described his working relationship with the head:

> I work as a team with Mark [the head], who will come to me and say: 'I want to do this sort of thing, what do you think?' I look at the financial implications and say 'yes' or 'I wouldn't do it quite like that' until we come up with a mutual agreement as to what is best . . . This morning I have to go through all the staffing salaries and see whether we can afford to increase the number of incentive allowances.

The Harrimore head mentioned in the 1993 re-interview that in his appraisal senior staff thought there should be more collective decision-making. His response was to have a formal monthly budget review where the bursar informed the whole senior team. The deputies could also access any information they wanted from the computer.

The other secondary head (All Saints) who acted as a budget manager was keen to retain his instructional leadership role by still teaching seven hours a week – 'to prevent me becoming divorced from reality, the staff and the kids'. But he felt unable to delegate budget management:

> In practice, delegating responsibility for LMS depends on the situation within each school. At the time it would have been impossible to delegate because of the nature of the people within the jobs and even with the two new deputies the time involved in training would have been too time-consuming. Some of the things that I was doing are now being done well by the deputies and so I am not spending the time that I used to picking up the pieces.

This head, despite acting as the budget manager, was less interested in and involved in budget management than the other secondary headteachers who had delegated it to a deputy. One reason for this was that budget management was partially undertaken by a very active governor, an accountant who chaired the finance committee. Also, the development of a rational approach to resource management was less evident in this school than in the other secondaries. A head of department commented:

> There has been little change in the management structure and that seems a wasted opportunity. LMS is a chance to improve efficiency and effectiveness but there has been no attempt or desire to change anything here. Long-term planning is of the essence but also does not seem to be in evidence.

The teacher noted tight staffing and lack of staff development, while he observed resources being wasted in other departments.

In the primary sector, it was very difficult for headteachers to delegate budget management. Three primary heads and one middle school head were active and competent budget managers, and two of these were well supported by a highly competent finance officer. The Waterton headteacher did not formally delegate budget management, but part of this role, together with the finance officer role, were performed by a head of department who had non-contact time for the job, with three other teachers now covering part of his timetable. He had volunteered for the job of 'finance officer' and was one of four senior teachers who were very influential in running the school. He described his work:

> I put everything into the computer as the secretary is shy of computers. She will take invoices and send them off and do the necessary

paperwork. There is the reconciliation disk to do and then the big job of reconciling the two sets of figures and then fielding queries, preparing print-outs for governors. I cannot do this in the time allocated. I am here from 7.45 to 6.00 and often work on these after school. I take the computer home during the holidays and do some finance work. Once it dominated everything, but now I do various things in chunks. I feel that the secretary could do more but one does not want to pressure her into leaving as the school may collapse. It relies on my goodwill; they wanted it done on the cheap and it has been done on the cheap. I asked if they would make me a deputy but that did not materialize, and I am not getting interviews although I am doing more than many deputies.

The headteacher, who later took early retirement, did not play a central role in budget management. As he remarked: 'If a major problem occurs then I am consulted, but it does not happen very often so there is little need for me to be consulted except in formal meetings'. Waterton was one of the schools where rational resource management seemed least well developed. It was, however, in a middle-class catchment area and popular with parents. In addition, as it had received a large increase in its budget as a result of formula-funding, it was under no pressure to attract more pupils or to maximize the value obtained from its resources.

The other middle school head at Gracelands acted as budget manager and did a considerable amount of the detailed financial figure work as well. He took prime responsibility for making budget decisions and drawing up the budget, but fully consulted the staff by giving them a lot of budgetary information and sounding them out about alternatives. The workload was considerable:

I spend far more time than I should on financial issues. The budget figure arrived on the telephone on the last day of term and the paperwork during the holidays. I started work on it when I got back and devoted most of my time until five, refusing to take it home. It took me three weeks to get it into the computer and produce the final paper and have it ready for governors. What now consumes the time is checking with County Treasury because I do not think they are getting it right.

In 1993, budget preparation was still complex and time-consuming because of the impact of further delegation of services to schools:

It was very difficult to work out how badly off you were . . . It took a long time for schools to work out where they were because there was so little comparison with the year before. We were one of the first schools to realize where we were – we were £30,000 in the red. I had to read all the paperwork on compulsory redundancies.

This headteacher had delegated curriculum and pastoral responsibilities to a deputy and also to a senior teacher, referred to as a deputy. In a relatively small school he was still able to maintain contact with staff and pupils and believed in extensive consultation of staff. He was held in high regard by staff, who recognized his skill in bringing resources into the school. Site management was undertaken by the caretaker, but the head was also a skilled handyman. For 1994 he had negotiated an ingenious early retirement scheme on health grounds to save the school making compulsory redundancies. He would work as site manager/caretaker, since the caretaker was retiring, and also act as budget manager.

The Yellowstone headteacher was similarly perceived by staff as a good manager. He saw his role thus:

> I am a mixture of chief executive and finance officer to the subcommittees, as I put forward proposals and recommendations which are not always taken on board . . . I am a negotiator and then an arbitrator able to work with an overview of the whole school, so apportioning is even-handed. If finance were delegated, something would have had to be lifted from the deputy who is carrying a heavy workload. It is very important that the head should be in the forefront of a development which is integral to the whole working of the school.

The headteachers at Pentland and Horsefield similarly acted as budget managers. Both felt unable to delegate this role to their deputies. The problem of coping with budget and site management is particularly severe for heads of small primary schools who have a major teaching commitment. The heads of the two small primaries in our sample had at most a day a week non-contact time. The headteacher at Candleford, who resigned early on in our study, was reported to have done all the budget planning herself with no direct involvement of others. The new headteacher (interviewed in 1993) realized that the burden on her secretary was so great that she increased her teaching time from four to four and a half days in order to release money to pay her secretary on a higher grade for five hours a week to do the financial work. The head initially had to put in extra time catching up with the backlog of budget work. She now relied on her secretary to act as a finance officer cum bursar who made decisions on her own initiative. The headteacher at Fishlake delegated budget management completely to a highly competent female parent-governor, who was paid on an hourly basis for acting as both budget manager and finance officer:

> I feel it is important to be more in touch with the children and so do minimal work on LMS. I want to be more accessible to parents so they can see me as someone closely involved with the children, rather than being locked away in an office and thus set apart.
>
> (Fishlake headteacher)

Instructional leadership

All the headteachers, but especially those who had not delegated budget management, were very conscious of the diversion of time away from teaching and daily contact with pupils and staff. Teachers tended to be critical of this aspect of local management. Of course, merely having such contact is no guarantee that instructional leadership is provided by the headteacher. Nor is it the case that a school with a non-teaching head lacks instructional leadership, since this in part can be delegated to other staff and promoted by building up teacher teams concerned with developing and evaluating the curriculum. Headteachers can act as instructional leaders through developing a school culture and management style conducive to effective learning, rather than through teaching a regular timetable.

The time demands of local management were cited by 65 per cent of senior managers in the eleven schools as a drawback to LMS and was the negative feature most frequently mentioned by staff at all levels (Marren and Levačić 1994). Concern at the lack of contact with classroom teaching was, not surprisingly, greatest among the primary heads:

I am becoming more and more some sort of line manager, much more so than a headteacher. I do very little teaching. I still feel guilty about my lack of contact with the children. I am sure that parents would prefer a head who was seen more in the classroom.

(Horsefield headteacher)

Heads are now much more line managers and I am not sure all heads are happy about this. Most headteachers are there because they are good teachers and show good practice in the classroom and like interacting with and teaching children. They had a timetable where they were able to balance their management expertise and take their teaching expertise to the classroom and support staff in the classroom. Now that has been almost wiped away overnight, as we are spending so much time in chairs over documentation and there is a feeling of guilt that we should be doing more in the classroom. Being optimistic, this may be a temporary phase as we get our own time-management sorted out and as we get a firmer grip of what is asked of us and thus speed up the processes, but we are learning quite major professional skills and the sacrifice is the interactions which happened previously. Heads are stressed because they are trying to do the old job as well as coming to grips with the new demands. Financial planning and budgetary control are a large part of this.

(Pentland headteacher)

Classroom teachers in most schools expressed concern about the impact of local management on the headteacher's role as professional leader. However, in Yellowstone, where the 'good practice' model for local management seemed most developed, teachers were much more positive.

The head is enjoying LMS thoroughly. He works very hard. He gives the staff positive messages about it. The headteacher is the main motivator of staff.

(Teacher A)

I think the effects of LMS depend on how well the head manages the budget. Here he does a marvellous job, but I wonder whether other heads I've worked with could manage.

(Teacher B)

The evidence reveals the changed nature of the role of head and the different ways in which the headteachers responded to the need to determine a balance between the now expanded requirements of their post. For a secondary head, delegating the budget manager role to a deputy head while retaining a central interest in resource management and making decisions collectively within the senior management team is probably the most effective response. However, Maychell's (1994) survey found that in only just over one-third of secondary schools did a deputy head have a major responsibility for finance. Primary headteachers are not in a position to delegate budget management. Very few primary deputies in Maychell's survey had financial responsibilities. Thus primary heads, if they are to manage effectively, must have a capable finance officer to undertake financial control and be able to advise on expenditure decisions. Consequently, primary headteachers in all but the smallest schools must develop the capacity for instructional leadership in other staff members. There is some evidence that the deputy head's role in the primary school is becoming much better defined in management terms and is focused on providing curriculum leadership (Maw 1994). One possible implication of this is that women will not be attracted to progressing beyond deputy headship in primary schools, as the headteacher's role requires less involvement with teaching and much more with external networking and resource management.

There were some indications by 1993 that headteachers had overcome the initial workload hump, had learned how to operate the system, and to delegate. Finance staff had become more skilled and the LEA was now providing a bursaring service which small schools could buy into, thus benefiting from economies of scale.

The deputy as budget manager

Delegating the budget manager role still leaves unresolved the question of how best to allocate these tasks, whether to a teaching deputy or to a non-teacher bursar. None of the schools studied had employed a bursar or 'general manager' in a senior post, as have an increasing number of schools elsewhere. What I have classified as a finance officer was referred to as a bursar in two schools.

At Fenmore and Peacehaven, the deputy who was the budget manager was also in charge of premises matters. One taught 15/40 periods a week and the other was on a half timetable. The Fenmore deputy was also in charge of health and safety, reprographics, trips and INSET. At Peacehaven, the deputy's duties included receiving and deciding on quotations for small building works, refuse collection, and furniture and fittings, receiving salespeople and dealing with the County Property Department. It was as he described it, 'boring and nitty-gritty', but he was reluctant to agree that a non-teaching staff member could deal with these issues because of the accountability. Because of 'problems with the software', the Fenmore deputy had been 'preoccupied with menial and day-to-day financial management'. Both deputies' workload had increased:

> I'm not only working longer hours but trying to get more out of the hours that I do work . . . I'm not teaching awfully well – few heads and deputies are. I'm teaching worse than ever I was; my marking is difficult to do well. There are times of the year when the workload is very heavy and what suffers is the kids and it should be the other way round. But I feel a management responsibility for £1.4 million pounds and for a board of governors who are responsible through me for that.
>
> (Peacehaven deputy head)

These two examples of deputy roles indicate the problems that arise when the budget manager role is not clearly separated from the site manager and finance officer roles. The budget manager role, because of the need to gather, filter and analyse (often informally and intuitively) information relating educational objectives to resourcing, is probably best undertaken by someone with teaching experience. However, the finance officer and site manager roles, which are concerned with operational support services, do not need teacher-based knowledge. A deputy head who performs both budget and site manager roles is likely to be overloaded with maintenance tasks and therefore unable to concentrate sufficiently on development issues, personal teaching or on better communication with all staff members. It is questionable that site management is most efficiently undertaken by a deputy head whose professional background does not encompass training in the necessary technical matters.

Another issue is the possible impact of the budget manager role on the prospects of women reaching headships. While female deputies tend to specialize in pastoral and personnel issues, the budget manager role tends to be assigned to a male deputy. Thus women will not obtain the all-round management experience at deputy level required for headship if they do not put themselves forward as budget manager and/or are not selected for this role. In the primary sector, three of our five schools had female headteachers. They appeared to be just as capable as the men of taking on the budget manager role when required to. However, as already noted, if women are put off primary headship by the resource management dimension of the role, this will adversely affect the proportion of headships held by women.

The role of the finance officer

The new role of finance officer has now become crucial to the effective management of schools. If headteachers or other senior teachers acting as budget managers are also to function effectively in the other aspects of their jobs, they need the administrative aspects of financial management undertaken for them. In primary schools, the tasks of financial record-keeping and reporting has mainly fallen to the school secretary, whose job has been radically altered by the advent of local management. Similar role extension for the school secretary has occurred in secondary schools. At Peacehaven, for example, the head's secretary became the bursar assisted by a clerk for inputting data into the computer. School secretaries were thus required to learn new skills in both accounting and computing, and handle new systems which were not yet working well. The experience of Horsefield's school secretary was typical:

> The training courses have been reasonable, but it was a case of too much too quick. If I ring up the school's finance officer he is never there, so I ring up Helen [another secretary] who has proved invaluable. There is an informal network whereby we help each other . . . I do at times take work home. I cannot concentrate with the office distractions . . . Most staff are appreciative of what I do, but some take it for granted and just expect it to be done . . . The job is enjoyable and challenging but it does rely on my goodwill.

Common themes of the finance officers were the problems they had with interfacing with the LEA's computerized financial system, in particular the difficulty of reconciling the monthly accounts and their need to constantly check for accounting errors. A particular problem was the difficulty of getting sufficient uninterrupted time away from other tasks in order to concentrate on the financial work. Senior staff appreciated the value of a good finance officer, who could save the school money by his/her knowledge of the accounting system and by vigilance. Not all the case-study schools were fortunate enough to have secretaries who had coped well with the additional demands. Even in one case where the finance officer was held in high regard, she resigned because of the pressures of the job. Without the support of a competent finance officer, the budget manager (head or deputy) was driven into spending a lot of time on routine financial administration, which is an inefficient and ineffective use of their time.

As in Crawford's (1994) study of ten primary school secretaries, those in the case-study schools were all married women with families, attracted to work in schools at relatively low pay because of the convenience of the hours. They considered themselves poorly paid, even after some increase in pay in recognition of their additional responsibilities and workload. As with Crawford's sample, they undertook a varied and wide selection of other duties and relied considerably on self-development in the job. Their relationship with the headteacher was crucial to the effectiveness with which they felt they could do their jobs. In secondary schools, where a larger number of administrative and clerical staff are employed, it is more common for the finance officer post to be a specialized one for a trained accountancy clerk, usually filled by a woman, except for more senior bursar posts.

Local management has therefore had a significant impact on the school secretary/ finance officer. Its smooth implementation has been highly dependent on the women filling these roles, who mostly provide a high degree of skill at a lower rate of pay than in other sectors because of the non-monetary attractions of the job to women with dependent children. Their role has become more influential in the school, which has on occasions met with resentment from teachers.

Class teacher involvement in financial management

The issue of teacher involvement in financial management is salient to the extent that there is a relationship between teachers' ability to control their work and the effectiveness of teaching and learning. There is no clear evidence regarding the degree of teacher control or empowerment which promotes the greatest degree of motivation or of the links between motivation, job satisfaction and teacher performance. A predominant theme in the current educational management literature is that effective teaching is promoted by collaborative decision-making in schools and by headteacher leadership, which is facilitative rather than authoritarian. Facilitative power on the part of principals/headteachers is defined by Dunlap and Goldman (1991) to involve:

- acquiring or arranging material resources that support staff and their aspirations;
- creating effective teams;
- feedback and reinforcement systems;
- networks to link the school with the outside world.

Local management has a dual aspect with respect to headteachers' exercise of facilitative power. On the one hand, it has increased headteachers' powers by redistributing to them powers which used to belong to the LEA. On the other hand, it provides headteachers with greater opportunities to 'acquire or arrange material resources to support teachers' and greater pressures to develop external and supportive networks. The encouragement to develop a rational approach to resource management in which outputs are more transparent is consistent with developing feedback and reinforcement systems. And the effective conduct of headship, given its expanded responsibilities, requires the creation of effective teams within the school. However, as Chapman (1990: 213) notes, 'the influence of the principal remains fundamental in determining the extent, nature and pattern of teacher participation in the decision-making of schools', and that no direct relationship has been demonstrated between teacher involvement and improved practice.

An influence on decisions and the power to make decisions are quite distinct. As professionals, teachers have a degree of power, which varies between education systems and schools within the same system, to make decisions which affect their work. These decisions may be made as autonomous individuals or collectively. There is clearly a trade-off between a teacher's individual power and that of the teacher collective. Teachers may influence decisions but not have the ultimate power to determine them. Headteachers who consult teachers and take notice of their views give teachers influence but not power over decision-making. There is considerable advocacy nowadays of collaborative or collegial management, which is closely related to the concept of facilitative management by headteachers. Collaborative or collegial management (Wallace 1989; Nias *et al.* 1992) implies that headteachers develop teacher teams to whom collective power may be delegated on particular issues or with whom the headteacher seeks to negotiate a consensus. When management arrangements are flexible and fluid, there is no clear designation of who has authority to take decisions over pre-specified matters.

A useful framework to apply in determining when teacher participation in decision-making is effective because it improves the quality of decisions and promotes cooperation has been put forward by Hoy and Tarter (1993), building on the seminal work of Barnard (1938). For determining whether a decision lies within teachers' 'zone of acceptance' (i.e. they can accept not being involved), two main criteria are proposed.

- *Interest*: do teachers have a personal interest in the decision?
- *Expertise*: can the teachers provide expert knowledge to inform the decision?

If the decision is neither of interest or in an area of teacher expertise, then teacher participation in the decision would be ineffective, as teachers would resent the time involved, especially if their lack of expertise meant their views had no impact. If teachers have an interest and expertise, then participation is called for and the decision is outside the zone of acceptance. The other two permutations are marginal to the zone of acceptance and teacher participation is only sometimes called for depending on the nature of the issue. Two other relevant factors which affect the appropriate degree of participation are the amount of time required for participation relative to the amount available and the degree of teacher commitment to school goals. In a school with considerable conflicts over goals and extensive micropolitical activity, participation in decision-making can exacerbate tensions and certainly requires considerable headteacher skill to negotiate a satisfactory conclusion to the exercise.

The Hoy–Tarter framework is of considerable value in explaining the IFFS findings on the nature of teacher participation in budget decision-making. Teachers had little influence in making decisions about the overall budget, though the extent to which they were consulted varied from school to school. The greatest degree of involvement was in deciding on allocations for curriculum support resources and then determining their own spending within an allocated budget. Thus teacher participation was greatest in relation to that part of the budget where teachers had a direct interest and expertise. By and large, teachers did not seek a greater degree of involvement in overall budget-setting, expressing both a lack of interest and expertise. They saw financial management as lying within the domain of senior management who have the necessary expertise. Typical statements were:

> Look, I have the greatest respect for the way in which the deputy has been involved in delivering LMS. And the reason I don't know very much about it is because I don't need to worry about things. You've enough work to do without getting involved in things that don't concern you.
>
> (Peacehaven teacher – clearly exasperated at being interviewed about LMS!)

> We have a say in what happens but not in overall financial planning. There is confidence in management here and so no cause to worry. I do not think a lot of staff would want to bother about being party to these decisions.
>
> (Harrimore teacher)

Other teachers responded:

> I know very little apart from how my department is affected. I have no wish to know more.

> I am not really aware of the financial situation within the school. We are made aware, but it is not really my area.

> I do not spend time on financial matters as I do not think it important to do so.

The greatest involvement the staff as a whole had in overall budget-setting in any of the eleven schools consisted of being presented at a full staff meeting with a draft of next year's budget and being consulted on alternatives. This occurred at Yellowstone, Fenmore, Graceland, Pentland and Fishlake, though in a very small school such consultation is much

easier. It is interesting to note that the two schools with the most constrained budgets and which faced the prospect of staff cuts were among the
group which consulted the most. Clearly, teachers' interests were more at
stake than in schools with expanded budgets. The Graceland head noted:

> . . . the restructuring went through a very lengthy process of demo-
> cratic discussion with the staff ending up with a secret ballot with a
> number of models being put forward. There were staff meetings and
> even interviews with individual members of staff.

At schools with less formal consultation of the whole staff, particular
staff who took an interest in finance or related matters would be consulted
and could acquire knowledge and influence, for example by joining an *ad
hoc* advisory committee. However, the use by senior management of consultative committees and internal networks in determining budget priorities did not necessarily give staff an overall picture of how and why decisions
were made. As one head of department at Peacehaven said:

> . . . decisions are being made and we are not really aware of how they
> come about. I get the feeling that decisions are being made where we
> are given the feeling we are in a process of deciding, though the head
> and his deputies are already pretty clear as to what they would like the
> outcome to be.

Teachers did not always appreciate the new ways of participating in the
financial decisions which their headteacher enthused about:

> I find LMS tedious. In the old days, money was always found. Now
> you have to bid at the beginning of the year. You are given a list at
> staff meetings of where there is funding and hope the head can find it,
> or it goes to finance committee and that can be time-consuming.
>
> (Pentland teacher)

As predicted from the Hoy–Tarter framework, teacher involvement was
greatest with respect to curriculum support materials, but it had not changed
significantly as a result of local management in most schools. This was
particularly the case in the secondary schools where non-promoted teachers
were not budget-holders. The situation of heads of department being budget-
holders for departmental allocations had not changed. If anything there was
a trend to less budgetary autonomy for heads of department due to centralization of decision-making within the senior management team and a
greater emphasis on addressing whole school priorities. Previously, heads
of department could go to LEA advisers for pockets of money quite independently of their headteacher. In the secondary schools, other than All
Saints, which were more actively changing their decision-making in response to local management, there was a trend to making heads of department more accountable for their spending. Formulae were being replaced
by a bidding system as part of a general move towards greater integration

of departments and tighter coupling. Pressures for departments to produce development plans, which aligned with the school development plan and which were used to justify resource bids, were already evident. These have been further strengthened by the Office for Standards in Education (OFSTED) inspection recommendations (Levačić and Glover 1994a,b).

In the primary schools in our sample, there was more evidence of an increase in individual teacher empowerment. In the three larger primary schools, teachers had been allocated more money to spend at their own discretion. At Horsefield, this was in the order of £300 each, but it was £1000 at Yellowstone. Here teachers were grouped in twos or threes as 'partners' who taught classes in the same year group. Each partnership was given an annual budget out of which they had to purchase everything required for their classes. The curriculum consultants also had budgets to spend on their subject area. Once the budgets had been allocated, there was no expectation that more could be obtained. The arrangement was popular with the teachers:

> My partner and I think we have done very well out of this system because it has given us the freedom to choose where we think we need to spend the money. In the old days it was a much smaller amount. We now spend a lot of time looking at catalogues. You have to agree with your partner what you will buy and this makes it a lengthy process.

Each curriculum consultant is responsible for deciding what to buy with his or her budget in consultation with other staff on the working party for that curriculum area. The consultant is responsible for making other staff aware of what resources are available and how they can be used, and staff meeting time is set aside for this.

How much money to put in the budget for curriculum support and how to allocate it were decided at Yellowstone after consulting staff. The curriculum consultants put in bids to the senior management team (head, deputy and heads of infant and junior sections), who considered the implications of these bids for the amount left over for the partnership budgets, given all the other likely claims on the budget. This information and the bids were then discussed at a staff meeting and agreed. Partnership class budgets were arrived at by dividing equally among all the classes the amount left over from the curriculum support budget after deducting the curriculum consultants' budgets. Following this discussion, the head prioritized the bids and put them to the governors' curriculum committee together with a report on the overall financial situation. Using the information it received in the course of the year on curriculum policies developed by working groups, which included resource implications, the curriculum committee made recommendations to the finance committee as part of the overall budget plan. In practice, the committee was unlikely to revise the bids in any significant way.

While the teachers were fully consulted and had an influence on the decisions, the headteacher still retained the predominant influence. In his view:

> It would be untrue to say there is no authoritarianism, but not in the old way. There have been times when decisions have not always gone in the direction I would like to see, but I stand back and say: 'These people are leading their own lives and they will live by these decisions'.

The teachers at Yellowstone were far more positive about local management than the teachers at the other schools and far more aware of increased resourcing as a result of local management. There was also a tendency for the primary teachers to be less negative about local management than the secondary teachers. Tentatively, one can conclude that there is a positive relationship between the extra (but in many cases relatively small) degree of empowerment over resource allocation and teachers' perceptions of the benefits of local management (for more detail, see Marren and Levačić 1994). A larger survey by Maychell (1994) found some increase in teachers' involvement in financial decision-making: more teachers were budget-holders and teachers were being consulted more about the size of their curriculum support budgets.

The headteacher as buffer

One of the functions of management highlighted by the open systems model is to act as a buffer which protects the technical core of the organization from the turbulence of the external environment. The role of management is to secure and allocate the resources required to sustain the technical core, while leaving it to concentrate on the productive purposes of the organization. From this perspective, financial management is a specialized task overseen by the school's managers, with specialist support from staff who are not part of the technical core (i.e. non-teachers). Teachers' perceptions of their lack of expertise and interest in finance (except when job security is threatened) is wholly consistent with this view of the relative roles of teachers and senior management teams in resource management and budgeting. The head's role as buffer and its incompatibility with staff involvement were summed up by Harrimore's head:

> I am torn between wanting to make people more financially aware and saying 'Well it's not your problem really'. It is so easy for the headteacher and deputies to forget what it is like to see things as a mainstream classroom teacher, so I want them to be involved in these sorts of decisions to the extent that they want to be and not to add to their worries.

The head of Graceland, a strong believer in staff consultation or 'democracy', reflected on the loneliness of his primary role as decision-maker, buffer and mediator with the outside world:

> I consider myself the person making quite a lot of important financial decisions at stage one of the decision-making process . . . recruiting as many as you can get from the feeder schools is a damage limitation exercise . . . This requires me to have greater skills in management, to be more subtle, making decisions before I throw them into the ring. I have to see all these things because I cannot allow other people to see them, even the governors – with parent and teacher governors . . . At what point do you tell them about projected doom and gloom? I tell them as little as I can in that quarter.

Most teachers accepted and even welcomed the headteacher and senior management acting as buffers and taking the decisions. The few who expressed some unhappiness at the lack of teacher involvement tended to be at two schools where the headteachers were not perceived to be providing effective and active budget management, either themselves or via delegation.

The finding that financial management becomes concentrated within the senior management team in schools is also reported in other research findings on the impact of local management on schools (e.g. Bowe and Ball 1992; Broadbent *et al.* 1992). However, these researchers, interpreting the effects of local management from a critical perspective, present senior management specialization in resourcing issues and its attendant time demands as divorcing senior managers from classroom teachers. This divorce is seen as being due not only to a lack of time spent by senior managers interacting with teachers and pupils, but also to a more fundamental cleavage between educational and 'entrepreneurial' values. It was, however, difficult to sense any such difference in educational values between headteachers and deputies and classroom teachers in the eleven schools in our study. The tensions between the collectivist values of the educational service and self-interested competitive institutional behaviour which is perceived to harm the system as a whole were evident in headteachers' reflections and represented genuine dilemmas. These had two principal foci, one outward and the other inward. The outward looking concern was with the conflict between acts of institutional self-interest which harmed schools collectively, such as 'poaching pupils' or going grant-maintained (GM), both of which were frowned upon. The inward tensions were between balancing different conceptions of value – educational value and monetary value – particularly with respect to staff recruitment. Schools were still adjusting to deciding resource allocation issues which had previously rested with the LEA or which had never been explicitly confronted before but which were now made transparent by local management.

The absence of teacher involvement in resource management decisions, apart from some participation and discretion to spend in limited areas where they possess expertise, makes it difficult to conclude that local management can improve educational standards through the greater empowerment or energizing of classroom teachers. If it does have such effects, then it must be due to its impact on how the school functions as an organization and on its leadership.

The role of the governing body

As pointed out in Chapter 4, in the official model of local management the governing body acts as a board of directors with the headteacher as the chief executive. In this model, the governing body sets school goals and objectives, determines policy, allocates resources, monitors school performance and holds the professional managers to account. It has a number of specific duties, including senior staff appointments, salaries, staff discipline and dismissal, pupil suspensions, implementation of the national curriculum and implementation of collective worship. The governing body is itself held accountable to parents and to the LEA, which can, in extreme circumstances, withdraw delegation. The board of directors model was first brought in by the 1988 Education Act and has been strengthened by subsequent legislation. The inspection process implemented under the Education (Schools) Act 1992 has given greater prominence to the accountability the governing body renders to parents, to the community and to central government. The inspection framework includes an evaluation of the management oversight of the governing body and makes it responsible for the action plans which must be drawn up in response to the key issues raised in the inspection report. The governing body of a school, which inspectors designate as being 'at risk of failing', can be replaced by an 'education association' appointed by the Department for Education (DFE) to manage the school and turn it round.

However, as Golensky (1993) argues with respect to non-profit organizations, whether the board or the executive is in control depends less on the formal structure of authority than on factors which influence the ways in which board members and the executive interact. These interactions depend on the resources the different parties command, their interests, perspectives and values, as well as on the decision issues with which they are dealing. Thus the nature of the relationship between board and executive can change over time and with respect to different issues. Golensky concludes from her own and other studies that an important factor in determining the nature of the board–executive relationship is clarity over their respective roles.

The lack of role clarity is a salient factor in Kogan and co-workers' (1984) analysis of school governing bodies based on a detailed study of eight of them. They point out that:

... it is expecting a lot of the members of any institution that they should operate as rulers, advisers, mediators and assistants at one and the same time and doubly difficult when they belong to an institution that is as spasmodic in its operation as a governing body.

(Kogan *et al.* 1984: 164)

Sallis (1991: 217) confirms the continuation of role ambiguity: 'Most governors who write to me say, in different ways, that they are confused about their role, whether they are in effect supporters, inspectors, ambassadors or go-betweens'.

The taxonomy of types of governing body, defined in relation to their main purpose, which Kogan *et al.* (1984) developed in the days when governing bodies had little formal power and were ambiguously placed in the line of accountability between school and LEA, is still relevant. The four models are:

1 The *accountable governing body*, whose purpose is to ensure the school is working effectively within the policies set by local and central government. At the time, Kogan *et al.* noted that none of their eight governing bodies corresponded to this model. However, transposed out of the LEA line of accountability, and charged with being responsible for ensuring the efficient and effective operation of the school, the accountable model now corresponds to government expectations.

2 The *advisory governing body*, whose purpose is to provide a forum in which the professionals report back to laity and are responsive to their views. While Kogan *et al.* found this a common mode of operating, it was in a form in which the professionals did not accept that they had an obligation to report about educational issues or to respond to lay opinion.

3 The *supportive governing body* exists to support the school by providing it with resources (such as volunteers' time) and networking on its behalf. This type of governing body accords unquestioning trust to the professionals.

4 The *mediating governing body's* purpose is to represent the diverse interests which have a stake in the school, promote consensus among them and enable them to influence the school. This was not a common model, because interests did not see using governing bodies in this way as being effective.

While governing bodies are officially expected to operate as accountable bodies and now have far more formal power through legislation, there are still many obstacles in their way. These obstacles were evident in the eleven governing bodies studied and have much in common with the factors affecting board–executive relationships in non-profit organizations in general. To act as an accountable body, the governors need to be in control of the executive and thus exercise *de facto* power in relation to them.

However, headteachers have many more resources at their disposal to retain the power to control what goes on in school. As Golensky (1993) points out, the executive possesses professional expertise, administrative authority, full-time commitment, access to and control of information flows, and relationships with key individuals. In contrast, governors are lay people, have limited time to commit themselves to getting to know the school, each other and the relevant decision issues, and are dependent on the headteacher for information. If governors wish to assert their accountability role and it is resisted by the headteacher, then the resulting conflict over power is likely to impede the effective management of the school. Most governors are probably reluctant to press hard for accountability if this is the cost to the school. Headteachers tend to favour the supportive governing body, since it brings in resources to the school at no threat to their positional power. As Kogan et al. (1984) concluded, governors are confused about their role because there are elements of all four roles in their work as governors. It is therefore much easier for governors, who are unsure of their expertise, lack time, are unwilling to resist the denial by professionals of the legitimacy of their accountability role and reluctant to create unproductive conflict, to acquiesce to the supportive role.

None of the eleven governing bodies in the IFFS study was operating in a full accountability mode. They were largely advisory and supportive. However, some of the governing bodies were closer to the accountability role than others. The major factors influencing governing bodies towards adopting the accountability role appeared to be governors' expertise and their belief that they should operate in this way. According to the headteacher of All Saints, voluntary-aided and controlled school governing bodies had always wielded more power than those in the maintained sector, but the latter would now have to change:

> Voluntary-aided heads have always had governing bodies with real power whether or not they use this power or the heads are able to manipulate them. This has not been true in the rest of the state sector, where schools have been pretty well totally run and managed and policy made by heads and heads generally getting their way. You could certainly not do that here on any major policy decision. Heads will now have to adapt to managing people and negotiating, even on things such as appointments. This will bring the rest of the state system into line with the sort of things that have always existed in the voluntary-aided sector.

In this school, the chair of the governors' finance committee, an accountant, possessed expertise and information (provided for him by the finance officer) and controlled the meeting in which he presented a draft budget plan which he had drawn up. According to the head, the draft budget was prepared on the basis of information fed in by managers and heads of department. The head saw the committee as responsive to the school rather than dictating to it, though governors did not always take his advice on staffing.

The Harrimore head described himself as 'line manager' to the governors ever since his appointment a few years previously. The chair of governors possessed considerable resources, being well connected in local networks and himself a senior manager in another public service. By now the head noted: 'We have got rid of any suspicion of each other and trust has been established'. Trust was important in enabling the governors to accept the professional advice given. The finance committee consisted of governors with accountancy and business backgrounds, who asked probing questions and expected heads of department to be accountable for their budgets. However, the headteacher controlled budget preparation and felt that ultimately he was responsible for the final decisions. The governors at Waterton, in a middle-class area, also included men with business and accountancy backgrounds, who sat on the finance committee and asked probing questions about financial issues when reviewing a draft budget presented to them by the senior staff. These governors were becoming more assertive and were appointing a new headteacher on the early retirement of the current post-holder. At Yellowstone, too, the governors were actively involved and seeking to become more so, and the finance committee governors were also from business backgrounds. The relationship between head and governors was good and based on mutual respect. The governors had insisted on the procedure of setting a standstill budget with which to open the new financial year. The headteacher, however, retained a high degree of influence in determining the budget and expected to get most of his proposals, negotiated through the internal structures, approved.

At some of the other schools, the governors played a much more low-profile role in budget decision-making. The governors lacked expertise and/or commitment and this was associated with their social background. The head at Gracelands stated:

> We have always kept the governors informed and tried to involve them in the school, but in reality they do not come in. One lacked the confidence to come into the classroom and the staffroom. I do not know that I would welcome governors coming into school and I do not know if I could find the time to put aside for governors. The governors trust my decision-making, so see no further need to become further involved.

The headteacher's description of how the budget was approved by governors was confirmed by observation:

> I present my recommendations to governors with an education officer present and they all clap and say wonderful. I take them all carefully through it. But I expect they would have grave difficulty in picking up anything if I chose to twist the truth. The sad truth is that most

schools are like that: the head makes all the decisions and then sells it to them.

However, the governors were much more involved in the first year when the size of the budget meant that the school had to negotiate voluntary redundancies.

At four other primaries, the headteachers referred to the difficulty of getting governors involved in the school or doing more than rubber-stamping their decisions. At Candleford, 'the governors had not been involved in the budget' according to the first headteacher. The Horsefield head reported that he had taken over from an authoritarian head, the governors had been used to a non-participatory role and he was finding it difficult to get them to be more active:

> They mostly have full-time jobs and do not have time to pop into school: even the parent-governors. The chair has a very demanding job and I tend not to hear from him. I feel as if I am dragging them kicking and screaming into the new era.

The Pentland head was having more success in encouraging her governors to become more active and challenge her recommendations, though they also lacked time and confidence, and were largely acceptant of budget recommendations.

The Fenmore head also referred to the dependence of governors on the headteacher:

> Philosophically, I am inclined to share and enable them to fulfil their role and help them manage and they cannot do that without the information. However, I do not want to relinquish day-to-day control of management . . . Governors do not interfere in that and we sometimes have useful discussions as to where the borderline between an overview and long-term policy and day-to-day management lies.

The maintenance of the headteacher in the driving seat was clearly articulated by the Peacehaven head:

> We don't delegate decision-making to governors either. I know the governors take full responsibility for LMS but clearly they have to rely on guidance from us. They are closely involved with us in how it works, but they know that they are in partnership with us and trust the things we say.

While there were several governors who took an active interest in finance and sat on the LMS (finance) committee, the full governing body, drawn from an affluent rural area and who were generally active within the school, approved the proposed budget with very little questioning except on relatively minor financial matters. The chair of governors, a professional man, confirmed this stance:

> The governors have a lot of confidence in the head, deputy and bursar. They are happy to accept the figures they put in front of us . . . If things seemed to be going badly adrift, I could see us stepping in and being critical.

The governors interviewed were the more active ones, since they were either chairs of the governing body or of the finance committee. They expressed having problems with lack of time, information and expertise and felt the need for more training. The importance of their trust in the headteacher was reiterated. Some felt uncomfortable with the degree of formal power possessed by governors, while others sought to extend their accountability role. For instance, the Yellowstone chair of governors had pressed for more governor involvement in the development plan:

> This school is very open. But even so, it is very difficult for the governors to plan anything that will affect the day-to-day running of the school. Being involved in the school development plan may mean we can be more involved in the day-to-day running of the school.

The evidence from these schools shows that governors were mainly acting in advisory and supportive roles and that they were in an unequal partnership with headteachers. This is fully consistent with the findings of Burgess *et al.* (1992), who conducted nine case studies of resource allocation in Sheffield schools and found:

> . . . only one instance . . . where governors were actively involved with the head teacher in reaching decisions on resource allocation. The common practice across all sites was one whereby governors had delegated all decisions concerning resource allocation including financial decisions to the head.
>
> (Burgess *et al.* 1992: 3)

However, as Golensky (1993) concludes with reference to non-profit organizations, the working style of the board is not always constant but can change with the issues before it. A crisis situation produces a different response, as was the case with Graceland when staff reductions were required. Governor resources of expertise and time are important in determining the role they take on. Headteachers at this time valued governors with accountancy and business training. Most though not all schools had finance committees which scrutinized budgets in order to fulfil their stewardship role for public money. Governor expertise lay with premises issues, where they could act to improve value for money, but they were unable to, or even unaware of, the need to evaluate the efficiency or effectiveness of educational provision. In our particular sample, not much in the way of conflict was observed between governors and headteachers, or between governors. Clearly, the potential for greater frequency of conflict exists as governors attempt to adopt the accountability model. Only about half the headteachers in the Bullock and Thomas (1994) survey welcomed increased governor involvement. Slowing down decision-making and causing more work for headteachers were cited as reasons. The headteacher associations have reported an increasing number of instances of conflict particularly in the primary sector. Conflict was also found in some governing bodies in a study by Deem and Brehony (1993).

Therefore, the evidence broadly points to governing bodies performing supportive and advisory roles rather than operating the accountability model of official expectations. This is corroborated by the findings from Maychell's (1994) seven case-study schools that governors were not usually involved in budget planning. This is further supported by the Bullock and Thomas (1994) survey finding that only 23 per cent of governing bodies were involved in the school development plan. The broad conclusion is therefore that governing bodies' working style has been considerably affected by LMS and is still evolving towards an accountability role. The ability of governors to do this depends very much on their individual expertise, competence and commitment, and on the willingness of the headteacher to recognize the legitimacy of the governors' accountability role and to permit it or encourage it to develop.

Governors exercising their accountability role, and particularly interpreting it to include intervention in day-to-day management, are likely to provoke conflict between themselves and the headteacher. Mutual trust and respect, and clarification of the respective roles of board and executive are essential if governors' efforts are to bring benefits both to their school and to the education system as a whole. Earley's (1994) study of governing bodies similarly concluded that to be effective they needed governors willing to make a substantial time commitment and to work collaboratively together and with the headteacher and staff. In turn, the headteacher needed to value the role of the governors as 'critical friends' rather than as a quiescent rubber-stamping group of supporters.

Headteachers' responses to local management

All the headteachers in our eleven schools, and all the other senior managers – except two who were not involved in resource management – responded positively to local management even if their school had been a budget loser.[3] Ninety-five per cent of the twenty senior managers interviewed mentioned greater school autonomy as a principal benefit of local management: 'We are able to do far more than we would have done two years ago' (secondary headteacher).

The other major benefits of local management reported by at least 80 per cent of the senior managers were greater financial awareness and flexibility, more efficient use of resources and improved planning. Headteachers at schools which had been budget losers were also favourably disposed to local management, though their endorsement was not so unqualified as that at schools which had gained from formula-funding. For example, the head at Graceland, which had been severely constrained by its budget, despite increasing its pupil numbers, and had to resort to voluntary redundancies, felt positive about it: 'This is the delightful side of LMS, being able to decide how to spend your money even though you know you are going to be worse off'. After three years he felt that:

> Had we had the same amount of money cut anyway we would have been a lot worse off without the flexibility of LMS to allow us to do our own manipulating. I feel happy about this: it may be strange. I'm happy because we've managed the cuts: it's satisfying to resolve a problem.

Even the two small village primary schools were considerably more positive about local management after three years than they had been after one year. While Candleford's head acknowledged the advantage of spending on what the school needed, she was very conscious of the workload. The finance officer at Fishlake, which had enjoyed a substantial rise in its roll, was more enthusiastic: 'The advantages are very strong. We have much more control over what we want to do and getting resources for our development plan and projects'.

These findings are endorsed by those of a much larger survey (Bullock and Thomas 1994), which reported that by 1993, 81 per cent of the 191 primary headteachers surveyed and 93 per cent of the 40 secondary headteachers would not welcome a return to the previous system. However, the usual undesirable aspects of LMS were reported by these headteachers, in particular the time demands and the diversion of their attention away from teaching and learning. Headteachers' responses in the Bullock and Thomas study to the generally agreed impact of more efficient resource management and greater autonomy, combined with the costs of time spent on issues other than direct educational matters, ranged from enthusiasm to concern with the greater complexity of the job through to considerable unhappiness with the lack of time for direct instructional leadership.

Conclusion

It can therefore be concluded that local management has significantly enlarged the role of the headteacher and made it more complex. It has increased the power of headteachers, both *de jure* and *de facto*, as they, in practice, exercise the power given by the legislation to governing bodies. Local management has empowered headteachers and by and large they like it. On balance, many headteachers consider local management beneficial to schools, though they are concerned about the costs in time and possible diversion of focus away from teaching and learning. However, these judgements are dependent on headteachers' conception of what their role should be and on the circumstances of the school, though personal values and attitudes are probably more important than the school's financial position.

Classroom teachers in post have on the whole not been directly affected by local management, except when tight budget cuts have required staff cuts. Particularly when budgeting is undertaken in the traditional way, with no explicit link made between the budget and educational objectives reflected in teaching and learning, classroom teachers perceive themselves to be neither interested or to have expertise in resource management and regard this as the proper role of senior management. These perceptions may change if budgeting is better integrated with the school's educational activities and associated learning objectives. If classroom teachers become more actively involved in planning and developing teaching approaches and in experimenting with different types and mixes of resource use, their expertise would be much more relevant to resource management. The need for middle managers in secondary schools to link their departmental policies to whole school development planning, and to improve the efficiency with which they plan and use the resources at their disposal, has been quite frequently commented upon in OFSTED inspection reports. If classroom teachers' practice is not affected by local management, other than being given a few more resources to work with as a result of the school management's efforts, then it is difficult to see what other channels there are by which local management could secure improved school effectiveness with respect to pupils' learning.

The impact of local management on resource allocation: Efficiency, effectiveness and equity

Introduction

Having now considered the financial decision-making process and the roles of key personnel, this chapter examines the outcomes of these decision-making processes. The chapter assesses the resource allocation decisions made by locally managed schools and from this evidence attempts to reach conclusions about the impact of local management on efficiency, effectiveness and equity. The main evidence is drawn from the eleven case-study schools and is compared with the findings of other reports on the implementation of local management. Before examining evidence from the individual schools studied, the financial context at the national level and within Barsetshire are considered.

Educational expenditure in England during the period of implementation of local management of schools

As noted in Chapter 2, local management has been attacked as a ploy intended to make it easier for central government to reduce spending on education by placing responsibility, if not blame, for cuts in schools' resourcing on the shoulders of governors. This critique is almost invariably made without considering the empirical evidence. The perception in education, as in other public services, that resources are being cut, is quite often not accurate. It is derived from both providers and clients naturally

Table 7.1   Real expenditure per pupil in English LEAs

	Primary per pupil (£)	Secondary per pupil (£)	Deflator	Primary per pupil in real terms (£)	Secondary per pupil in real terms (£)	Primary: real change (%)	Secondary: real change (%)
1989–90	1214	1728	0.94	1286	1832		
1990–91	1293	1851	1.00	1293	1851	0.54	1.05
1991–92	1423	2070	1.06	1342	1953	3.81	5.52
1992–93	1545	2202	1.13	1267	1948	1.85	−0.24
1993–94	1582	2194	1.15	1375	1908	0.53	−2.18

Source: House of Commons (1994), Vol. II, p. 169 for first two columns.

wishing to have more spent, and from an annually repeated rhetoric whereby as part of the public sector budget negotiation process, the future budgetary position is made out to be graver than actually materializes. This rhetoric encourages scrutiny of expenditures in order to reassess their benefits in relation to costs and makes the final settlement seem more satisfactory to budget spenders when the outcome is better than initial indications.[1]

Changes in the financing of schools and in their organizational structure, such as the growth of grant-maintained (GM) schools, and the official presentation of statistics makes it difficult to determine how educational spending in the different sectors has changed over time. A further problem is determining how the amount of real expenditure per pupil changes over time. Government statistics deflate nominal expenditures by the gross domestic product (GDP) deflator rather than by cost indices specific to each sector, which would take into account increases in staff costs which occur at a different and usually higher rate than the general level of prices.[1]

On examining the statistics on central and local government spending on schools, a mixed picture emerges of differential experiences of local education authorities (LEAs), which is particularly dependent on whether their spending, both overall and on education, was in excess of their standard spending assessments (SSAs) for all services and for education.[2] The financial situation for local authorities became more constrained in the later years of implementing local management than in the first two. Noting these problems, Ranson and Travers (1994) estimate that school expenditure (including primary, secondary and GM schools) increased by about 8.5 per cent in real terms between 1987–88 and 1992–93, remaining almost static in 1993–94. Over the same period, overall pupil numbers increased by 3 per cent. Other analyses of the schools expenditure data also suggest a general increase in real terms, particularly in the first two years of local management. Table 7.1 shows data produced by the Association of County Councils on the overall expenditure per pupil by English LEAs in nominal terms,

Table 7.2 Changes in real expenditure per pupil in a sample of LEAs

	Comparison between 1991–92 and 1990–91		Comparison between 1992–93 and 1991–92	
	ASB per pupil	GSB per pupil	ASB per pupil	GSB per pupil
Average % real change	2.75	−0.83	2.05	0.08
No. of LEAs in sample	60	60	72	72
No. of LEAs cutting expenditure	8	38	14	34

ASB, aggregated schools budget (the amount delegated to schools); GSB, general schools budget (the total spending on school education by the LEA).
Source: Education Statistics Estimates 1990–91 to 1992–93, CIPFA.

which I have adjusted to real terms using a constructed price deflator.[3] The expenditure shown here is thus equivalent to the general schools budget, as it includes LEA direct expenditure as well as the aggregated schools budget (from 1990). From this evidence, it would appear that spending per primary pupil rose in real terms while that per secondary pupil rose until 1991–92 and then fell. The number of primary pupils grew over the period by about 6 per cent, while the number in the secondary sector fell in 1991–92 and then rose again. The decline in real per pupil secondary expenditure therefore came about from a failure to raise total spending in line with pupil numbers, while the growth in primary pupils was more than offset by the growth in real total spending. However, in 1994–5, LEA education budgets were further squeezed by failure to raise SSAs in line with teacher pay awards.

However, the aggregate changes mask differences in expenditure changes experienced within different authorities. Changes in real per pupil expenditure were estimated from the Education Statistics Estimates (CIPFA 1990–91, 1991–92, 1992–93) for those LEAs which had supplied data. Table 7.2 shows the average percentage change in per pupil spending for these LEAs and the number of LEAs experiencing real cuts or real increases. There were more LEAs in the third year of local management having to cut the aggregated schools budget per pupil in real terms. Around half the LEAs in the sample cut their general schools budgets in real terms in both 1991–92 and 1992–93, though the majority succeeded in protecting schools' budgets from real cuts in per pupil funding. However, such cuts in real per pupil funding are not made transparent to schools, since they are issued with a total budget in current prices.

From these data it can be concluded that local management of schools

Table 7.3 Changes in pupil–teacher ratios and average class size since introduction of local management

	Pupil–teacher ratios		Average class size		Primary classes with 31–35 pupils (%)
	Primary	Secondary	Primary	Secondary	
1989	22.0	15.3	26.1	20.6	16.8
1990	22.0	15.3	26.4	20.7	17.5
1991	22.2	15.5	26.8	21.0	18.9
1992	22.2	15.8	26.7	21.2	18.7
1993	22.4	16.1	27.0	21.4	19.9

Source: Department for Education (1994).

was not introduced in a universal context of budget reductions. Whether schools actually experienced cuts in real funding per pupil depended on which LEA they were maintained by and which sector they were in. Schools going grant-maintained gained financially in the initial years, and clearly the financial incentive to opt out depended on the financial situation within their LEA. In later years, cuts in real expenditure per pupil became more widespread as central government pressure on LEAs not to spend in excess of their SSA mounted and pupil numbers grew.

The net impact of changes in the level of funding on schools' real resources and the resulting decisions at school level has been rising pupil–teacher ratios and average class size as shown in Table 7.3. It should be borne in mind that average class size and pupil–teacher ratios in the secondary sector were at a historically low level in 1989 following a period of declining numbers which was then reversed. The rise in the pupil–teacher ratio and in average class size was greater than the change in per pupil funding would have projected. As we shall see later, there is evidence that this could be explained by increased spending on responsibility allowances to teachers and on heads' and deputies' pay, and by some increase in non-contact time for primary teachers, albeit from a very low base.

Education spending in Barsetshire

Barsetshire was a relatively high spending authority, with expenditure on schools exceeding its SSA. In the first two years of local management, Barsetshire was able to increase its education budget in real terms.[4] The real percentage increases in per pupil funding (the primary and secondary aggregated schools budgets divided by the respective number of pupils) are given in Table 7.4. The most notable item is the 5 per cent increase in real terms in primary funding. The secondary aggregated schools budget (ASB)

Table 7.4 Increase in real per pupil funding (the aggregated school budget) in Barsetshire

Change in per pupil funding	1990–91 compared to 1989–90 (%)	1991–92 compared to 1990–91 (%)
Primary	4.96	2.36
Secondary	3.16	0.60
Overall	3.51	1.40

was increased by only 0.9 per cent, but the decline in the number of secondary pupils made for a higher percentage increase per pupil in 1990–91. The members initially increased the primary ASB by £1.2 million, but raised it by a further £1.6 million in response to a well-argued case by the local primary headteachers' association.

The amount of budget share received by a school depends on both the authority's ASB and the formula by which this is allocated. In common with other LEAs (the LMS Initiative 1992), Barsetshire wished to ensure that the introduction of formula-funding did not cause sudden and large changes, particularly downwards, in schools' budgets. The formula to be implemented in 1990–91 was arrived at by simulating 1989–90 school budgets and comparing these with the 1989–90 'historic budget', which was the actual expenditure on each school in that year as far as the LEA could assess this figure. In order to reduce the change in school budgets as a consequence of formula-funding, the Department for Education (DFE) permitted a four-year transitional period in which LEAs could adjust the formula in ways which would not be permitted once LMS was fully implemented. Hence in assessing the impact of formula-funding on schools, one needs to distinguish between the 'pure formula' and the 'transitional formula', which is the pure formula adjusted to ease schools' transition to the new funding regime. The main adjustment to the pure formula in Barset was to pay schools the actual salaries of teachers who had been in post before 1990, so as not to disadvantage schools with staff high up the salary scale or who had protected salaries due to previous school reorganizations. The percentage of the difference between actual and LEA average teacher costs given to schools was gradually reduced over the four-year adjustment period. Schools with high staff salary costs benefited from the transitional formula at the expense of schools with low staff salary costs.

The impact of introducing the formula on school budgets holding all other factors constant, which the LEA modelled for 1989–90, is shown in Table 7.5. The first column in Table 7.5 shows the mean percentage difference between the schools' historic budgets in 1989–90 and the pure formula they would have got had it been implemented that year. The third column shows the mean percentage difference between the historic 1989–

Table 7.5 Percentage budget change in real terms comparing formula budgets with historic budgets, 1989–90

Type of school	Pure formula		Transitional formula	
	Mean	Standard deviation	Mean	Standard deviation
Secondary	−0.63	3.69	0.05	2.66
Middle	−1.45	6.18	−3.24	6.35
Primary	0.22	6.81	−0.09	6.06

Table 7.6 Percentage real budget changes comparing 1990–91 formula budgets with 1989–90 historic budgets

Type of school	Pure formula		Transitional formula	
	Mean	Standard deviation	Mean	Standard deviation
Secondary	−0.20	5.43	0.91	4.27
Middle	8.91	5.42	8.16	5.89
Primary	4.57	10.41	4.80	9.35

90 budgets and the transitional formula, simulated for that year. The transitional formula had the effect of reducing the mean budget change and its standard deviation for both primary and secondary schools. Middle schools were disadvantaged by the formula because their year 5 and 6 pupils now had to be funded at the same level as those in primary schools. Even with the transitional formula, the percentage changes for some schools would have been large, being at the extremes +30 per cent and −25 per cent for primary schools and +10 per cent and −14 per cent for secondary and middle schools. In the event, the budget cuts were not so great because of the increase in the primary and secondary ASBs.

The actual percentage difference between the formula budgets allocated to schools in 1990–91 and the previous year's historic budget is shown in Table 7.6. Because of the favourable impact of the LEA's increase in its ASB, schools in all phases gained on average. The larger gains by middle schools are in part due to the amalgamation of four middle schools into two new schools, to make them financially viable.

Still over a third of the LEA's schools experienced a cut in budget in real terms in the first year of local management. However, all but thirty of the primary schools still had their budgets managed by the LEA, receiving delegated budgets over the next two years. The budget changes experienced by the case-study schools are shown in Table 5.1. Only two of the second-ary schools actually experienced a real budget cut.

Implications of the funding formula for efficiency

The DFE requirement that at least 75 per cent (raised to 80 per cent in 1993) of the ASB must be allocated according to the number and ages of pupils favours larger schools, since these have a smaller proportion of fixed costs in their cost structure. Local education authorities can and do support smaller schools through either a lump sum, which all schools get regardless of size (used by Barset), or by additional allocations for schools with low pupil rolls. Small schools (or small classes within schools, often sixth-form groups) are not cost-effective, unless there is a significant saving in transport costs in rural areas, or considerable improvements in learning relative to larger schools. Official guidance indicates that the minimum efficient size for a primary school is two forms of entry, or about 240 pupils for a junior school, while six forms of entry (around 850 pupils) is the minimum effi-cient size for a secondary school (Sheffield City Council 1992).

Given these considerations, a funding regime which discourages small school or year group sizes promotes cost-efficiency at the system level. In Barset, percentage losses in school budgets due to the formula were asso-ciated with small size and under-utilization of capacity (Levačić 1993a).[5] The tendency for small schools to lose out under formula-funding has also been found in studies by Bullock and Thomas (1992) and the LMS Initia-tive (1992). Whether the bias against small schools arising from formula-funding actually results in greater cost-efficiency by the system as a whole depends on LEAs (or the Funding Agency for Schools) reorganizing schools into larger units. The pressures in government policy towards creating more efficient sized schools are contradictory, reflecting the conflict be-tween a planner's view of cost-efficiency as determined by the size of the production unit and the market process view of allocative efficiency which requires competition between producers in response to consumer choice, implying an element of spare capacity and a diversity in school size. Both the Audit Commission (1991) and central government (DFE 1992) have urged school closures to remove spare capacity and reduce the number of small schools. However, LEAs became more reluctant to venture into the hostile political waters of school closures because schools could threaten to go grant-maintained to avoid reorganization and were supported in doing so by the DFE even when some of these schools were not fully viable in financial terms. The DFE has permitted some GM secondary schools to open sixth-forms, which are likely to be of inefficient size and to take pupils from other providers, while Office for Standards in Education (OFSTED) inspectors have been critical of small sixth-forms (Levačić and Glover 1994a,b). Some LEAs, such as Warwickshire and Sheffield, have responded to central government pressure to reduce education spending in line with their SSA by implementing school closures and reorganizations. Others, like Barset, which instituted a review of primary provision, have decided not to pursue the matter, except for a few cases. For instance, the governors of one small village primary in Barsetshire requested closure on the grounds that the school was not educationally or financially viable.

Implications of the funding formula for equity in relation to social and educational disadvantage

The equity implications of formula-funding are even less clear-cut than those of efficiency. As far as procedural equity is concerned, the formula scores in that it makes transparent the rules for distribution and minimizes the scope for LEA officer and local politician discretion with respect to individual schools. A number of respondents in our study approved of this aspect of formula-funding. In relation to distributional equity, the main issue with reference to vertical equity (see p. 32) is whether socially and educationally disadvantaged pupils have received proportionately less resourcing as a consequence of local management. The formula guidelines enable LEAs to allocate through the formula additional funding to schools for educationally and socially disadvantaged pupils, provided the LEA can devise 'objective' indicators of these needs. My own detailed analysis of three authorities' formulae (Levačić 1992c, 1993a) did not produce evidence to support this. However, the LMS Initiative (1992) reported that schools suffering more than a 10 per cent budget loss had higher than average proportions of special needs pupils, but no statistical significance for the data was given. It also reported that LEAs found it difficult to support inner-city schools as favourably. However, the example of Sheffield, which maintained its positive action policies, spending between £170 and £350 more on pupils in inner-city schools (Sheffield City Council 1992) shows that, given the political will, schools could still be differentially funded for social and educational disadvantage.

Another potential source of reduced funding for non-statemented special needs is further delegation, which is the requirement (DES 1991a) that LEAs increase the proportion of the potential schools budget (PSB) delegated to schools to at least 85 per cent.[6] This requirement, combined with central government's financial penalties on LEAs spending in excess of their SSA, has forced most LEAs, including Barset, to disband centrally provided special needs support services. Given the same level of funding in real terms and schools' desire to fund non-statemented special needs from their own budgets, further delegation of itself would not reduce special needs provision and could improve it by giving schools more control over how the resources are used to meet their pupils' needs. However, the continued squeeze on education budgets and the possible imposition of a common funding formula for GM schools based on SSAs do not bode well for the future funding of non-statemented special needs. A countervailing factor is the 1993 Education Act, which provides for governors to ensure that pupils' special needs are met (the duty of the LEA with respect to special educational needs), and a supporting code of practice, and OFSTED inspection of schools' special needs provision. Thus regulation is used in an attempt to counter the potential impact of market forces on special needs provision. How individual schools responded to their increased responsibility for special needs provision is considered later in this chapter.

A further vertical equity implication of local management arises from the impact of parental choice on the resourcing of schools and whether schools in socially disadvantaged areas lose pupils and hence resources to schools in more socially advantaged areas. The equity implications of such a shift in school populations are not clear-cut. For such a shift to harm those pupils who remain in their local schools depends on these schools being less effective in achieving educational outcomes than the schools which have gained pupils, once differences in pupils' social class and ability have been taken into account. There is now considerable evidence that schools can contribute between 7 and 15 per cent to differences in examination grades, with a few making larger differences. There is also evidence that examination grades depend not only on the social background and ability of individual pupils, but also on those of their peer group (Willms 1992). Given these considerations, pupils whose parents are able to exercise the choice of an alternative and more effective school, may well diminish the effectiveness of their local school if it consequently experiences a declining roll, a falling budget and an increased concentration of low-ability pupils. However, preventing pupils from attending schools out of their catchment area advantages those whose parents can select a more effective state school by choosing to live in its catchment area. One way of testing whether the hypothesis that more open enrolment and pupil-driven funding discriminates against schools with higher concentrations of educationally and socially disadvantaged pupils is to see whether school budget gains and student recruitment are negatively associated with the percentage of pupils with special needs, which can be measured using the index of special need in the LEA's funding formula. Statistical tests of this hypothesis for three county LEAs including Barset (Levačić 1992c, 1993a) found no support for it. However, later work (Hardman and Levačić 1994b) indicates that in a metropolitan LEA with an inner-city area of considerable social deprivation, changes in pupil enrolment and the proportion of places filled in schools were negatively related to the percentage of socially disadvantaged pupils.

Equity in relation to the differential between primary and secondary funding

One of the arguments in favour of formula-funding is that it enhances accountability for public financing decisions by making them more transparent to service users and taxpayers. Transparency, by providing information that was previously unavailable in the public arena, stimulates public debate about the relative merits of different funding options. The long-standing differential between the funding of primary and secondary schools, which stems from larger class sizes, the much higher teacher contact time traditionally accepted in primary schools and a small percentage of promoted posts in primary schools, has come under increased scrutiny and criticism as a result of the transparent difference between cash allocations for secondary and primary aged pupils. One outcome of public pressure on this issue was a report by the House of Commons Committee on Education (1994) recommending that primary funding be increased so that it is on a par with secondary funding. The report showed that over the last ten years or so, secondary pupils have been funded roughly 40 per cent more than primary pupils. Individual LEAs fall either side of the 40 per cent differential, which is also roughly the difference between the central government's SSAs for primary and secondary education. The disparity, which has its roots in the historically low status of elementary compared with selective secondary education, is even more difficult to justify when the 1988 Education Reform Act has extended the range of subjects primary teachers have to cover and required far more assessment of pupils' work and its reporting. The House of Commons Committee on Education recommended that primary teachers should have similar time in the school day to secondary teachers for 'monitoring and curriculum support' activities and similar class sizes, funded by a gradual increase in education spending being directed towards primary schools. LEAs have already begun to respond to the funding needs of primary schools. The percentage difference in England between primary and secondary unit costs fell from 53.7 per cent in 1989–90 to 46.3 per cent in 1991–92. Since 1990, an increasing number of LEAs have improved the cash allocations of primary pupils relative to those for secondary pupils. Though there has been a general increase in pupil–teacher ratios in both sectors since 1990, pupil–teacher ratios have risen more in secondary than in primary schools (Hardman and Levačić 1994a).

The disparity between primary and secondary funding is debated both as a matter of inequity between pupils of different ages who have educational needs which require equivalent resourcing and in relation to effectiveness. If children are not given a good grounding in basic literacy and numeracy in their primary years and become demotivated by school, they fail to benefit fully from their secondary education, leaving them inadequately prepared for further education and employment. In the words of the House of Commons Committee on Education Report (1994: xxxix): 'if any particular phase of school education is funded at a disproportionately low level, children of all ages will suffer, and in the long run the nation as a whole suffers'. However, the committee stopped short of the contentious issue of whether it would be more cost-effective to shift resources into primary schools at the expense of the secondary sector.

The impact of local management on equity is both a contentious and complex subject, since its assessment depends both on how equity is defined and perceived, and on a host of interrelated factors, which are likely to differ in their effects on schools and pupils according to the local context.

Resource allocation decisions by schools and their implications for efficiency and effectiveness

The *raison d'être* of local management is the ability of schools to take their own distinctive resource allocation decisions. If local management as an organizational design succeeds in promoting efficiency and effectiveness in resource use, this must in the end be due to the decisions made by individual schools as much as the financial and regulatory systems set up by central and local government. The open systems model developed in Chapter 3 provides a useful analytical framework for assessing the resource allocation decisions made by the sample of schools studied. The main points made there are that efficiency is a measure of input in relation to output, but that there is a complex sequence of processes between decisions made about inputs and the consequent effects on educational outputs. Knowledge about this linkage is largely a matter of professional judgement of a personal nature, rather than documented technical knowledge. Knowledge about the effectiveness of the school is similarly handicapped by ambiguity about what educational outputs are desired and the extent to which they have been attained.

In examining the resource allocation decisions made by schools, I will start at the initial stages of the input–output process within the open systems model, which is the translation of the financial budget into real resources. The clearest evidence in favour of local management stimulating improvements in efficiency is in relation to the production of intermediate outputs. These provide the operational and administrative services required to support teaching and learning activities. All the case-study schools except Waterton, which had been a very large budget gainer, made considerable efforts to secure value for money in their operational services.

Operational services

Operational services include the budget headings of buildings and ground maintenance, cleaning, utilities, supplies and general services. The first three headings were subject to the compulsory competitive tendering provisions of the 1988 Local Government Act, under which local authorities were required to put out these services to compulsory competitive tender. Local authorities were forced to reorganize their own workforces into 'direct service organizations', which tendered for contracts to undertake the services in competition with private firms. Initially, when local management was implemented in 1990, schools were obliged to continue with LEA contracts which had already been entered into, and could not choose to employ their own workers or engage private contractors. With further delegation coming on stream in 1993 and the demise of existing service contracts, schools gained more freedom in their choice of service provider. The government also enabled schools with fewer than three full-time equivalent employees engaged on these services to employ their own workers. Local authority schools with more than three full-time maintenance staff were still obliged to engage in compulsory competitive tendering either on their own account or via the LEA.

The case-study schools were largely critical of the inefficiency and poor quality of the authority's contractual services, in particular cleaning. Cleaners, employed on low wages by a contractor, had no loyalty to the school and were not under its direct control. Enforcing agreed contractual standards was tiresome for schools due to indirect, slow and ineffective channels of communication. The schools considered that they could obtain better value for money by employing their own contractors or employees for grounds maintenance, repairs, small buildings work and cleaning, but were limited in their ability to do so by the compulsory competitive tendering legislation and existing contracts. Where schools were able to organize their own services, they were very satisfied with the results both in terms of quality and lower cost. Peacehaven School was unusual in being in a district which had not yet taken out local authority contracts for grounds maintenance and began to employ its own groundsman. This did not cost less but resulted in a much higher standard of grounds maintenance. A number of the schools employed local handymen for odd jobs. Improvements in speed, flexibility and cost compared with the previous administrative system of using the authority's maintenance staff were experienced. A report on LMS by Her Majesty's Inspectors (1992a) also noted 'the fact that minor works can be carried out quickly has removed a major source of frustration from staff'. The small village primary schools were particularly successful at obtaining various services from the local community, either paid or voluntary. Fishlake's finance officer claimed that they could 'maintain the environment for half the price and put the rest of the money into the classroom'. At Candleford School, a parent replaced broken windows without charging for his time. Improvements to the school's physical environment, in particular redecoration, were favoured by schools provided they could be afforded after essential staffing and services had been paid for. Schools also made considerable efforts to save on water and energy by installing devices such as thermostats, heating zone controls, toilet flushing regulators and water meters, carefully monitoring usage and economizing. This finding is confirmed by the Audit Commission (1993), which found that primary schools had been particularly successful in reducing the proportion of their budgets spent on running costs.

An obvious consequence of local management was that schools increased their employment of financial and clerical staff, both by paying for more hours and upgrading the member of staff (almost always a woman) taking on the finance officer role. Local management provided greater flexibility, since job roles and consequent grades and pay were no longer set by the LEA. Clearly, the extra financial work required additional staff hours, but more clerical staff were also employed, particularly in the secondary schools, to relieve teachers of clerical tasks associated with preparing teaching materials and keeping records. Fenmore, which was financially constrained, created additional flexibility by employing extra clerical hours for peak periods. The small primary schools in our sample were concerned with the number of administrative staff hours they could afford. As already mentioned, the Candleford head decided to teach an extra half day in order to pay for more hours for her secretary.

A general increase in office staff hours was also reported by 80 per cent of schools in the NFER study (Maychell 1994): three-quarters of secondary schools and one-third of primary schools had employed a bursar or finance officer. The average increase in office staff hours was ten per week in primary schools and thirty in secondary schools; size of school correlated positively with the increase in office hours. However, considerable differences in the number of administrative hours per pupil in schools of similar size were reported with some concern by the Audit Commission (1993). These variances and the inability of the Audit Commission to do more than query the practices of some schools, is a good example of the ambiguity concerning what are efficient ways of using specific resources in schools.

Overall, these schools responded to new opportunities in altering spending patterns on operational services and indicated a strong desire to secure value for money in order to put the consequent 'savings' into resources used directly in the classroom. Schools were limited in their ability to do this by the complexities and consequent costs of engaging in compulsory competitive tendering. In larger samples of schools subject to financial audits, the Audit Commission (1993) with regard to LEA schools and the National Audit Office (1994) with respect to GM schools discovered some schools failing to ensure value-for-money procedures in purchasing or engaging in questionable transactions which involved some personal financial interest. 'Overall', the Audit Commission (1993: 22) concluded, 'the picture is one of a commitment to securing value for money and most headteachers and governors are gaining experience gradually and safely'.

Decisions regarding teaching and classroom support staff

Schools are labour-intensive operations, so decisions regarding staffing, which generally account for around 80 per cent of a school's budget, are of prime importance. Not only were schools able to determine their own staffing establishment under local management, but the opportunity cost of these decisions was deliberately placed at school level by the controversial average-in-actual-out salary principle in the funding formula.

The quality of the teaching staff, the match of their expertise with the needs of the curriculum, and the morale of staff were regarded as key factors by the schools' managers. Fenmore, for example, adhered to a 'tradition that good staff are the core of our strength'. The key variables upon which the budgets were based in the secondary schools were the pupil–teacher ratio and non-contact time for teachers. For example, at Harrimore, these were set at 16 and 20 per cent, respectively. Peacehaven, with a rising roll, expanded staffing to maintain its current pupil–teacher ratio and made some increase in non-contact time. In the primary schools, the key variable was the number of classes to run, which was determined by the maximum desirable class size and the extent to which the head was willing to have mixed age classes. So Yellowstone kept class sizes down to twenty-six or below by mixed age grouping, while Gracelands (a middle school) kept to single year group classes but refused to countenance classes of thirty, as this size 'is out of the question when eighty per cent of the pupils have below normal reading ages'. So when their intake rose from seventy-five to ninety, they decided to run four classes and so still found the financial situation very tight. The other middle school, Waterton, which was larger and in a more affluent area, ran classes of thirty or more and consequently felt much less financial constraint, despite lower per capita funding. Fishlake also responded to an increase in their total roll from seventy-three to ninety by creating an extra class, which reduced the range of age groups per class from three to two. However, all these decisions were made on the basis of qualitative professional judgement, accumulated through personal experience. There was no hard evidence that the chosen way of using resources was more effective or efficient in terms of pupils' learning than alternatives which had not been considered or had been considered and rejected. Nor did schools appear to undertake any formal or systematic evaluation of the resulting outcomes of these decisions. They were evaluated, in so far as they were, through intuition and judgement.

The schools in our sample, which were designated as losers from formula-funding and which felt tightly constrained by their budget allocation, gave primacy to maintaining the level of staffing and in particular to avoiding compulsory redundancies. By 1993, despite increasing constraints on the education budget, no school in the LEA had yet declared compulsory redundancies. Harrimore and Graceland coped in the first year by the early retirement of expensive staff. At Harrimore a deputy was not replaced, while at Graceland, where the budgetary position in 1990–91 initially seemed to threaten a deficit, two senior staff took early retirement and a deputy on a protected salary who got a headship elsewhere was replaced by a senior teacher on a C allowance. Again in 1993–94, when LEA budget cuts created another potential deficit, the caretaker and headteacher took early retirement. The head devised a package whereby he retired on grounds of disability but returned as site manager with budget manager duties included. This meant that class sizes could be maintained and compulsory redundancies avoided. Nationally, however, teachers have been made redundant, though the annual number from 1989–90 to 1991–92 remained fairly constant at around 2700, before rising to 4000 in 1992–93 (when transitional funding arangements were ending). Early retirements have increased. Teachers Pensions Agency data show that between 1990–91 and 1993–94, the number of heads and deputies retiring because of redundancy rose from 101 to 505. The number of deputies retiring through redundancy rose ten-fold. This would appear to be mainly in the secondary sector. A third of secondary schools in the NFER survey (Maychell 1994) had reduced deputy head posts compared with 2 per cent of primary schools. At the national level, total teacher retirements due to health and in the interests of efficiency were around 12,000 a year between 1988–89 and 1992–93. However, the number retiring in the interests of efficiency and hence due to LEA reorganizations declined, while the number retiring for health reasons increased, so that by 1994 just over half of teacher retirements were officially recorded as being due to ill-health (Rafferty 1994). This may reflect a change from LEA- to school-initiated staff cuts rather than an actual increase in ill-health.

Fenmore was an example of a school which had no retirements and decided to carry on with a staffing establishment which in 1990 was two more than required. As pupil numbers rose in the next three years, this surplus was gradually absorbed. Mismatch between subject requirements and the expertise of existing staff was bridged by a few part-time appointments and by the use of student teachers. Money received from the initial teacher training institution was used to fund additional part-time teaching hours in departments with shortages, while the students were allocated to departments with some staff slack. Despite financial tightness, free staff meals and cover after one day were retained in order to maintain staff morale. As a consequence, Fenmore was initially unable to implement a newly agreed salary incentive structure and had to limit expenditure on INSET and curriculum support materials. Harrimore, in contrast, which had lost two staff in 1990, felt much less straitened in subsequent years and was able to spend more on premises, grounds and information technology (IT). It was also able to retain items previously funded by the LEA, such as a community tutor, family room and home–school links. These two examples illustrate how schools which were similarly placed adopted different expenditure priorities, partly fortuitously and partly by choice.

As well as the number of teachers to employ, governors under local management have greater discretion in how much to pay them, with the financial consequences felt directly by the school. One of the main criticisms of the average-in-actual-out salary funding rule, is that schools will respond by employing less experienced and hence less competent teachers, rather than the best candidate. The headteachers and governors in the case-study schools stated that they wished to pay the rate necessary to get the right candidate and this was observed in appointments. Young teachers were in demand, not just for cost reasons, but in order to get fresh ideas into the school and to achieve a balanced age profile of staff, though this was much more difficult to achieve in small schools. Graceland was forced to go for cheaper teachers, such as a licensed teacher, and was unable to pay the market rate for incentive allowances, thus making it more difficult to recruit and retain staff. Other studies indicate that the market criteria of cost began to influence teacher appointment decisions. Sixty per cent of headteachers surveyed by Bullock and Thomas (1994) believed this. An Audit Commission (1993) study of 100 schools found that the average point on the teachers' pay scale at which schools appoint had fallen from point 7 prior to local management to point 6 by 1992–93. However, it must also be borne in mind that schools were no longer forced to take redeployed teachers, which would have increased the scale point at appointment. The Audit Commission also found that schools had increased their teachers' pay bill but were employing fewer teachers in relation to pupil numbers. This was explained by incremental drift up the pay scale and increases in incentive allowances. This finding provides some explanation for the rise in average class sizes and pupil–teacher ratios even when real per pupil expenditure was rising, which was noted at the start of this chapter.

The greater flexibility of delegated budgeting enabled the case-study schools to employ more part-time staff in order to meet year-by-year variations in specific curriculum needs or class sizes. The two small village primaries benefited considerably from this flexibility, which enabled them to employ particular teachers on a regular basis, but vary their hours and commitments from term to term. For example, Candleford employed a part-time teacher for both supply and special needs; she also did two additional mornings with a class which had temporarily increased in size.

Schools coped with the fluctuations in staffing requirements and uncertainties over future funding levels by appointing at least one member of staff on a temporary contract or awarding temporary incentive allowances. Some headteachers, such as Graceland's, disliked temporary contracts on principle and others, such as Fishlake's, used them as a probationary period after which it was hoped to make the appointment permanent. Schools obviously need at least one temporary appointment if there is some probability that the budget will be cut in the future or if specialist needs are likely to change. A report on 60 schools by HMI (1992a) also found an increase in temporary and part-time appointments, as did Bullock and Thomas (1994) and Maychell (1994), who reported that over 40 per cent of schools had increased their use of temporary contracts compared with 10 per cent which had reduced them. There is thus considerable evidence that local management has promoted the development of a dual labour market in teachers, where the bulk of staff are on permanent contracts with the needed flexibility secured by part-time and temporary appointments. This mirrors similar developments in other sectors of the economy. Particularly in teaching, the secondary labour force consists largely of women who seek part-time and irregular employment because of child-care responsibilities. The other source is retired teachers.

Apart from formula-funding and delegated budgeting, government-inspired changes in the pay and conditions of teachers have created greater flexibility in the salary structure. Teachers and headteachers' salaries need not be completely determined by the administrative criteria of length of service, qualifications and group size of school, but can be enhanced by the governors for additional responsibilities or good performance (Interim Advisory Committee 1989, 1990, 1991; School Teachers' Review Body 1992). The headteachers studied were conscious of operating in a market for teachers and the need to pay at the appropriate scale point and incentive allowance to get the specialism and expertise required. Evidence of this developing nationally was reported by Marr (1992). However, there was no movement at all in the case-study schools towards using the new pay flexibilities to relate pay to performance in the classroom as the government has urged. Incentive allowances were granted for specific responsibilities. A handful of heads and deputies were moved up the salary scale in those schools with money to spare. The reluctance to move towards relating teachers' pay to performance in the classroom has also been observed by Marr (1992), HMI (1992a) and the School Teachers' Review Body (1994). There is little substantive evidence that pay linked in a detailed way to quality of performance (as opposed to responsibilities) improves motivation and hence productivity in the public services, especially when the amounts on offer would be quite small. Teachers are generally hostile to performance-related pay and heads remain largely unconvinced, fearing it would create staffroom divisiveness, in part because of the difficulties of finding widely accepted measures of teacher performance. Governors are unlikely to take an independent line on this, except those who are confident that private sector performance-related pay schemes are transferable to schools. So far, only a handful of schools have tried operating a variety of performance-related pay schemes, a number of which seem more akin to rewards for extra time and effort expended (Merrick 1994).

One flexibility which schools have availed themselves of is the appointment of classroom support staff, in particular classroom assistants (or learning support assistants) in primary schools, particularly for the younger classes. In secondary schools, the practice is less well developed and is usually used to support special needs students. In our sample, Horsefield in its first year of local management provided a good example of taking advantage of the new flexibility. The headteacher chose to run a year 6 group of forty-six as one class rather than two by employing 1.5 teachers and a classroom assistant. All the primary schools increased the number of classroom assistant hours. Other new appointments were a qualified librarian at

Peacehaven, a parent helper to run a parents' room at Fenmore and an IT technician at Harrimore.

The Audit Commission (1993) also found that the number of classroom assistants has increased significantly since budget delegation, as did Bullock and Thomas (1994) for primary schools. Mortimore *et al.* (1992) report a number of case-study examples of the benefits of using support staff. Maychell (1994) found that almost half of primary schools had increased their use of classroom assistants after budget delegation, compared with just over 10 per cent of secondary schools. Two-thirds of secondary schools increased the employment of support staff, equally spread over technicians, librarians and classroom assistants. Thus local management has stimulated the growth of a para-teaching force in schools.

Delegated budgets also give schools much more control over staff development. While teacher appraisal has been introduced through compulsion and funded by earmarked grants, schools can supplement these grants out of their own budgets and determine their own schemes. In-service training, also funded through earmarked grants, is now determined at the school level and has become more tightly bound up with the corporate needs of the school as LEA funding for individual teacher secondments on courses and LEA provision of courses provided free to teachers have disappeared. As a consequence of 'further delegation', LEAs have restructured course provision and advisory services on a commercial basis with schools as paying clients. When this occurred in Barsetshire in 1993, after an extensive process of consultation, the headteachers interviewed were satisfied with the quality of service and with the improvements secured by the schools playing a key role in shaping the services provided. Consequently, schools can integrate a whole range of resources, including INSET courses and external consultants, into their school development planning. A particular curriculum development can thus be supported through internal staff time using supply cover, off-the-peg courses and external consultancy. Such developments are consistent with a more efficient and effective deployment of resources, through using local knowledge to assess school needs and the best ways of meeting them.

None of these examples of staffing decisions in the case-study schools (or elsewhere cited) contains hard evidence on the consequent beneficial effects on students' learning. There is evidence, however, of schools making staffing decisions that were not available to them prior to delegation, and basing these decisions on professional judgements that the most beneficial learning outcomes would result from this particular use of resources. These changes in resource mixes are consistent with schools seeking more efficient ways of using a range of different kinds of staff. Clearly, these benefits are to some extent offset by the costs of additional administrative and management time in schools and no evidence has been gathered here on the savings in administrative time of LEA personnel; it was considered that reliable data could not be gathered within the resource constraints of the project.

Table 7.7 Case-study schools carry-forward, 1990–91

School	Carry-forward (£)	Carry-forward (% of budget share)
Harrimore (loser)	70,905	5.0
Fenmore (loser)	26,137	2.1
Peacehaven	77,866	5.5
All Saints	105,349	11.7
Waterton	68,966	12.6
Graceland (loser: only by formula)	47,254	9.8
Yellowstone	39,182	8.4
Pentland	19,050	6.2
Horsefield (loser: only by formula)	30,155	6.5
Fishlake	8,655	11.2
Candleford (loser: only by formula)	1,989	2.8

Discretionary expenditures

While schools spend some undefined minimum on essential repairs and curriculum materials, these items and in-service training tend to be discretionary items. Because they do not involve long-term contractual commitments and can be dispensed with for a while, these items are used to absorb the gap between the actual budget share and essential expenditure. They are cut back by schools when in budget difficulties and expanded when a positive budget carry-forward from the previous financial year is available. Maychell (1994) also found that the most popular items acquired using accumulated savings were curriculum resources, furniture and premises improvements. These items, like temporary staff contracts, provide a buffer against the uncertainties of both budget revenues and unexpected expenditure requirements.

Reserves

Caution in the face of budget uncertainty has led schools to accumulate reserves by underspending their budgets. In 1990–91, almost every school in Barset had a positive carry-forward figure, as had all the case-study schools, as shown in Table 7.7. Graceland maintained a reserve of £50,000 (around 10 per cent of its budget share) over the three years. With the staffing budget reduced by a further round of retirements in 1993–94, a lot more could be spent on curriculum support. By 1993, with a much tighter budgetary situation in the authority, many schools were reported to be drawing down their reserves. The experience in Barsetshire mirrored that in other authorities. The Audit Commission (1993) found that only 9 per cent of schools had run budget deficits and that financial reserves were 5 per cent of the budget in primary schools and 3.5 per cent in secondary schools. However, there were considerable variations, as with the case-study schools, in the size of the reserve balances. The NFER study found that only 6 per cent of primary schools had end of year deficits over the three years since 1991, but that the proportion of secondary schools over-spending rose from 9 per cent to 16 per cent.

Apart from accumulating savings for a large capital project, the holding of excessively large balances (say in excess of 5 per cent of the budget for primary schools and 3 per cent for secondary schools) means that resources have not been used for the educational benefit of the children for whom the funds were allocated by central and local government. Such excess balances indicate a failure of schools to use their resources effectively unless justified by the need to accumulate reserves in order to maintain staffing levels when government expenditure cuts occur at some future date. Though the sample is very small, it is nevertheless interesting to note that the case-study schools with the highest percentage carry-forward (All Saints and Waterton) were those which had moved least in the direction of the rational approach to budgeting. The high carry-forwards of Fishlake and Graceland can be explained by their greater concern at the possibility of running a deficit.

Income generation

Under local management, schools have a financial incentive to make com-mercial use of their assets and thereby make more efficient use of school buildings and equipment that would otherwise lie idle. For most schools, income generation, apart from parent–teacher association (PTA) activities, involves renting out premises and the use of equipment therein. It was noticeable that among the case-study schools, it was those in tight financial circumstances which made efforts at income generation. Fenmore, for in-stance, made £10,000–£15,000 more than its neighbour, Harrimore, and used the money to fund a teacher. Other schools, in particular Harrimore, Yellowstone, Horsefield and Peacehaven, felt the time involved was not worth the extra money. One school was in the unusual position of having a farm for rural studies. As LEA funding for it was cut, the school found it very difficult to generate enough income to cover its costs. On a national scale, the LMS Initiative (1992) reported that secondary schools in particu-lar are 'marketing their services quite heavily and seconding teachers full-time to marketing'. HMI (1992a) report that between 0.1 and 1.7 per cent of schools' budgets was raised by income generation. Income from lettings was generated by 90 per cent of secondary schools and half of primary schools in the NFER survey; sponsorship and donations were the next most frequent source of additional funds.

Business sponsorship was also sought by some of our case-study schools. Fenmore and Harrimore, situated in the same town, set up a trust with their primary feeder schools to obtain business sponsorship for arts events and IT equipment for the smaller schools. Funds raised were modest. The Graceland head was successful in citing the social deprivation of the pupils when approaching local business to fund a minibus. As already noted, the village primary schools were particularly successful at securing resources from their communities, which to some extent offset the financial disadvantages of their small size. A number of the schools became good at cash management and securing the best return on cash deposits, particularly when school chequeing accounts became available. Parent–teacher associations made significant contributions to school funds. At Graceland, though parents could not contribute much individually, they supported school fund-raising events. Fund-raising and working voluntarily in school are valuable ways for many parents to support their child's school and develop links with it.

Some equity implications of resource allocation decisions in schools

Evidence on the equity implications of resource allocation decisions in the case-study schools relates mainly to special needs provision. Barsetshire members, in particular the Labour Group, took a considerable interest in special needs and voted about £500,000 or 4.5 per cent of the ASB to be allocated for special needs. Barset opted for an index which measured social disadvantage only and so was not a direct measure of the educational need of individual pupils, but a predictor of their incidence in each school. The index was complicated and not well understood in schools. Its main component was a set of variables from the Registrar General's census data on the social disadvantage of geographic areas. The census variables used were the number of five- to fifteen-year-olds in 1981 in households which lacked basic amenities, whose head was unemployed, a single parent or in socio-economic group 4 or 5. In 1990–91 these census data were attributed to the school according to its catchment area, but in 1991–92 they were related to the addresses of the pupils by postcoding addresses and mapping postcodes to census districts. Headteachers, governors and some officers had little knowledge of why the particular index was chosen. However, it was a direct development of an existing index used to allocate additional teachers, which was introduced in 1986 for secondary schools and in 1987 for primary schools. As well as using the existing index, the House of Commons Committee on Education voted in April 1989 to add pupils entitled to free meals, with English as a second language, with single parents or with some form of social service care. For the 1990–91 formula, free meals taken was included in the census data. Entitlement to free meals was implemented in the 1992–93 formula. English as a second language and single parents data were collected for the 1991–92 formula by means of a questionnaire to schools. Headteachers were unhappy about collecting such sensitive information but, with money at stake, only a handful of schools failed to submit the data. Schools were advised to deduce single parenthood from there being only one adult registered in the school records at the same address as the pupil. Officers suspected that some returns were overestimates. In order to construct an index of the number of pupils at each school for whom additional funding for special needs was allocated, the census measures of social deprivation were given a weight of 1, single parenthood a weight of 0.25, a pupil in care a weight of 2 and English as a second language a weight of only 0.1 because it attracted additional Section 11 funding. The percentage of special needs pupils at each school was then standardized so that the LEA total was 6.8 per cent of pupils, since it is this percentage of the age-weighted pupil allocation that members voted to fund at double the normal rate. When new measures were introduced into the 1991–92 special needs index, schools' special needs funding was redistributed. Some attempt was made by members to limit this redistribution by selecting a suitable weighting of census and non-census variables, but some schools received quite different allocations from the previous year.

There was a considerable degree of dissatisfaction with the index among senior teachers and governors.[7] The most common criticism was that pupils with special educational needs do not necessarily have single parents, live in areas with poor housing or come from socio-economic groups 4 and 5. Schools with a large proportion of service children, who suffer disruption to family life, complained that their pupils' needs were not recognized by the index. There seemed to be little awareness of evidence justifying social disadvantage variables as predictors of educational need. Because Barset did not use authority-wide testing of pupils, it did not have in place a mechanism for gathering educational test data on reading or non-verbal reasoning. The most common view was that nobody liked the index but they could not come up with a better one. A number of headteachers felt that the additional funding their school received for special needs did not adequately reflect the extent of social disadvantage at their school relative to others.[8]

As a result of further delegation and the squeeze on the authority's education budget after 1991, the LEA's special needs support service was considerably reduced. However, the authority did endeavour to monitor schools' special needs policies and expenditure on special needs – the one area where educational monitoring for accountability occurred. Most of the case-study schools increased spending on special needs teachers and support staff in order to make up for the loss of central services. A number of the schools claimed to spend more than their formula allocation for special needs. Yellowstone was able to appoint a special needs teacher for four days a week and Candleford employed a special needs teacher for an extra morning. Peacehaven employed more classroom assistant hours for special needs. However, when faced with a potential budget deficit in 1990–91, Graceland ended a part-time special needs teaching contract. Once it had weathered its first difficult year and emerged with a surplus, a new temporary part-time special needs appointment was made. Special needs staffing is thus likely to be vulnerable when schools are in financial difficulties and give priority to mainstream teaching. Similar findings for fifty-four schools visited in 1990 and 1991 were reported by HMI (1992b); special needs staffing was reduced by LEAs in response to central government pressure on their spending and to falling rolls rather than as a direct result of local management.

Another equity concern raised in relation to local management is whether schools engage in 'cream-skimming' by selecting pupils according to their ability and motivation, and getting rid of disruptive pupils. There was little evidence of selection by the case-study schools, given the general reluctance to compete for pupils and the inability of schools to fine-tune entry requirements, except in the case of voluntary-aided schools. However, the head of Graceland felt that schools like his, situated in areas of social deprivation, could not hope to attract pupils from outside the estate, and would be unable to recruit all their catchment area pupils because some parents preferred to send their children to schools off the estate.

There was some indication that schools were becoming more reluctant to continue putting up with disruptive pupils. As one secondary head remarked: 'We now view pupils giving us major disciplinary concern as costing us money and that is quite an effective argument with parents'.

Barsetshire had made exclusion less attractive to schools by providing in their scheme that schools had to pay the home tuition costs of excluded pupils. Subsequently, the DFE required schools to pay back cash allocated for excluded pupils. Nationally, the number of exclusions is reported to have risen since 1989, though there is a lack of reliable data. However, the equity and efficiency implications of exclusions are not clear-cut, since the removal of disruptive students benefits the learning of their classmates, and some excluded pupils have ceased to benefit from attending their school. Nevertheless, there is concern that some schools may be excluding pupils too readily, rather than making efforts to resolve the problem and secure improved pupil behaviour. High rates of exclusion are now viewed critically by OFSTED inspection teams.

The extent that financial and market pressures of local management lead schools to serve pupils with special needs less adequately than previously is dependent on the professional values of teachers, in particular headteachers and deputies, and on the attitudes of governing bodies. The headteachers of the case-study schools expressed concern for the welfare of pupils with special needs and seemed genuine in their desire to fund additional teaching and pastoral time for servicing these needs, once basic mainstream provision had been resourced.

Winners and losers

The differing fortunes of schools which gain from formula-funding and more open enrolment compared with those which lose raises an issue of horizontal equity, in that pupils' education can be affected by the financial viability of the school they attend. This type of inequity is impossible to avoid in any system of resource allocation, which is even partially subject to market forces. Nor is it the case that pure administrative allocation can ensure identical allocations of inputs for all students with the same educational needs. Certainly, this was not the case in Britain, as the principle of local democratic choice justifies different spending decisions by different communities. The local differences in funding persist even with the extension of central government power over schooling. However, government policy, while ensuring equal cash allocations for pupils of the same age in the same authority for at least 75 per cent of expenditure, has created greater differences in the financial fortunes of schools in the same authority, in particular between GM and LEA schools.

The differences in the fortunes of schools which gained and those which lost as a consequence of formula-funding can be illustrated by comparing the experiences of two of the case-study schools, Graceland and Waterton, both 9–13 middle schools (i.e. taking years 5–8). Graceland, as a school in one of the most socially deprived areas in the county, had in the past received generous allocations of staff from the LEA. It had been through a long period of contraction, which left it with highly paid staff. It was also a smaller school than Waterton. All these factors meant that its unit costs were considerably higher than Waterton's (as shown in Table 5.1). Graceland would have lost 12 per cent of its budget had the formula been applied in 1989–90, while Waterton would have had an 8 per cent budget increase. In the event, Graceland did not lose budget to this extent because of the increase in primary funding and because of various temporary expedients in the formula, including the LEA overestimating its pupil roll for the next academic year by thirty pupils. The school also received £58,000 from the social deprivation index in the formula. However, Graceland's initial 1990–91 budget allocation issued in March 1990 was lower than the one eventually allocated after the final adjustment in March 1991. The school was thus threatened with a budget deficit, not only because of its lower pupil–teacher ratio but also because of high salaries.

Anxious to avoid mixed age classes or classes of thirty-five pupils or more, given the pupils' educational needs, the headteacher decided to run twelve classes for 281 pupils. This gave an average class size of twenty-four and a pupil–teacher ratio of 17 to 1. The head had considerable difficulty in balancing the planned budget for 1990–91. Spending on INSET was suspended for a term and purchases of books, materials and equipment restricted until the end of the financial year. The head felt aggrieved that he could not pay 'the market rate' for teachers. He could not offer the incentive allowances for posts which neighbouring middle schools did and had to employ an instructor for music rather than a qualified teacher. Support staff hours were also cut by thirty. Every part of the budget was carefully scrutinized to see what savings could be made. Staff costs were brought

Table 7.8 Differences in unit costs between Graceland and Waterton, November 1990 prices

	1989–90 teaching cost per pupil (£)	1990–91 teaching cost per pupil (£)	1990–91 premises cost per pupil (£)	1990–91 curriculum materials cost per pupil (£)
Waterton	796	882	159	37.2
Graceland	1066	941	222	37.5

down from 82 per cent of the budget to 76 per cent. In the event, the school finished the first year of delegated budgeting with a carry-forward of £47,000, some of which was then used to fund a part-time temporary special needs teacher as well as extra incentive allowances.

In contrast, Waterton, in the same town as Graceland, but in a more affluent area, ran larger class sizes and had a pupil–teacher ratio of 19 to 1. Flush with money, it appointed 1.5 additional teachers, bought in more cover for INSET, promoted the head of science to a B allowance, increased its special needs teaching by a part-time appointment, spent £10,000 on new computers, redecorated parts of the school and improved the grounds. The deputy and head of maths were given additional non-contact time for management duties and the headteacher placed on the highest salary point prior to his retirement. The differences in cost components are shown in Table 7.8.

This example illustrates how schools which have difficulty balancing their budget are not necessarily funded any worse than other schools or suffer from falling rolls. Graceland's problems were due to a high unit cost structure, both due to its smaller size compared with Waterton and in particular to its higher staffing ratio, justified by the educational needs of its pupils. The main strategy for Graceland was to bring down its teaching costs, not by increasing the pupil–teacher ratio but by employing cheaper teachers.

Conclusions: Efficiency, equity and effectiveness

Efficiency

My conclusion from the evidence presented above is that local management has improved efficiency on the *input side* of the education production function. School managers are seeking and finding new ways of using and combining resource inputs. In particular, local management is more successful than LEA administrative allocation in concentrating the resources available to schools on direct teaching and learning. The delegation of LEA centrally provided education and administrative services has enabled schools to express preferences over what is supplied, thus promoting efficiency. Against this is the loss of economies of scale in the central production and allocation of such services and the contracting costs of market transactions. These are avoided by schools purchasing packages of contracts organized by the LEA, where schools judge these to be more cost-effective than direct production by themselves, or by purchasing directly from private contractors.

The most significant efficiency gains appear to be in the areas of utilities and property services, where local authority contractual arrangements are much less satisfactory than those for educational and administrative services. Money saved by schools on operational services and utilities is channelled into direct support of teaching and learning. Local management also enables a more flexible use of staff which is cost-efficient. However, this would seem to be more evident in the case of support staff rather than teaching staff, where the main effect so far has been to promote the development of a dual labour market. The flexibility of local management is leading schools to develop a cadre of support staff who work with teachers in promoting learning. The development of the dual labour market enables the education system to adjust teaching costs more rapidly in line with changes in pupil numbers and as a part of the overall budget constraint. It is, however, on present evidence, impossible to conclude on whether this is a cost-efficient practice. One has to balance the benefits of spending the money thus saved on non-teacher inputs against the potentially harmful impact on teacher motivation and the ability of the service to attract and retain good teachers.

The efficiency gains due to local management are less pronounced the smaller the school. Small schools are disadvantaged by economies of scale in teaching and in management. The headteacher of a small school, who has to undertake class teaching as well, has fewer staff to whom management functions can be delegated. Despite these disadvantages, the two small primary schools in our sample felt much more positive about local management after three years than at the beginning. The headteachers had succeeded in delegating the financial work and the schools received more support from their communities than larger schools, with people willing to fit in with the school's needs. The LEA still served a vital function by providing a range of services which schools contracted to buy in bulk. This saved schools considerable time and effort in search and monitoring costs. Schools in Barset were developing partnerships with each other, supported by some LEA funding, for the joint provision of services, such as special needs teaching. Vertical partnerships of a secondary school and its feeder primaries were developing to replace a previous system of clusters of small village primary schools. Clustering has been proposed as a solution to diseconomies of scale, though the evidence of its success is mixed; the

Exeter small schools survey indicates that only a half to a third of schools entered into such arrangements (Keast 1992a,b).

Equity

The evidence examined in relation to equity is somewhat limited, so that only very tentative conclusions can be drawn. This in part reflects the complexity of defining equity and reaching judgements about it, and also the limitations of the research design, which did not focus in a concentrated manner on the equity issue. Evidence on changes in the provision for special needs pupils in the case-study schools was given by headteachers and some special needs teachers; direct measures of the resources allocated to specific pupils or the impact on the learning of these pupils were not obtained. The tentative conclusion is that given the professional values of headteachers, pupils with special needs are not disadvantaged by local management *per se* but only by lack of funds, since schools will tend to give priority to basic mainstream provision before resourcing special needs. In assessing this conclusion, it must be borne in mind that the experiences of statemented pupils were not investigated, and only the broad category of special needs was addressed when gathering evidence. A further caveat concerns pupils with emotional and behavioural difficulties. The sample of schools studied was very small, the schools were not actively competitive, and the evidence gathered from teachers and governors on their policies towards pupils is potentially biased.

Effectiveness

If local management is to improve school effectiveness, then it must impact on the classroom. One way for this to occur is that local management leads to a more cost-efficient deployment of a given quantity of resources, which I have argued is the case. However, it is unlikely that the effect of a modest increase in resources on educational outputs could be picked up statistically when major externally imposed curriculum change is occurring at the same time. Since research shows that process variables are more important determinants of school effectiveness than moderate differences in resourcing (Rutter *et al.* 1979; Purkey and Smith 1983; Hanushek 1986; Mortimore *et al.* 1988; Reynolds 1992; Willms 1992), the impact of a relatively small increase in resources for supporting teaching and learning is not of itself likely to bring about more than a minor improvement in schools' educational productivity.

A second possible channel whereby local management could increase educational productivity is by stimulating those processes which are associated with school effectiveness and school improvement (Chubb and Moe 1990; Malen *et al.* 1990).[9] These issues were examined in Chapters 5 and 6. The most that could be concluded in favour of local management is that in some schools it is beginning to stimulate or facilitate the development of these processes, which are largely related to leadership, staff motivation, school culture and coordination – all focusing on teaching and learning. These possible benefits are to a greater or lesser degree offset by the greater uncertainty facing schools and the additional management time expended by schools, especially those suffering from budget cuts. While the 'losing' schools in our sample responded by a more careful consideration of their priorities than some of the 'winning' schools, none of them suffered a marked decline in pupils and staff.

A key process through which delegated budgeting impacts on school effectiveness is linking budget planning to the educational purposes of the school. The difficulties schools experience in doing this, observed in this study and in others, follows from the ambiguous nature of the relationships between inputs and outputs in the education production function. This ambiguity lies at the heart of the problem of trying to get a purchase on the causal links between school-based management and improved educational outcomes. When we examine other evidence on the possible and actual impacts of local management on school processes, the tentative conclusion is that so far the evidence of any resulting improvement in educational standards is relatively sparse. For instance, HMI (1992a: 11) conclude:

> There is little evidence yet of LMS having any substantial impact on educational standards, although specific initiatives have led to improvements in targeting of resources and staff and so to improvements in the quality of educational experience.

Malen *et al.* (1990: 323), in surveying the North American literature, conclude that 'the link between school-based management and the evocation of effective schools is fragile at best'. Bullock and Thomas (1994) are also cautious about the beneficial effects of local management on children's learning, which they assessed by surveying headteachers' opinions on this question. The number of headteachers perceiving benefits to learning as a result of local management had risen over the three years of the survey to about 50 per cent, and to 80 per cent for heads of large secondary schools. In contrast, only 30 per cent of heads in small secondary schools perceived benefits and only 30 per cent of teachers agreed that learning had benefited. Bullock and Thomas infer that the financial position of the school is the chief determinant of whether heads perceive learning benefits. This suggests that it is through additional resources that learning benefits are derived rather than through improved decision-making processes and changes in school culture. This conclusion accords with our study to the extent that perceived benefits were derived mainly from changes in resourcing, rather than from cultural change in schools promoting more effective learning strategies. However, the clear distinction between the perceptions of headteachers in budget gaining and losing schools in the Bullock and Thomas study was not found in our sample. Even the head of Graceland thought that the flexibility of local management had benefited the school, given the cuts would have come anyway. He was optimistic that 'we are now getting away from heads worrying about cleaning contracts and broken glass and balancing budgets, but concentrating on the curriculum'. The headteacher at Harrimore, which was resourced at a similar level to that before local management, was, like two other heads, an enthusiastic advocate of its beneficial effects on educational provision:

> We are providing more resources for children and a better environment in which to work. It has taken a lot of administration duties away from teachers and given them to support staff. There is much improved teacher support. Governors are now aware of how well schools run and on how little they have to run on. This leads to councillors voting for more money for schools.

Quasi-markets and management control

Introduction

Local management of schools is but one example of the movement away from administrative hierarchy as the dominant form of organization for public services to a quasi-market framework (Le Grand and Bartlett 1993). The distinguishing characteristics of a quasi-market for a public service are the separation of purchaser from provider and an element of user choice between providers. The quasi-market remains highly regulated. The government continues to control such matters as entry by new providers, investment, the quality of service (as with the national curriculum) and price, which is often zero to the user, as in schooling. In this book, I have so far applied theoretical frameworks for analysing local management which focus on the school as a single unit. The purpose of this chapter is to widen the focus by examining theories drawn from institutional economics and organizational theory in order to analyse inter-organizational relationships within the quasi-market. Within this framework, the changed relationships between central government, local education authorities (LEAs) and schools are considered. The salient features of these organizational changes are increased central government control, the redefinition of a reduced LEA role and the development of locally differentiated patterns of inter-school relationships. One of the most interesting features of schools' responses to the dismemberment of local authority administrative and political control is the development of different kinds of networking arrangements between schools. The main line of argument developed here is that the new institutional arrangements for schools replicate similar organizational forms in the private sector, and can be similarly analysed as the abandonment of bureaucratic administration as an inefficient organizational structure. Market and networking relationships between schools, their suppliers and their 'customers' are developing alongside new forms of regulatory state control.

The models I propose to use for analysing local management and thereby examining its organizational impact have a common basis. They conceive of local management as a control device – that is, as a means for attaining particular ends. The term 'control' is used to refer to the range of structures, processes and personal interactions that are used in an organizational system to ensure that the organization fulfils its purposes (Anthony and Herzlinger 1989). Control in this sense is broader in meaning than its common usage and includes the creation of organizational cultures which promote the attainment of organizational purposes. Coming largely from an economics perspective, the models used here focus attention on the transactions or exchanges that take place between different parties, the knowledge which the transactors possess about the likely future outcomes of the transactions and the motivations of those engaged in transactions. People's (or, more technically, agents') decisions to engage in any particular transaction are determined by the perceived relative costs and benefits of doing so. A key variable is thus the cost of transactions. This means that those organizational structures and processes which possess lower transactions costs are more efficient and will be preferred over those with higher transactions costs. Consequently, it is predicted that the more efficient organizational form will eventually emerge as the dominant mode of coordination for any particular set of transactions.

Principal agent theory

Principal agent theory offers the broadest framework for interrelating the various dimensions of local management and analysing it as a control device. A principal–agent relationship arises in exchange whenever one person (the principal) depends on another (the agent) for some action which the principal wishes to have undertaken. The theory of principal–agent relations is succinctly summarized by Pratt and Zeckhauser (1985: 2–3):

> Whenever one individual depends on the action of another an *agency relationship* arises. The individual taking the action is called the *agent*. The affected party is the *principal* . . . The challenge of the agency relationship arises whenever – which is almost always – the principal cannot perfectly and costlessly monitor the agent's action and information.
>
> Relationships vary in the degree of informational asymmetry they involve. At one extreme we have the fabled perfect market transaction, with standardised products and all information fully shared. At the other end of the continuum are situations in which the agent has full discretion and is not observed at all by the principal.

Much of the work on principal–agent theory has been related to the separation of corporate ownership from management, where the shareholder is principal and the firm's managers are the shareholders' agents. In the political arena, citizens are the ultimate principals: they elect politicians in order to pursue policies or values which they favour. In turn, politicians take on the role of principal and have to rely on public sector workers to implement their policies. A major difference between principal–agent relationships in the private and in the public sectors is that citizens' preferences are far more diverse than those of a firm's shareholders. The issue of what are the best constititutional arrangements for reflecting voters' preferences and supporting democratic ideals is thus much wider than that relating to corporate governance and stock market operations. However, principal–agent theory seems particularly applicable to the UK's unwritten constitution, since it provides for the dictatorship of the majority political party in an essentially single-chamber legislature rather than a counterbalancing of plural interests.

A salient aspect of principal–agent theory applied to the public sector is the hypothesis of provider dominance over the interests of service users. Public choice theory, which has developed over the past thirty years (for surveys, see McLean 1987; Mueller 1989; Levačić, 1990a), has sought to demonstrate the inefficiency of collective choice mechanisms and public sector bureaucracy provision and has been a major influence in fermenting critical attitudes to the public sector. The underpinning assumption that individuals are self-interested rational utility maximisers is applied to the public sector as well as the private sector. It therefore follows that if public sector employees act in their own interests, then the government, as principal, has a problem controlling its agents – the public sector providers. It cannot rely on them to deliver 'good performance' as defined by the government, ostensibly on behalf of service users. There must therefore be put in place a set of institutional arrangements which provide appropriate incentives and sanctions to ensure agents' compliance with the principal's policy objectives.

If principals and agents could share all information at no cost and had the same preferences, there would be no transactions costs involved in setting up and conducting exchanges between agent and principal. When these ideal conditions do not exist, the principal needs to make use of devices for 'controlling' the agent to ensure that it acts in the principal's interests. These control mechanisms incur costs and therefore give rise to an *agency loss* or *agency cost*.[1] 'Control mechanisms' in the sense used here cover a range of distinctly different devices, most of which do not imply coercion except as a last resort. Four broad but distinct control devices can be usefully distinguished:

1 A market relationship is one under which the principal makes *contingency payments* to the agent if certain conditions are met. The nature of the

contract determines the conditions which need to be met for payments to be made. Because of uncertainty about outcomes, there is risk for both agent and principal and the contract determines how risk is shared between principal and agent. Uncertainty arises because the outcomes are not wholly dependent upon the agent's actions and the principal cannot distinguish outcomes caused by the agent's actions from those due to other events.

2 The principal can exert hierarchical control over the agent by means of rules and commands (or authority) issued by the principal, who is in a superordinate position *vis-à-vis* the agent. In the case of the public sector, these rules usually have statutory backing. Hierarchy is the distinguishing control mechanism of administrative bureaucracy.

3 Under political control, principals vote agents into and out of power.

4 Ethical codes of accepted behaviour can guide agents' actions and establish trust between principal and agent. Public service agencies are distinguished from most commercial enterprises by the key role the various 'professions' play in service delivery. As Matthews (1991) points out in his discussion of professional ethics as a low-cost instrument of regulation, professionals are motivated by self-interest in maintaining a high professional reputation, as well as by more altruistic 'internalized morality'.

Another way of looking at the different control devices is as modes of accountability. The classification of control devices given above maps quite closely to the different modes of accountability distinguished by Kogan (1986), who classifies them as professional, consumerist and public accountability. Kogan's main stress within public accountability is managerial accountability through bureaucratic structures but embedded within a system of local political control. His consumerist accountability in education is subdivided into free market and partnership. I would classify the latter under professional ethics, since partnership with parents, for example, depends on teachers' respecting and valuing parents' involvement.

'Professional ethics' or more broadly 'trust' between those engaging in transactions reduces transactions costs both in markets and within organizational hierarchies. Efficient market transactions depend on buyers and sellers acting honestly, since reliance on trust is much less costly than resorting to legal enforcement of contracts. The more principal–agent relationships are governed by trust the less need there is for costly legal enforcement which would inhibit transactions from taking place. As Matthews (1991) argues, trust between principal and agent is of particular importance in the relationship between a client and a member of a profession exercising expertise and so providing a service, the quality of which it is difficult for the client to judge. In such cases, there is information asymmetry, with the agent possessing more information than the principal. Trust in the form of professional ethics is important when the principal has inadequate knowledge to assess the quality of the service being provided by the agent, as is often the case in the relationship between parent and teacher. Trust benefits both parties. Without trust the market demand for professional services would be less because clients would have great difficulty in distinguishing between poor and good practitioners and would have to take out insurance against malpractice. Alternatively, if legal sanctions protect clients, then professionals have to take out insurance which increases costs.

A further consideration is that some professionals provide public goods and so may on occasions need to judge between their obligations to society and the interests of an individual client. These wider social obligations, as conceived by the profession, lead it to embrace a 'professional ethic' or 'internalized morality', which may not accord with the preferences either of individual clients or of government. Professional codes of conduct usually include restrictions on competition. In part, this is to prevent conduct which would be to the longer-term detriment of clients because of the use of deception to attract custom, but it can also be misused to give the profession's members less need to perform well and satisfy client preferences, while protecting their incomes from competition due to price-cutting among themselves or by unlicensed practitioners.

Professional values are therefore important for ensuring that agents serve principals well. However, the mechanisms that protect professional values, in particular freedom from hierarchical rules directing professionals' work and restraints on competition for monetary rewards, depend for their efficacy on the ethical code being maintained through professional acculturation and self-regulation. Conflicts will arise when the values of a profession clash with those of its principals, in particular when the immediate principals are politicians who have considerable power conferred on them by a system of elected majority dictatorship.

Applying principal–agent theory to the school system, local management is analysed as a change in the control devices used by central government with respect to education sector employees. Table 8.1 shows the complex hierarchy of principal–agent relationships with respect to state schools. The control mechanisms which have been strengthened since 1988 are indicated in bold type and those which have been weakened are shown in italics. Citizens are the ultimate principals with both central and local politicians as their direct agents. The control device is political (i.e. voting). Local management has been associated with an increase in the political representation of parents through elections to governing bodies and of the community through co-options to school governing bodies.

A further change in control devices brought about by the 1988 Education Reform Act was replacing LEAs' hierarchical administrative control of schools by a quasi-market in which schools receive payments which are contingent on their success in attracting pupils. In this quasi-market, LEAs act on behalf of parents by purchasing educational services from schools. This mechanism thus provides an element of control through the market

Table 8.1 Modes of control of agents by principals: State schooling since 1988[a]

Agent	Principal					
	Citizen	Parent/child	Central government	LEA	School governing body	Headteacher
Central government	Political					
LEA	Political	Political	**Authority**			
School governing body		**Political; Market choice; Public service ethics**	**Authority; Public service ethics**	*Authority* (none for GM schools); **Public service ethics**		
Headteacher		**Market choice;** Professional ethics	**Authority;** *Professional ethics*	*Authority* (none for GM schools); professional ethics	**Authority; Contingency payments;** Professional ethics	
Teacher		**Market choice;** Professional ethics	**Authority;** *Professional ethics*	*Authority* (none for GM schools)	**Authority; Contingency payments;** Professional ethics	**Authority;** Professional ethics

[a] In 1988, the 1986 Education Act, which enhanced the powers of governing bodies and increased the representation of parent and co-opted governors at the expense of LEA-appointed governors, was implemented.

Note: Enhancement in mode of control indicated by **bold font** and diminution by *italics*.

choices of parents. In this way, parents are used to control schools by giving schools an incentive to respond to parental preferences. However, the link between school performance and pupil recruitment is moderated by the degree of competition, which varies according to local circumstances.

Governors' potential powers as principals with respect to staff employed in schools have been considerably enhanced. Governors can use authority in determining school policy, the spending of its budget and in managing staff. The government has made further attempts to extend control via contingency payments by enabling governors to introduce performance-related pay for teachers. Local management has also considerably increased the powers and responsibilities of headteachers. As the research evidence indicates, much of the enhanced power and influence of headteachers stems from their exercising in practice the *de jure* responsibilities of the governing body. In contrast to the position of LEAs, central government has considerably strengthened its central hierarchical control through the national curriculum, testing, inspection, the funding rules imposed on LEAs, and by the direct funding of grant-maintained (GM) schools.

In summary, then, local management is a change in the mechanisms by which central government, as principal, attempts to control its agents – the LEAs, school governors, headteachers and teachers – mainly by introducing a greater element of contingency payments and an increase in its use of authority. It is important to note that while local management of schools has increased the number of financial signals to which school managers are expected to respond and constrained them with a new set of hierarchical rules about the curriculum, it still depends for its efficacy on the public service and professional motivations of governors and teachers.

Local management as a model of multi-divisional organizational structure

Set in a web of principal–agent relationships, decentralized resource management is located within the hierarchical span of control which runs from the Department for Education (DFE) to the LEA or Funding Agency for Schools (FAS) and then to the school. There appears to be an apparent paradox noted by a number of writers (Campbell *et al.* 1987; Coulby 1991), that increased central control of the curriculum has been accompanied by decreased control of resource management. However, the equivalent organizational change in the private sector – that of the multidivisional or M-form firm replacing a centrally controlled, functionally specialized corporate structure (U-form firm) – has been explained as a means of enhancing top management control and hence efficiency (see Levačić 1993b).

Prior to local management, local authority education services were organized along U-form lines. In a U-form organization, the specialist functions, such as finance, personnel and purchasing, are organized into separate departments supplying services to the operational units which produce the final output or services for the market. There is a single peak coordinator – chief executive or board of directors – to which the managers of the functional departments report. Top management exercises detailed bureaucratic control of the functional and operational areas. The old-style local authority was organized into operational departments such as education, social services, transport and housing, and functional departments such as finance, property and personnel. The functional departments serviced the operational areas, which had little control over the services received. The finance department, for example, did the accounting for the education department. Teachers' salaries were recorded in a single account, regardless of the school at which they were employed. Similarly, utility invoices were dealt with in another account and not attributed to the building which incurred the heating or water costs. The property department serviced and maintained all the authority's buildings and thus the authority, not the schools, decided what maintenance work would take place.

The U-form firm was the original structure adopted in the nineteenth century. Its particular advantage is that specialist functional departments can achieve lower costs through the division of labour and economies of scale. However, it is generally argued (Chandler 1966) that as the U-form firm grows in size and complexity, top management loses the capacity to coordinate the entire enterprise. The relationship between top management and other employees, in particular middle management, is another example of a principal–agent relationship. Hence the inefficiency of the U-form structure is attributed to the costs of its detailed bureaucratic control structure.

In contrast, a multi-divisional or M-form organization is structured into operational divisions, based on products or regions, which are given a high degree of autonomy to manage themselves. They are controlled by the headquarters management by being set targets, monitored against these targets, and allocated resources in line with their success in contributing to overall company goals. The greater efficiency claimed for the M-form firm, which is reputed to have been originated by Alfred Sloan for General Motors in the 1920s, stems from the ability of top management to engage in strategic management rather than being immersed in detailed operational issues, as in the U-form structure. At the heart of the greater efficiency of the M-form division is the saving in transactions costs through more efficient use of information which is the key to management control. A major factor causing transactions costs is limitations to people's capacity to analyse and make sense of information. This human limitation in information processing is termed 'bounded rationality', an important concept orginating in Simon's (1947) *Administrative Behaviour* and developed further for the analysis of firm structure in the transactions cost approach of Williamson (1970, 1975). The advent of computers has not eliminated bounded rationality. Computers can store, analyse and present a mass of information, but it still has to be interpreted and made sense of by human intelligence.

Another key factor in creating transactions costs is the 'guileful pursuit of self-interest' or 'opportunism'[2] by people working in organizations. If top managers rely on detailed bureaucratic control of subordinates, they depend on the upward flow of information from subordinates to know what is happening in the organization in order to direct it. However, opportunistic subordinates distort the upward flow of information in order to serve their own ends, which may well be rooted in departmental rather than purely personal interests, but which are not congruent with the goals of the organization as conceived by top management. Opportunism is therefore an example of inadequate control of agents by the principal.

It is argued that the M-form division is better than the U-form in reducing the costs of principal–agent control in an organization thereby making it more efficient. In the M-form structure, the operational divisions and their managers are given much more responsibility for managing their own functions. The problem of bounded rationality is addressed by limiting the amount of information top managers need. Decisions which require knowledge of local market conditions and production methods are decentralized to the product divisions. Appropriate incentives are given to divisional managers through setting personal and divisional performance targets which promote company-wide objectives. Thus the self-interest of managers and divisions is harnessed for the benefit of the organization as a whole. The information required by top management is therefore restricted to that needed for monitoring the overall performance of managers and their divisions and for making strategic decisions about the development and direction of the business. The M-form organization is thus depicted as tight mission accompanied by loose means. Top management operates tight control through strategic management and performance monitoring, while leaving how the objectives are attained to middle managers and their divisions.

The analogy between the M-form model and the restructured LEA would have been quite close had the LEA retained and developed monitoring and strategic management functions. This analogy is set out in Table 8.2, where each of the characteristics of an M-form organization, as set out by Williamson (1970), is matched against the LEA equivalent.

While the constituent features of the M-form model correspond well to equivalent features of the restructured education service, the model as developed in the English school system at the time of writing lacks the clear lines of accountability between top management and the divisions which characterize the generic M-form model. The 1988 Education Reform Act specified key elements of the M-form model, in particular establishing schools as operational divisions managed as independent cost centres, and creating in the national curriculum and its national testing a means for assessing the performance of schools and holding them accountable. Implicit

Table 8.2 The local education authority as an M-form organization

The general characteristics of M-form as developed for business	M-form equivalent for the education system
A multi-divisional structure, in which the divisions are profit centres responsible for products or regions and have considerable management autonomy	Schools are the equivalent of operational divisions and are restructured as cost centres, funded by formula. Schools are responsible for managing their delegated budgets, staff and other resources
Top management and its general office are separate from the operational and functional divisions. They are concerned with the overall performance of the divisions, not their day-to-day management	Further delegation has forced LEAs to cease direct production of functional services for schools. LEAs have to contract to sell services to schools
The general office is primarily concerned with strategic management, involving determining organizational structure, planning, coordinating and allocating resources	LEAs have some strategic functions left for those schools they maintain: • determining the education budget within constraints; • devising and operating a DFE-approved funding formula; • allocating approved capital expenditure; • determining (with DFE approval) the number, type and size of schools; • determining criteria for admissions to schools
Performance monitoring. An elite staff within the general office provides research, advisory and auditing function in order to secure control over the operational divisions	Performance monitoring. Standards are set by central government through national curriculum, testing and OFSTED inspections. LEAs can develop their own performance monitoring systems

in the 1988 Act was the expectation that LEAs would strengthen their school monitoring function, which was held to be inadequate (Audit Commission 1989a). However, the creation of the Office for Standards in Education (OFSTED) in 1992 placed central government more clearly in the role of the M-form headquarters management. Furthermore, the creation under the 1993 Education Act of the FAS, clarified the Department of Education's role as headquarters management for GM schools.

Another feature of the education system which weakens the strategic and monitoring roles of the LEA (and FAS) is the powers of governing bodies, which are no longer part of the line of hierarchical control between school and LEA. Governors now act for the school in its dealings with the LEA and can be quite critical of the LEA, even when remaining within it, as reported in research by Deem (1993) and Arnott and Munn (1994). A further factor is the public goods nature of education, which means that LEAs still act on behalf of the customers of education, while also being providers of education services, though not on the scale they were prior to the 1988 Education Reform Act. Under the 1993 Education Act, LEAs have been given the task of representing parental interests with respect to children with special needs in seeking to ensure that these are met by schools or other means. In the wake of the torrent of educational legislation, LEAs have been forced to redefine their role (or roles) and are doing so in different ways (Cordingly and Kogan 1992; Ranson 1992, 1994; Riley 1994). Local education authorities have always varied in their political and organizational characteristics; these historical factors have played a major part in determining how each LEA has redefined its role and justified its existence since 1988.

The role of the LEA

The LEA modelled as an M-form organization would have the headquarters functions of performance monitoring and strategic management. The general office would oversee the operational divisions (the schools) and the functional divisions, such as finance, personnel, property services, educational advice, welfare, in-service training, music, library and museum services. The latter, organized as cost centres, sell services to schools. In providing these services, the LEA is acting as a producer which operates an internal market for allocating resources between its divisions. The operational divisions are purchasers, the functional divisions suppliers. Thus the internal market replaces bureaucratic administration as the mode of coordination within the M-form LEA.

However, the M-form analogy taken from the private sector breaks down with respect to the principal–agent relationship in the LEA, since the principals are, when translated into private sector equivalents, both customers and shareholders. Under the restructured system, central government has put itself more strongly in the role of principal in relation to the LEAs and schools, acting on behalf of individual customers of education as well as asserting its right to define the public goods aspects of education through the national curriculum. This stance places LEAs more firmly in the role of providers. At the same time, those LEAs asserting collectivist values see their role as that of acting on behalf of the community's interest and of the interests of certain groups within the community and hence acting on behalf of customers. In taking this stance, LEAs seek to limit the cost to the perceived collective interest of self-interested behaviour by individual parents and schools. In this role, LEAs act as principal on behalf of the collective interest or on behalf of individual parental interests, in relation to schools as agents. Even central government, under the 1993 Education Act, has placed LEAs in the role of protecting certain consumer interests, notably those of children with special needs. A range of statutory duties in the field of education remains from long-standing legislation as well as that specified in recent Acts (Morris 1994). Thus redefining the roles of the LEA and developing new working relationships to fulfil these roles are complex issues. One aspect of this complexity is that the roles of strategist, school performance monitor, service provider and protector of consumer interests are not separate but are interwoven. Not surprisingly, LEAs have developed these roles in different ways since 1988, as a number of studies have shown (Ranson 1992, 1994; Riley 1994). The variety of LEA response is of itself an interesting example of mediation of policy in the process of implementation.

The application of the M-form model to LEAs indicates four major areas in which LEAs can redefine their rationale and role. These are strategic leadership of the local education service, quality assurance or performance monitoring, service provider to schools and upholding the interests of education service users. All but the last function would be performed by an M-form firm acting in the interests of its shareholders. These roles encompass the six proposed by the Audit Commission (1989a): those of educational leader, planner of facilities, partner and banker to schools, provider of information for users, and regulator of quality. Local education authorities, despite the creation of the quasi-market with its separation of purchaser and provider roles, have still been left to function both as purchasers of services on behalf of parents and as providers of services to schools. In principle, a LEA could realign its role so as to act only on behalf of education customers by privatizing all school support services and by acting as a regulatory agent in providing parents with information on schools' performance, rather than in the performance monitoring role of the M-form firm's top management. Where the LEA continues to act as a provider as well, the performance monitoring function is then an internal function, undertaken to inform schools' managements and to be used by the LEA in its own quality assurance work.

The strategic role

The strategy of the LEA refers to the general principles and supporting policies which broadly define the type of educational service the LEA provides and the political values which underpin it. At one extreme is the model of the enabling LEA, where the LEA merely ensures that statutorily prescribed public services are provided in the locality by the private sector or non-governmental, quasi-autonomous agencies. In contrast to this passive, reactive strategy, a pro-active LEA articulates clear values and broad aims for the local education service and translates these into its service provision, over which it retains considerable influence. The strategies LEAs have pursued in response to delegated budgeting, opting out and the strengthening of central government inspection have determined the ways in which the other three functions – quality assurance, service provision and customer support – are undertaken. Two important aspects of the strategic role are the determination of the funding formula, including the total budget to be allocated, and overseeing – subject to DFE approval – the structure of the local schooling system (the number and sizes of schools, admissions policy and the capital programme). Clearly, a LEA with a high proportion of GM schools cannot sustain a pro-active strategic role, as it has lost command of the necessary resources.

Local education authorities have differed quite considerably in their strategic response to the legislative changes since 1988, thus increasing the differentiation between them. These differences have depended upon existing political values and the historical factors which affected a particular LEA's relationship with its schools, its financial position and the extent of competition between schools due to surplus places. The extent to which the LEA has been able to retain its schools has been highly dependent on these existing factors, as well as on the subsequent strategic response of the LEA. By the mid-1990s, it appeared that the wave of opting out was diminishing and that many LEAs were consolidating their position within a redefined relationship with their schools.

In a study of LEAs restructuring over the five years since 1988, Ranson (1994) distinguished four models of LEA management, with specific LEA examples of each model. At the minimal end of the spectrum is the 'contractor' model, under which the LEA manages contracts to supply services to autonomous schools, both from private sector providers and its own remaining service units, which are run on a fully commercial basis. The market is thus the dominant mode of coordination in the contractor LEA. The next is the 'enabling' LEA, which provides advice and support to a loosely coordinated network of schools. Contractual relationships between the LEA and schools are underpinned and supplemented by inter-organizational and interpersonal relationships of influence. These relationships are stronger still in the 'partnership' model. Here the LEA provides educational leadership and promotes active cooperation between schools and between schools and the LEA. While further delegation has required the LEA to put many of its services on a contractual basis, the partnership LEA develops these in consultation with schools. There is a clear expectation that schools need to support these services in order to preserve them in the collective interest. Barsetshire falls into the category of the partnership LEA, since it has retained most of its schools and has undertaken further delegation after elaborate consultation with schools. Schools were still largely buying into the LEA services, including advisory services. The headteachers in the case-study schools valued the role of the LEA and considered that services had improved as a result of delegation. At the other end of the spectrum is the 'civic provider' – the LEA which has retained all its schools and preserves its pre-1988 purpose as a comprehensive provider of all educational needs in its locality, with a particular emphasis on the needs of the less socially advantaged. It also takes on an active role in monitoring performance and quality assurance. Delegated budgeting is now accepted as managerially efficient, but the commercialization of its support services has been restricted as far as possible. In all four models, but to an increasing degree as one moves from the civic provider to the contractor, the balance of power in the relationship between headteachers and the LEA has shifted to the former. Local education authorities now have to cultivate the goodwill of their headteachers and prove their value to schools.

Performance monitoring

Performance monitoring of schools is a function which LEAs have increasingly developed as part of redefining a role for themselves. Various forms of benchmarking or making inter-organizational comparisons across a range of performance indicators are being developed by LEAs as a service which they can provide for schools (Morris 1994; STRB 1994, para. 125). Much of the benchmarking data are at the school level and concern financial variables, student enrolment and characteristics, and comparisons of examination results with contextual data, such as the percentage of pupils entitled to free school meals. A small but increasing number of LEAs are developing value-added pupil level data on school effectiveness (Hill *et al.* 1990). In this way, LEAs are taking on the performance monitoring role of the M-form firm's general office and thus supplementing or improving upon the monitoring provided by central government through the league tables of raw examination results. However, as Morris (1994: 20) concludes: 'The law of education is now unsatisfactory in a crucial respect, that the legal basis of LEA responsibility for quality in schooling, i.e. the effectiveness of the pedagogy and the soundness of the curriculum, is confused and unclear.

This lack of clarity is reflected in the variety of approaches by LEAs to the management of school quality. Four such approaches are distinguished by Riley (1994) using interview evidence from seven LEAs on their management of quality assurance with respect to schools. The four types correspond quite closely to the four models distinguished by Ranson. The interventionist LEA actively monitors school performance and takes action to improve performance. The interactionist LEA, such as Barsetshire, is less interventionist and instead develops a strong partnership with its schools for monitoring quality. The responsive LEA reacts to schools' expressed needs but is not pro-active in seeking to undertake monitoring, while the non-interventionist LEA treats schools as autonomous and does no monitoring of its own.

Service provider

In the first wave of local management from 1990 to 1992, LEAs concentrated on developing a DFE-approved funding formula. Because of the large information requirements, this took several years. For most LEAs some aspects of the formula were only approved for an interim period of two years (see Thomas and Levačić 1991) Barsetshire, for example, was unable to work out a sub-formula for energy initially because of a lack of data and was allowed to use historic costs for the first two years. Other aspects of the formula needed fine-tuning, as with fixed costs and the pupil count data in Barsetshire. In the second wave from 1993, LEAs were required to undertake further delegation, so that 85 per cent of the potential schools budget (PSB) was delegated to schools. This resulted in considerable upheaval in central services, as these needed to be put on a commercial footing now that schools could buy from them using their delegated budgets. This period was also one of greater financial stringency, so that many LEAs, including Barsetshire, reduced the amount available for allocation to schools for the purchase of central services.

Local education authorities have been relatively successful so far in retaining schools as purchasers for their services, though this varies by service. School meals and cleaning have largely gone to private contractors. However, LEAs' educational services (e.g. advisory, library and even music), for which gloomy prognostications abounded, have survived with schools buying in. Many LEAs have offered schools packages of contractual services. This is particularly attractive to primary schools, because they do not possess the managerial resources to devote time to market search. The financial viability of such services depends on a critical mass of schools purchasing them; hence there is some collective pressure on individual schools, particularly larger ones, not to take their custom elsewhere and so jeopardize the availability of LEA services to smaller schools. Despite the survival of LEA services in the newly created internal market, there have been profound changes in the working conditions of LEA central staff whose jobs are now dependent on market demand. There has been a considerable shake-out of staff, with some retiring and others becoming self-employed. The LEA no longer offers such an attractive career structure to tempt teachers out of schools, a trend likely to diminish the future supply of inspectors. However, as far as the evidence gathered in Barsetshire indicated, headteachers considered that the quality of services had improved as a result of the internal market, though concern was expressed at cuts in the resources available to purchase them.

The M-form education authority: The case of stengthened control in Edmonton

In the English context, the M-form education authority does not demonstrate more efficient control over its school than the U-form structure, because of the deliberate weakening of the LEA's powers by central government. The LEA can only retain influence and survive largely intact with the consent of its schools. This depends on the political outlook of governors and headteachers, as well as the value schools place on the LEA's leadership and service functions. In part, the role of the M-form headquarters has been grasped by central government through the DFE and its agencies – the School Curriculum and Assessment Authority, the FAS and OFSTED. However, other systems can provide examples of the way in which decentralized resource management, as part of an M-form structure, has enhanced the controlling capacity of the education authority.

One such system is to be found in the Edmonton Public School District in Canada (see Levačić 1992b).[3] In the late 1970s, Edmonton chose decentralization as a deliberate strategy for securing better managerial control by the Board of Trustees and the superintendent (the top appointed official). The previous structure had been U-form, with extreme centralization of functions organized around a planning, programming-budgeting system. The function of the school principal was to coordinate the resources provided by many disparate central officials and to represent staff and community views to Board officials. Decentralized budgeting was chosen as the means to initiate a fundamental restructuring of the organization. From allowing schools to determine the spending of 2 per cent of the education budget in the late 1970s, by 1990 a total of 75 per cent was delegated by a pupil-driven formula. Parents could opt to send their children to out-of-catchment schools, but did not receive free transport if they did so. Consequently, there could be considerable year-by-year fluctuations in rolls, which were dealt with by the district redeploying teachers to schools with vacancies.

The continually reiterated management philosophy of the district was that the Board and its officers were concerned with results not school processes. The district clearly stated its objectives and had strong line management accountability, passing from the superintendent to six associate superintendents, each responsible for about thirty school principals based on the view that each person should have only 'one boss'. The Board and its officers had resisted proposals for school councils with power because this would have blurred the line of accountability and fatally weakened their management control system. The superintendent and his associates monitored the performance of principals and their schools and held principals accountable for their results. Since 1980 schools have been assessed by means of an annual attitude survey of staff, pupils and parents, and since 1987 by tests of pupils at grades 3, 6 and 9 in language, arts, maths, science and humanities as well. The associate superintendents undertook with each principal an annual review of his or her school's performance indicators as measured by the tests and attitude surveys, as well as pupil recruitment. Areas for improvement were then agreed. These reviews meshed in with the district annual planning cycle followed by each school. Principals who performed badly on these criteria were eased out and the district was evolving succession planning for principals. There appeared to be a strong organizational culture, reflected in catchphrases ('tight mission', 'easy means', 'the golden rule is gold rules', 'celebrating growth') which reinforced the more overt control mechanisms. Thus Edmonton provides a counter-example to the English system of how an M-form structure can lead to more effective top management control than the U-form structure.

School cooperative networks

In the English context, schools have experienced differing degrees of autonomy and of potential or actual isolation, since they are no longer cocooned in the protective if restricting embrace of the LEA. The flip side of the freedom and flexibility of local management for schools is the threat to performance and survival from inadequate resources and a hostile external environment. For some schools, the potential disadvantages of isolation in an uncertain environment cannot be assuaged by the presence of a protective LEA, because the LEA cannot or chooses not to function in this way. For other schools, the protective embrace of the LEA would be too stifling to be an attractive solution to the dangers of isolation. A noticeable response by schools to the attentuated role of the LEA is the growth of stronger cooperative networks, often building on previous school groupings organized by the LEA and now given active encouragement to develop further and more independently. Where successful, these cooperative groupings evolve over time and expand the range of collaborative activities in which the schools are engaged.

The development of cooperation among schools seems on the face of it at odds with the competitive market which the legislation has promoted. However, cooperation within the context of market relationships is well developed in the private sector. The organizational network as a mode of coordination which supplements market relationships has been given increasing attention as a contemporary organizational form, developed in response to firms' seeking greater flexibility and speedier adaptation in a world of rapid change. A key feature of an organizational network is that its members are horizontally related, in contrast to the vertical hierarchical relationship of bureaucratic control. They are predominantly social relationships reliant on trust, unlike the pure market relationship in which traders do not know each other. Organizations in networks engage in joint decision-making and the exchange of different kinds of services. Alter and Hage (1993) propose three types of cooperation – limited, moderate and broad. Limited cooperation involves the exchange of information and mutual support, moderate cooperation encompasses activities such as joint purchasing, borrowing and marketing, while broad cooperation extends to joint production of goods and services. Alter and Hage posit that competitive cooperation among organizations in the same sector is less likely to be long-lasting and deeply embedded in organizational functioning than is 'symbiotic cooperation' among organisations from different sectors, such as that between customer and supplier firms. Translated to schools, this suggests that cooperative networks between secondary schools and their feeder primaries are more likely to flourish than those between schools in the same phase and which are thus in competition.

Schools would seem to be predisposed to cooperation as one of the factors promoting cooperative networks in a culture which values cooperation and perceives its advantages. For many schools, collaboration is an expression of a public service ethos, in which schools exist to serve the needs of all children in the local community, while competition by schools for pupils is perceived as potentially harmful for the less advantaged. Of course, this ethical justification for collaboration can also, from a different perspective, mean collusion on the part of schools as producers to create cartels, thus protecting poorly performing schools and teachers from the consequences of competition. In general, cartels – that is, cooperative agreements between firms producing for the same market to restrict competition – are prone to instability because of the potential benefits to any one member of breaking the agreement. Early research on the development of school networks within the quasi-market (e.g. Busher and Hodgkinson 1994; Levačić and Woods 1994) indicates that many aspects of organizational network theory are applicable. Cooperative networks of schools in close proximity to each other are developing, often assisted by the LEA. The trend seems more pronounced with respect to 'family' networks of a secondary school and its feeder primary schools. The secondary school often provides some additional resources to the primaries in the form of administrative support for the network and supply cover. Because of their small size, primary schools in particular need cooperation to secure additional resources, whereas the secondary school is anxious to improve the quality and consistency of the learning achieved by its intake pupils and to secure the recruitment of pupils through good relationships with its local primary schools.

Such partnership schools are now sharing parts of their budgets in order to undertake joint purchases of services and so take advantage of lower unit costs through economies of scale and scope. Economies of scale occur when the average cost of a product or service (such as property maintenance or payroll administration) falls as more is produced. For example, it is cheaper for five schools to employ one special needs teacher for one day a week each than for them to employ five teachers one day a week each. Economies of scope apply to the reduction in unit costs that occur by undertaking more activities which require similar skills. A headteacher of a small primary school has insufficient time to manage all the aspects of a school's resourcing needs and cannot therefore secure economies of scope in the way a group of schools pooling their resources can. The most common areas for joint resourcing are marketing, in particular leaflets, collaborative in-service training and curriculum development, joint specialist teaching appointments, shared personnel for property maintenance and, less commonly, financial recording and reporting. This degree of cooperation is most appropriately classified as moderate, as it requires some sharing of budgets. Much more joint curriculum development and teaching would be required to develop broad cooperation. The costs of cooperation are largely the time involved: examples include £900 a year for a primary headteacher's time and £4500 for a secondary school teachers time.[4] Another cost is that of compromising the individual interests of the school in order to gain the benefits of cooperation. Clearly, if this cost becomes too marked, then tensions become manifest and may lead to the breakdown of cooperation.

As trust is a fundamental prerequisite for successful inter-school networks, these are less likely to develop where schools are in competition with each other. Thus factors such as the prevalence of surplus places and the existence of a substantial number of GM schools are likely to inhibit collaborative networks. Schools in such local environments would have to look outside their locality for networking relationships, which are less easy to develop and sustain when geographic distance makes interpersonal communication more costly. Schools which have remained within the LEA perceive the mutual support of their networks as an important factor in this choice. However, there are also examples of GM schools, as in Milton Keynes, which have bought into the LEA's network support provision.

The increased importance of vertical networks was apparent in Barsetshire. The LEA had previously supported clusters of small rural primaries. This network had now superimposed on it the vertical partnership of the secondary school and its feeder primaries. In most cases, this network was a strengthening of previous vertical links, encouraged by the LEA providing a small amount of matched funding for collaborative projects set up by the partnerships. Four secondary school heads interviewed were enthusiastic about the partnerships and saw their role as collaborating with the primary schools to improve the quality of the primary curriculum, particularly in the case of small schools. The two village primary schoolheads seemed less enthusiastic and tended to regret the lessened importance of the primary cluster, which shared common problems. Two secondary schools in one town engaged in some collaboration, such as raising funds from local business and discouraging competition for students. There was considerable pressure in the network groupings for members not to desert the LEA and opt out. One primary school was persuaded not to have a ballot and another, which went grant maintained, was thrown out of the partnership despite being a feeder primary school.

Conclusion

Local management has had profound effects on inter-organizational relationships in the school system which are still evolving. There is a range of organizational theory by which local management can be usefully analysed. A major theme of the analysis developed here, drawn from principal–agent theory and institutional economics, is that local management is an organizational form for securing greater efficiency and stronger organizational control. The pure M-form organizational structure combined with an internal market, as in Edmonton, provides an education authority with enhanced control over school performance compared with administrative bureaucracy. In the English context, control by the education authority is diffused and diluted by the overlapping roles of a number of agencies: the DFE, the FAS, OFSTED and governing bodies. The stream of legislative change since 1988 – which has continually redefined, but left partially ambiguous, the roles of the various agencies with responsibility for school performance – reveals policy-making on the hoof rather than the implementation of a well-conceived organizational design. Thus the theoretical approaches developed here are used to analyse the restructuring of the school system, not to suggest that a blueprint for organizational design was in the minds of policy-makers.

A related theme developed in this chapter is that the restructuring set in train since 1988 has increased the differences between organizational structures and cultures across the country. This is not only because market forces have worked themselves out differently in different places, but, possibly even more importantly, because of the divergence in political and organizational responses by schools and LEAs. Both LEAs and schools have responded according to a range of models, distinguished by the different emphasis given to autonomy and individual interests at one extreme and collaboration and the collective interest at the other. Both individual interests and different conceptions of the collective interest have legitimate claims which need to be attended to through the mechanisms of choice in education. It would be futile to suppose that schools could ever be organized in a way which removed controversy about these fundamental political issues. However, one can hope for a greater degree of tolerance between competing positions and a willingness to operate within structures designed to balance different individual interests and different conceptions of the public interest. In this way, greater stability would be achieved in schools' organizational environments, which are in any case subject to continual disturbance by generally experienced economic, social and technical change.

Local management: An overview

Introduction

This book is an attempt to assess local management of schools, largely from economic and organizational perspectives. These perspectives are crucial to understanding local management, since it is a change in the institutional arrangements for allocating resources to schools. However, other perspectives not developed here, such as a micro-political or a cultural perspective, would also have valuable insights to offer. In this final chapter, I aim to provide a summary of the findings and conclusions discussed in the preceding chapters concerning what is probably now known about local management and then to raise issues concerning those areas where our knowledge of the effects of local management is still highly speculative and conjectural.

In this book, I have attempted to develop a theoretical framework for analysing local management and also to present empirical evidence which is interpreted through this framework. This chapter begins with a straight-forward summary of the evidence on the descriptive features of local management. It then proceeds to interpret the descriptive evidence using the theoretical framework developed in the book and thereby to assess local management against selected criteria, namely efficiency, effectiveness, equity and choice, responsiveness and diversity.

The impact of local management: A descriptive account

Local management has been a major change in the way in which schools are resourced and managed, and it has been implemented with considerable success, largely due to the efforts of local education authorities (LEAs) and staff and governors in schools. By success I refer not to whether its aims have been attained, but to the fact that the organizational changes required to implement the policy have been achieved. Local education authorities have succeeded in funding their schools through formulae and the very large majority of schools have coped with managing their own budgets. Local management is supported by the majority of headteachers and few would wish to return to the previous system. There is political consensus to retain local management, though some of its features, like the average-in-actual-out salary principle, might well be revised. Grant-maintained (GM) status is similarly popular among those schools availing themselves of it, though there is far less political consensus concerning its retention. While the principle of formula-funding has widespread support, the system of central government funding of local government for its education services is widely seen to be in need of reform in order to relate funding more closely with schools' resourcing needs. Disparities between funding in different LEAs, between the maintained sector and the GM sector, and between primary and secondary pupils continue to excite debate. The school funding formulae are complex, however, because of the need to reflect variations in schools' resource needs, and because of continual changes in what is delegated. They are not simple funding rules which make resource allocation transparent and easy to understand by the vast majority of teachers and governors, let alone parents.

Most schools can manage their finances to the standards required for demonstrating financial probity and good stewardship of public money and can also operate within their budget constraints. Only around 6 per cent of primary schools so far are overspent, and though the percentage of secondary schools overspending is reported (Maychell 1994) to have risen in 1993–94, many of these drawing on past reserves. The vast majority of schools have accumulated reserves, some to an embarrassing degree, since the existence of such reserves could be interpreted as indicating schools are over-generously funded. Schools are making more efforts at income generation but are still subject to considerable financial uncertainty because of budget fluctuations, due particularly to changes in pupil numbers. Accumulating reserves has been one response to this. Another significant development is the increased trend towards a dual labour market, with at present probably around 10 per cent of teachers on temporary contracts.

The main impact of delegated budgeting on resource allocation decisions has been for schools to improve their physical environment and to vire money from operational services, which they have provided more cost-efficiently than the LEA, into direct support for teaching and learning. The administrative provision of services by the LEA to schools has been severely curtailed and replaced by contracting, either with the LEA or with alternative providers. Grant-maintained schools, having been allocated money in lieu of LEA central services, have been able to direct more money towards preferred alternatives, such as staff and premises (*Times Educational Supplement*, 7 October 1994). There has been a growth in support staff in schools, while pupil–teacher ratios have risen. Schools appear to be spending more in real terms on those teachers they retain in the permanent core and are reluctant to cut teaching staff unless forced to by budget deficits.

The post most significantly affected by local management is that of the headteacher. This is not due simply to the addition of financial management as a further responsibility but to the greater complexity of managing semi-autonomous schools in a quasi-market environment. The headteacher is the key link between the school and its environment and has prime responsibility for bringing resources to the school and then for overseeing their deployment within the school. The headteacher must attend both to the functioning of the technical core of the school and its organizational culture, and sustaining the core with resources. While the totality of the task is less complex for primary schools, the much smaller number of staff available to perform these tasks means that the headteacher has less scope for delegation. Almost all primary headteachers undertake the budget manager role. As a consequence of this and the national curriculum, it would appear that primary deputy heads are taking on a major responsibility for curriculum management and that it is also being dispersed to more staff, some of whom receive incentive allowances. Another consequence is that school secretaries or finance officers are crucial in providing primary headteachers with administrative support. There is also a marked trend in secondary schools for the enhanced management responsibilities now located in schools to mean a greater dispersal of management roles among more staff, a reduction in the number of deputy head posts in schools and hence the movement to a flatter hierarchy in some schools. Some secondary heads delegate the budget manager role to a deputy, though others do not, relying instead on a bursar or finance officer for major support, backed up by other office staff.

Financial management is a specialized task within schools. It is largely regarded by classroom teachers as one where they have limited interest and expertise. In their view, it is the headteacher's proper function to resource the learning core of the school and protect it from undue disturbance and information overload from the external environment. Most headteachers concur with this and do not seek teacher involvement in budgeting except in resourcing the curriculum and in keeping them informed about the general financial situation of the school.

Although governing bodies are legally responsible for managing school budgets and are assumed in official documents to play a major role in planning the budget according to their school's needs, in practice most governing bodies are heavily reliant on the headteacher and passively approve budget plans prepared by the headteacher or senior management team.

There has been a considerable growth in formalized school planning, strongly promoted both by central government agencies and by some LEAs as a means of developing their strategic and performance monitoring roles. There is some indication that this has been prompted as much by the Office for Standards in Education (OFSTED) inspection framework's emphasis on the efficiency of the school as on local management itself. There was, for example, not much evidence of formalized planning in the case-study schools in 1990–92.

I have given a summary of the descriptive findings of the impact of local management so that readers can reflect on these separately from the assessment of these effects against selected criteria. An evaluation of a policy is necessarily more subject to personal interpretation than an account of what has happened as a consequence of that policy. An explanation of what meanings are to be attached to the evaluative criteria has already been given. What follows is a summary of the evaluative conclusions already discussed, mainly in Chapters 5–8, and for which the evidence has already been presented.

An assessment of the effects of local management

Cost-efficiency

Of the four criteria which I have selected, cost-efficiency is the one for which there is most evidence that local management has been successful in achieving the aims set for it by government. There is a reasonably strong theoretical presumption that local management should promote cost-efficiency, whereas the theoretical arguments as to how school effectiveness, responsiveness and distributional equity are promoted by local management are much weaker. The theory of organizational form (Chapter 8) explains why the presence of bounded rationality and opportunism makes the M-form a more efficient organizational structure. Using the input–output open systems model (Chapter 3) enables one to trace resource allocation decisions through a set of sequences from the receipt of real and financial resources into the school into their transformation into operational services and into resources for direct support of learning. These are the decision stages at which schools can utilize the flexibility of local management to:

- economize by purchasing resources at lower cost for a given quantity or quality than the LEA did;
- improve efficiency by adopting resource mixes that were unavailable or difficult to achieve under bureaucratic administration.

The empirical evidence for this proposition is mainly presented in Chapters 5 and 7. In examining decision processes at the case-study schools, I conclude that the schools were thinking more carefully about their educational aims and objectives and how best to achieve them with available resources than they had prior to delegated budgeting. These processes were not by and large formalized into structured planning and resulting documentation, but were *ad hoc* and informal. Headteachers could on the whole justify their budget decisions in relation to their aims for the school and give examples of measures taken to improve cost-efficiency. Budget managers in schools were more aware of their responsibility for public accountability for resource use now that it had become more transparent and given greater attention through the budgeting process. When the resource allocation choices are examined (Chapter 7), the clearest evidence in favour of local management promoting cost-efficiency is in relation to schools' production of intermediate outputs – operational and administrative services. Compared with the bureaucratic administrative allocation, schools can provide these services to themselves more speedily, at higher quality and more cheaply. This does, of course, take up administrative time in school. Because of economies of scale and scope, the larger the school, the more it can benefit from providing its own operational and administrative services. At some cut-off point for size, it may be the case that the additional administrative cost of local management offsets its benefits. However, there is some degree of flexibility in the quasi-market which enables small schools to exploit economies of scale by having bulk service contracts with the LEA or partnership agreements with other schools to share resources. One aspect of the grant-maintained option is that it enables schools to make different judgements about the value of the LEA's services.

As well as improved efficiency through economizing, improved quality and instituting better value-for-money purchasing procedures, local management has also begun to stimulate changes in the mix in which resources are used. The most notable development is the increased employment of teaching support staff, mainly classroom assistants in primary schools and a wider range of support staff in secondary schools. In this way, schools can increase the ratio of adults to children while reducing the ratio of teachers to children. It is not possible without much more evidence to ascertain whether this development is cost-effective. If greater learning progress can be made from a given expenditure of money by employing a lower ratio of teachers and a higher ratio of support staff, then this is cost-effective. Headteachers making this choice consider that this is the case, but this is on the basis of professional knowledge rather than academic research.

Another area of increased flexibility is that schools can target a range of different resources to support a particular curriculum development. In-service training, curriculum support materials and minor buildings works can all be combined to achieve a particular curriculum objective. This example is moving away from pure cost-efficiency into cost-effectiveness. The latter criterion is assessed by having some measure of the effectiveness of using the resources in one way rather than another which can be compared with the cost of the resources.

Effectiveness

The evidence on the positive impact of local management on teaching and learning is far more tentative than that on cost-efficiency. The theoretical rationale for a positive causal link from local management to improved learning outcomes in schools is not well established. The input–output open systems model is useful in demonstrating the complex linkages between a more competitive external environment and delegated budgets on the one hand, and the consequent changes to learning outputs and outcomes on the other. The most basic linkage is that between a school improving the cost-efficiency of its operational services and thus having more money to spend directly on its technical core of teaching and learning. The most basic linkage assumes no change in the mix of learning activities but only a change in the quantity of resources used to produce the same type of learning activities. Schools which were not budget losers can perceive such gains in the resourcing of learning (Bullock and Thomas 1994). However, even schools which suffer a budget cut could operate more efficiently with a given quantity of resources than under administrative allocation, as was thought by the Graceland headteacher in our study.

The problem for discerning improved effectiveness is detecting any learning improvement as a result of more being spent directly resourcing it. There has been no research on local management designed to obtain objective evidence on the impact of changes in resourcing as a consequence of local management on value-added measures of school output. Therefore, one is left with the perceptions of headteachers and teachers about the impact of learning, such as those gathered by questionnaire in the Bullock and Thomas study, which reported that by 1993 about half of headteachers in both sectors perceived benefits to children's learning. As this proportion fell to 30 per cent for headteachers of small secondary schools, there is a clear indication that the perception of benefits is related to cost-efficiency and hence to the quantity of resources which could be released for supporting learning.

A more important potential source of improved learning is that local management stimulates changes in the core technology itself, rather than just delivering a few more resources to essentially the same learning and teaching process. In economic terms, this would be equivalent to a change in technology. In the education literature, one looks to generalizable knowledge about school effectiveness and school improvement. Instead of seeking evidence of greater productivity by measuring inputs against school outputs, one examines the processes within schools which are associated with effective learning and considers how these are affected, if at all, by local management.

In Chapter 3, I singled out seven factors that are commonly cited in the literature as being associated with school effectiveness:

1 Greater goal clarity concerning the educational purposes of the school.
2 A more integrated school culture where these goals motivate most staff.
3 More effective leadership.
4 More collaborative decision-making.
5 More highly motivated, professionally oriented teams.
6 A greater capacity to respond to the needs of external stakeholders.
7 A greater capacity for organizational learning, in particular in relation to improving educational productivity.

Having in previous chapters presented evidence of the impact of local management on school decision-making processes, roles and relationships, it is useful to review these against the seven factors. The key question is whether local management stimulates such processes and can therefore be said to have a part to play in securing more effective schools. This question in turn begs another, and this is whether processes which research studies have found to be associated with school effectiveness are actually causal factors. They would have to be if one were to infer that local management contributed to school effectiveness because it stimulated processes associated with it. The alternative interpretation of an association between local management and processes associated with effective schools, is that effective schools evince these processes and do so with respect to their resource management as much as they do with respect to other aspects of school management.

The official model of good management practice, discussed in Chapter 4, is at face value consistent with encouraging the seven 'effectiveness' factors. It places particularly strong emphasis on the first factor, goal clarity, and looks for effective leadership and responsiveness to external stakeholders. There is exhortation to evaluate resource use and thus engage in organizational learning about improving productivity. Collaborative decision-making with respect to budgeting and developmental planning is sought, particularly in relation to the headteacher working collaboratively with the governing body. The good management practice advocated by Her Majesty's Inspectorate and now OFSTED gives more emphasis to collaborative decision-making involving classroom teachers. OFSTED inspection reports commend and recommend integration of school decision-making so that heads of department understand whole school issues and respond to them in the management of their departments (Levačić and Glover 1994a,b).

While one can see features of the official good practice management model which correspond to the seven 'effectiveness' factors, this does not necessarily mean that adoption of the official model is a guarantee of improved school effectiveness. There is an inevitable tendency for such official advocacy of good management practice to result in a focus on the visible aspects of management, in particular formalized rational planning and committees which bring together classroom teachers, senior managers and governors. It would be quite possible to introduce these visible aspects of 'good practice' into schools without them actually creating a more integrated collaborative school culture or highly motivated professional teams, or a greater capacity for organizational learning. There is a danger that such lists of approved organizational characteristics are deceptively simple, and fail to reveal the complexities behind them. For example, more collaborative decision-making need not lead to improved school effectiveness *per se*, unless it is focused on understanding how learning outcomes can be improved. It may merely prove a cumbersome organizational ritual. Another problem of interpretation is that the characteristics of school effectiveness distilled from the literature are by and large not derived from schools with extensive resource management autonomy and are not focused on the resource management issues.

Given all the above caveats, it would appear that local management has facilitated and stimulated the adoption and development of the rational approach to resource management and the attendant features of the good practice model. However, evidence from the IFFS case studies, from OFSTED reports and other studies is that schools are at very different stages in the development of these practices, and that full coupling of budgeting with school development or management planning is still relatively rare. There is still a lack of empirically based evidence that sophisticated formalized processes for integrating educational planning and budgeting and for evaluating the cost-effectiveness of resource use are either necessary or sufficient for achieving above-average effectiveness or for instituting school improvement. At the other extreme, it would seem implausible that a school which is improving its effectiveness would not make use of its available budget flexibility to relate resource use to educational priorities.

Another key issue in relation to the contribution of local management to school effectiveness is its impact on the role of the headteacher and the additional burden of management responsibility placed on the school. These developments have made the role of headteacher more complex and demanding, though there has been some commensurate increase in pay. Headteachers report working longer hours, spending more time on management and administration, and being less in contact with the classroom, particularly those in primary schools. Headteachers have responded by sharing management responsibilities with a wider range of colleagues. The positive impact of this, if done effectively, is that it develops professionally oriented teams, collaborative decision-making and a more integrated organizational culture. Conversely, it may lead to more overburdened teachers and a less integrated school culture, as the values and work domain of headteachers are divorced from everyday teaching. The IFFS study provided no evidence of the latter proposition and only weak evidence in favour of the former.

Equity

As already indicated, equity has not been a prime focus of this study. This issue is an extremely complex issue, because of the different conceptions and definitions of equity and the difficulty of obtaining adequate empirical evidence. The examination of resource allocation issues in relation to formula-funding and decision-making within schools has not in this study revealed any bias towards a less equitable distribution of resources for students with special needs. However, the overall workings of the school quasi-market and its impact on the educational provision of students from different social backgrounds has not been investigated in the IFFS study reported here. There is an absence of hard evidence as yet on whether the school quasi-market has been distributionally regressive. On the basis of *a priori* reasoning and some case-study research (e.g. Ball 1993; Bowe *et al.* 1994a,b), the indications are that socially disadvantaged parents are less able to avoid ineffective schools for their children. There is also *ad hoc* evidence that schools in socially deprived areas have suffered a loss of pupils to other schools, while a few have been assessed by inspectors as ineffective.

The justification for the market as an allocative mechanism has always been its dynamic efficiency and not equality of outcomes. Inequality has to be reduced through government intervention, though this is not necessarily successful. The current funding mechanism is structured so that it would be relatively easy, given the political will, to channel more resources towards schools with high concentrations of students with special educational needs. However, such additional resources can only be used effectively if the school managements are competent. The structures needed to revive failing schools are not yet adequate to the task. They depend on the ability of LEAs to develop their quality assurance role and on how well the process for tackling failing schools set in train by the 1992 Education (Schools) Act actually works.

Responsiveness, choice and diversity

As initially noted, these issues have only been touched on in the IFFS study and are not a major focus in this book. The case-study schools were mostly in areas of muted competition. Where some competition was evident, the case-study schools did not appear to be actively seeking to respond to parental preferences. Peacehaven did not welcome excess applicants from neighbouring catchment areas. Graceland, in a socially deprived area and with excess capacity, looked to strengthen links with feeder schools and to relate well to its local community, but did not seek to change in any substantive way. Given this general stance, it is not surprising that resource allocation decisions did not appear to be directed at changing the type of educational provision in response to perceived parental preferences or thus to increasing the diversity of provision. However, the secondary schools did consider their examination performance important. Peacehaven perceived it as a crucial part of their success as a school, and Harrimore in particular improved its examinations results quite significantly. As noted in Chapter 5, the PASCI study, which does focus on school responsiveness, indicates that this, as predicted, relates to the degree and nature of local competition. However, schools are keener to promote themselves and their educational values and to be responsive to other schools in their local network, rather than to find out about and respond directly to consumer preferences.

Recommendations

Given the focus of the book on the cost-efficiency and effectiveness of resource management, the recommendations are focused on these issues. It is apparent that schools need greater budget (and curriculum) stability if they are to devote more time to planning, thus integrating budgeting more closely with educational objectives. Greater stability would also discourage hoarding reserves. Schools facing budget reductions have to devote management time to cutting back on resources. Negotiating staff cuts is particularly time-consuming. Schools experience budget fluctuations from two main sources: the main one is changes in pupil numbers, followed by changes in the LEA's aggregated schools budget (ASB), which is vulnerable to central government cuts to the authority's standard spending assessment (SSA). The latter source of instability could be reduced by reform to the central government funding formula for LEA grant, so that it was less subject to annual manipulation by government in pursuit of short-term local government funding objectives.

Instability due to pupil roll changes is more difficult to tackle, since the proposal to use a three-year rolling average of pupil numbers assists schools with falling rolls but means very tight resourcing for schools experiencing a rapid rise in rolls. A better solution might be to make it easier for schools to borrow temporarily from the LEA, using the excess reserves of other schools. Currently, part of the cost of adjustment is borne by teachers on temporary contracts. School rolls can fluctuate from year to year, with about one-third of schools experiencing a rise and fall in rolls over two to three years (Bullock and Thomas 1994: 35–6). In any one area, some schools will be experiencing rising rolls and others falling rolls. If the LEA is able to fund a pool of teachers who could take up short-term appointments at different schools, this would improve the financial returns from temporary teaching posts and make it easier to attract good teachers to them. The current willingness of teachers to take temporary posts probably reflects the fact that most are women with a partner in work.

Improvements are also required to the internal processes by which schools make their resource allocation decisions. While it is necessary to be sceptical of the potential net benefits from a highly elaborate and formalized process of rational decision-making, since there is an absence of confirming evidence, the traditional approach to budget-setting which many schools are still following has a number of disadvantages. If the headteacher's budgeting consists merely of incremental changes to the subjective budget heads, then there is no application of professional judgement to secure a cost-effective use of resources by taking advantage of increased flexibility in the mix of resources. It is probably the case that many headteachers who appear from the budgets presented to governors to be practising incremental subjective budgeting have got in their own minds a relatively clear educational rationale for the proposed spending patterns, which they may well have shared and developed with senior colleagues. However, this informal and orally communicated understanding of how financial decisions relate to educational purposes is not transmitted to governors. One advantage of a more formal and better documented rational process for budget-setting and subsequent evaluation is that this enables governors to understand the educational rationale that underpins the budget. This makes them better placed to discharge their accountability role.

If budgeting remains decoupled from the technical core of learning and teaching, as it is in the traditional approach, then it does appear to classroom teachers to be an area where they have no expertise or interest. If delegated budgeting is to have a positive impact on learning, other than via the ability of the senior managers to achieve cost-efficiency and direct more resources into the classroom, then it must involve teachers in becoming more aware of alternative resource mixes or alternative educational activities that they could try out and for which they can obtain the required financial backing. This kind of enhanced professional awareness of alternatives, combined with the willingness to experiment with them and evaluate the consequences so as to inform future decisions, can only develop readily in a supportive organizational culture. Teachers come to know about the most effective ways of using resources through either their own experience or that of immediate colleagues. Currently, there is little in the way of an academic research-based knowledge that they can draw upon. I suspect that it is not so much effective resource allocation processes that will improve the quality of teaching and learning, but that the processes associated with effective schooling will also produce effective resource allocation.

Future research issues in resource management

Two major areas for further research stand out: the funding formula and the relationship between resource use and educational effectiveness. The two are interrelated, in that allocating budgets to schools on the basis of their resource needs presupposes a judgement about the nature of the educational production function (i.e. the relationship between inputs and learning outputs and outcomes). There is currently considerable disparity between the funding level per pupil in different LEAs, but there is very little UK research evidence on the relationship between the amount spent per pupil and the consequent impact on learning outputs once differences in pupils' prior attainment and social background are taken into account. There is a strong belief among professionals and parents that more resources mean better outcomes, as evinced in the desire for smaller classes and better facilities. Because the relationship between the amount of expenditure and consequent learning outputs is mediated by many process factors that influence the quality of teaching and learning, it is difficult to establish from the statistical analysis of measures of inputs, process and learning outputs what these relationships are. It may well be the case that small and subtle variations in local conditions make for quite substantial differences in the input–output relationship. We need to improve our understanding of how educational professionals develop knowledge about the relationships between inputs, processes and outputs, as well as to undertake more statistical research into these relationships across samples of schools. It may in fact be impossible to detect any differences in educational effectiveness across a sample of schools due to small differences in, say, class size or of relatively modest changes in the ratio of support staff to teaching staff. If this is the case, then it is more important to develop teachers' own understanding of these interrelationships so that they can make better judgements of the cost-effectiveness of alternative uses of resources and be stimulated to generate such alternatives.

At the more aggregate level of resourcing schools, the absence of a well-specified education function implies that going down the road of devising very detailed needs-based formulae, built up from many sub-formulae relating to a wide range of assumed educational activities (e.g. the number of teacher hours spent on assessment and parent consultations, or the class size for PE in year 7), will absorb more time and energy than the returns from the exercise warrant. Relatively simple and robust needs-based formulae are appropriate (such as that developed by Sheffield City Council in 1992) for the linkage between the major resource needs of schools and the total sum available in the LEA or national schools budget to be better understood, when both the size and distribution of expenditure on schools is being determined. It is politically easier for governments to have this linkage obscured, creating in the words of the School Teachers' Review Body (1993, para. 19), 'the "fog" which surrounds the flow of funding to schools'. Further work is therefore needed on developing and implementing clear and nationally consistent principles for funding schools according to broad criteria of resourcing need. This would include ensuring that the impact of the quasi-market in disadvantaging schools in areas of social deprivation is offset by additional funding and that such schools can make cost-effective use of such funds.

The coming of local management has provided far more opportunities for both practitioners and researchers to expand their knowledge and understanding of the relationships between the quantity and patterns of expenditure and resource allocation in schools, the interrelated processes of decision-making and classroom practice, and the consequent gains to learning. The wealth of everyday practitioner knowledge of these links and the potential for finding out more have greatly increased in the last five years. We have come a long way in managing and learning about these relationships since the days when Hough (1981), after much painstaking work on LEA internal records, managed to obtain enough data to analyse the relationship between school level unit costs and school size and wrote what was then regarded as a path-breaking book on school costs.

Notes

Chapter 1

1 The Department of Education was, prior to 1992, known as the Department for Education and Science. I generally refer to it as the DFE, but early publications are cited under DES. The DFE is responsible for education in England. The Welsh Office implements a version of the same legislation in Wales. The Department of Education for Northern Ireland administers essentially the same legislation as that in England, but usually under different statutory instruments, so there are some differences. Scotland has separate legislation, which is administered by the Scottish Office Education Department (SOED).

2 The standard number for a LEA-maintained school was specified in the 1988 Education Act as the number of pupils a school admitted to its intake year in 1979–80. For GM schools, a similar planned admissions number is agreed on incorporation.

3 Free transport is only mandatory if a child attends his or her catchment area school and travels at least three miles to get there.

4 The last two are added as of 1995–96. Discretionary exceptions are school meals and transport, pupils' welfare support, governors' insurance, LEA initiatives and contingencies (DFE 1994).

5 Arrangements still in place in 1990.

6 Standard spending assessments (SSAs) are determined by a central government formula designed to reflect differential need in LEAs, but which uses inadequate indicators and which is subject to political manipulation.

7 This can be done in order to gain information not otherwise obtainable, which is required by the LEA to carry out its functions.

8 These are school councils.

Chapter 2

1 The definition of 'efficiency' is further elaborated in Chapter 3 and its appendix.
2 Public sector accountancy rather than economics makes this distinction between efficiency and effectiveness. In economic theory, allocative efficiency occurs when the allocation of resources which can be defined as socially optimal is achieved. Allocative efficiency is therefore dependent on an assumption of what is socially valued. This in turn depends on a set of assumptions about perfect competition and perfect information which enables prices to reflect correctly consumers' preferences. It also depends on making an assumption about what is a socially desirable distribution of goods. Le Grand and Bartlett (1993), for example, propose four criteria for evaluating quasi-markets: productive efficiency, responsiveness, choice and equity. Productive efficiency is equated to value for money. Thus their definition of productive efficiency is dependent upon the social value of output. This means that productive efficiency could appear to increase if costs fell and output apparently remained the same, but it could in fact have fallen if the social value of the output in question had fallen.
3 Le Grand and Bartlett (1993) use similar criteria for evaluating quasi-markets in a number of social services. However they do not distinguish between efficiency and effectiveness, and instead use the equivalent of value for money as a single criterion, which they call 'productive efficiency'. They treat choice and responsiveness as separate criteria.
4 Whether these procedures have been speeded up by the 1993 Education Act, which gave the Funding Agency for Schools (FAS) and the Secretary of State additional powers with respect to school restructuring, remains to be seen.
5 Unit costs are costs per pupil.
6 Many critiques come from within organizational theory rather than critical sociology.
7 While the rule is normally stated as 80 per cent, up to 5 per cent can be for pupils' special educational needs.
8 Local education authorities (LEAs) can, if they wish, retain this centrally as a discretionary item.
9 If such compensation of losers – to return them to their previous level of utility – were not possible, then the change in resource use would by definition not improve efficiency. A Pareto efficient allocation of resources is defined as one where it is impossible to make one person better off without making someone else worse off. So if it is possible to make at least one person better off without reducing the utility of anyone else, then a change in resource allocation which is efficiency-promoting is possible.

Chapter 3

1 Many such studies sprouted in education economics in the late 1960s but were on the wane by the late 1970s (Levin 1974).
2 In the UK system, state schools cannot compete in terms of price, except indirectly through insisting on expensive school uniforms. A genuine comprehensive school does not attempt to skew its intake towards a large population of high ability students by interviewing applicants. However, some non-selective voluntary schools and GM schools do use interviews for this purpose, as do CTCs.

3 This is, of course, deduced from a rational model rather than from empirical verification.

Chapter 4

1 Applies to England and Wales.
2 Greenfield's epistemological objections to organizational rationality are similar in their basic conclusions to Arrow's (1963) demonstration of the impossibility of deriving an aggregate community utility' function from the aggregation of individual preferences which has a consistent set of desirable properties.
3 OFSTED's 1993a handbook was amended by issuing replacement pages in May 1994. Hence references are to both versions.
4 Examples used by Hargreaves and Hopkins.
5 One school I have studied has exactly these characteristics.
6 Opportunity costs in this example are the benefits which would have ensued from the next best alternative way of using staff time.
7 This applies to most organizations. In not-for-profit organizations, the absence of economic calculus covers a wide range of decisions.
8 The 1986 Education Act reconstituted governing bodies to give them new powers, which subsequent legislation has further enhanced. The governing bodies of grant-maintained schools are independent trusts. Governors can be sued through the courts and, in certain specified circumstances, such as financial mismanagement or being deemed by OFSTED to be a school at risk, can have delegated powers removed in the case of LEA schools or have new governors appointed in the case of GM schools.
9 The headteacher can elect whether to be a governor or not.
10 'Classroom teachers' refers to all teaching staff other than the senior management team, and includes heads of department.

Chapter 5

1 Full delegation means that all the major budget heads had been delegated to schools as specified in Circular 7/88. Some LEAs opted for partial delegation and only delegated some items to schools in the first transitional years. Many LEAs, like Barset, staggered the entry of schools into full delegation. Schools without delegated budgets – usually primary schools – had their budget determined by formula but managed by the LEA. By 1993–94, all schools (except those in inner London) were required to have full delegation.
2 The SSA is the amount central government determines that local authorities need to spend given measured indicators of need. A SSA is calculated for each service, including education, and is further split into SSAs for each sector.
3 The LEA made provision for schools to claim additional funding in the event of a particularly rapid rise in rolls.

Chapter 6

1 In particular the North American and British literature, though not so consistently in the Dutch literature.
2 Years 7 to 9, that is twelve- to fourteen-year-olds.
3 These findings are reported in greater detail in Marren and Levačić (1994).

Chapter 7

1 'In real terms' means that the increase in costs due to salary increases and other price rises is deducted using a price deflator. Each LEA uses its own price deflator when calculating its education budgets, and a single index is not published by the Public Institute of Finance.

2 In Britain, local authorities receive a block grant from central government to cover all services, and are free to spend more or less on any one service than the SSA for that service, which is the amount central government deems the local authority needs to spend. The block grant is related to the SSA. Authorities have been penalized when spending more than their SSA.

3 The annual deflator is 0.75 times the increase in teachers' salaries (to reflect their relevant importance in education budgets), plus 0.25 times the GDP deflator from *Economic Trends*.

4 The cost deflators used here are those used by Barsetshire.

5 The statistical analysis supporting this conclusion is reported in Levačić (1993a).

6 The potential schools budget is the general schools budget minus capital expenditure, central government and EC grants, premature retirement and dismissal costs, educational psychology and welfare services (all these items cannot be delegated) and minus any discretionary items not delegated, including school meals, school transport, pupil support, governors' insurance, LEA initiatives, LEA contingencies.

7 Classroom teachers on the whole had very little knowledge of the formula.

8 In 1990–91, for example, Graceland – with a special needs index of 25 – received £185 per pupil, compared with the £133 per pupil received by Waterton, with an index of 14.7. Graceland's headmaster perceived his pupils as being considerably more socially disadvantaged than the pupils at Waterton.

9 As Reynolds (1992) points out, knowing what factors are associated with effective schools is not the same as knowing what needs to be done to improve a school.

Chapter 8

1 The national curriculum, assessment and publication of individual school performance indicators are thus agency costs.

2 'Opportunism' is the term used for the guileful pursuit of self-interest by Williamson (1975), whose work in developing the economic analysis of institutions has been seminal.

3 Evidence on the Edmonton system was obtained during a study tour in 1990 and is reported in greater detail in Levačić (1992b).

4 Figures are for 1992–93 (Busher and Hodgkinson 1994).

References

Alter, C. and Hage, J. (1993) *Organisations Working Together*. London: Sage.

Anthony, A.R. and Herzlinger, R.E. (1989) 'Management control in non-profit organisations'. In Levačić, R. (ed.), *Financial Management in Education*. Milton Keynes: Open University Press.

Arnott, M. and Munn, P. (1994) 'Devolved management in Scotland and England: Policy contradictions?' Paper presented at the *British Educational Research Association Annual Conference*, Oxford, September.

Arrow, K.J. (1963) *Social Choice and Individual Value*, 2nd edn. New York: John Wiley.

Audit Commission (1984) *Code of Local Government Audit Practice for England and Wales*. London: HMSO.

Audit Commission (1989a) *Losing an Empire: Finding a Role. The LEA of the Future*. London: HMSO.

Audit Commission (1989b) *Assessing Quality in Education*. London: HMSO.

Audit Commission (1991) *Rationalising Primary School Provision*. London: HMSO.

Audit Commission (1993) *Adding Up the Sums: Schools' Management of their Finances and Comparative Information for Schools*. London: HMSO.

Audit Commission/OFSTED (1993) *Keeping Your Balance: Standards for Financial Administration in Schools*. London: OFSTED.

Australian Schools Commission (1973) *Schools in Australia* (The Karmel Report). Canberra: Australian Government Publishing Service.

Bagley, C., Woods, P. and Glatter, R. (1994) 'Empowerment, effectiveness and marketing: The engagement of stakeholders in education'. Paper presented at the *British Educational Research Association Annual Conference*, Oxford, September.

Baldridge, J.V. (1971) *Power and Conflict in the University*. New York: John Wiley.

Ball, S. (1987) *The Micropolitics of the School*. London: Methuen.

Ball, S. (1993) 'Education markets, choice and social class: The market as a class strategy in the UK and USA'. *British Journal of Sociology of Education*, **14**(1): 3–20.

Barnard, C. (1938) *The Functions of the Executive*. Cambridge, MA: Harvard University Press.

Beare, H., Caldwell, B. and Millakin, R. (1989) *Creating an Excellent School*. London: Cassell.

Blackmore, J. (1990) 'School-based decision making and teacher unions: The appropriation of discourse'. In Chapman, J. (ed.), *School-based Decision-making and Management*. Lewes: Falmer Press.

Bottery, M. (1992) *The Ethics of Educational Management*. London: Cassell.

Bowe, R. and Ball, S. (1992) ' "Doing what comes naturally": An exploration of LMS in a secondary school'. In Wallace, G. (ed.), *Local Management of Schools: Research and Experience*. Clevedon: Multilingual Matters.

Bowe, R., Ball, S. and Gerwitz, S. (1994a) 'Parental choice, consumption and social theory: The operation of micro markets in education'. *British Journal of Educational Studies*, **XXXXII**(1): 38–52.

Bowe, R., Gerwitz, S. and Ball, S. (1994b) 'Captured by discourse? Issues and concerns in researching parental choice'. *British Journal of Sociology of Education*, **15**(1): 63–78.

Broadbent, J., Laughlin, R., Shearn, D. and Dandy, N. (1992) ' "It's a long way from teaching Susan to read": Some preliminary observations of a project studying the introduction of local management of schools'. In Wallace, G. (ed.), *Local Management of Schools: Research and Experience*. Clevedon: Multilingual Matters.

Brown, D.J. (1990) *Decentralisation and School-based Managment*. Lewes: Falmer Press.

Buchanan, J. (1986) *Liberty, Market and the State*. Brighton: Harvester.

Bullock, A. and Thomas, H. (1992) 'School size and local management funding formulae'. *Educational Management and Administration*, **20**(1): 30–39.

Bullock, A. and Thomas, H. (1994) *The Impact of Local Management on Schools: Final Report*. Birmingham: University of Birmingham/National Association of Head Teachers.

Burgess, R.G., Hockley, J., Phtiaka, H., Pole, C.J. and Sanday, A. (1992) *Thematic Report and Case Studies*. Sheffield: Sheffield City Council.

Bush, T., Coleman, M. and Glover, D. (1993) *Managing Autonomous Schools: The Grant Maintained Experience*. London: Paul Chapman.

Busher, H. and Hodgkinson, K. (1994) 'Co-operation and tension in the management of interschool networks'. Paper presented at the *British Educational Research Association Annual Conference*, Oxford, September.

Butler, R.J. (1991) *Designing Organisations: A Decision-Making Perspective*. London: Routledge.

Caldwell, B.J. (1990) 'Educational reform through school-site management: An international perspective on restructuring in education'. *Advances in Research and Theories of School Management and Educational Policy*, **1**: 303–333.

Caldwell, B.J. (1993) 'Paradox and uncertainty in the governance of education'. In Beare, H. and Lowe Boyd, W. (eds), *Restructuring Schools*. Lewes: Falmer Press.

Caldwell, B.J. and Spinks, J.M. (1988) *The Self-managing School*. Lewes: Falmer Press.

Campbell, J., Little, V. and Tomlinson, J. (1987) 'Multiplying the divisions? Intimations of educational policy post-1987'. *Journal of Education Policy*, **2**(4): 369–78.

Carnegie Task Force on Teaching as a Profession (1986) *A Nation Prepared: Teachers for the 21st Century*. New York: Carnegie Forum.

Chandler, A.D. (1966) *Strategy and Structure: Change in the History of Industrial Enterprise*. New York: Doubleday.

Chapman, J. (1990) 'School based decision-making and management: Implications for school personnel'. In Chapman, J. (ed.), *School-based Decision-making and Management*. Lewes: Falmer Press.

Chartered Institute of Public Finance and Accountancy (1990–91, 1991–92, 1992–93) *Education Estimates*. London: HMSO.

Cheng, Y.C. (1993) 'The theory and characteristics of school-based management'. *International Journal of Education Management*, **7**(6): 6–17.

Chrispeels, J.H. (1993) *Purposeful Restructuring: Creating a Culture for Learning and Achievement in Elementary Schools*. London: Falmer Press.

Chubb, J.E. and Moe, T.M. (1990) *Politics, Markets and America's Schools*. Washington, DC: Brookings Institute.

Cohen, M.D. and March, J.G. (1974) *Leadership and Ambiguity: The American College President*. Boston, MA: Harvard University Press.

Coopers and Lybrand (1988) *Local Management of Schools: A Report to the DES*. London: HMSO.

Cordingly, P. and Kogan, M. (1992) *Supporting Education: Matching National and Local Systems to Needs*. London: Jessica Kingsley.

Coulby, D. (1991) 'Introduction: The 1988 Education Act and themes of government policy'. In Coulby, D. and Bash, L. (eds), *Contradiction and Conflict: The 1988 Education Act in Action*. London: Cassell.

Crawford, M. (1994) 'The primary school secretary, a key part of the learning institution'. Paper presented at the *British Educational Management and Administration Society Annual Conference*, Manchester, September.

David, J. (1989) 'Synthesis of research on school-based management'. *Educational Leadership*, **46**(8): 45–53.

Deem, R. (1993) 'Governing schools in the 1990s: Autonomy or collaboration?' In Ranson, S. and Tomlinson, J. (eds), *School Co-operation: New Forms of Local Governance*. Harlow: Longman.

Deem, R. and Brehony, K. (1993) 'Consumers and education professionals in the organisation and administration of schools: Partnership or conflict?' *Educational Studies*, **19**(3): 339–55.

Department for Education (1988) *Education Reform Act*. London: HMSO.

Department for Education (1992) *Choice and Diversity*. London: HMSO.

Department for Education (1993) *School Governors: A Guide to the Law*. London: DFE.

Department for Education (1994) *Local Management of Schools*. Circular 2/94. London: DFE.

Department of Education and Science (1988) *Education Reform Act: Local Management of Schools*. London: DES.

Department of Education and Science (1991a) *Local Management of Schools: Further Guidance*. Circular 9/91. London: DES.

Department of Education and Science (1991b) *Development Planning: A Practical Guide*. London: DES.

Duckenfield, M. (1990) 'Kentucky ahead of the field on LMS'. *Guardian*, 3 July.

Dunlap, D. and Goldman, P. (1991) 'Rethinking power in school'. *Educational Administration Quarterly*, **27**(1): 69–92.

Earley, P. (1994) *School Governing Bodies: Making Progress?* Slough: NFER.

Evetts, J. (1993) 'Local management and headship: Changing the contexts for micropolitics'. *Educational Review*, **45**(1): 53–66.

Fitzgibbon, C. (1992) ' "A" levels: Corrective comparisons'. *Managing Schools Today*, **1**(2): 44–5.

Fowler, F.C. (1990) 'American theory and French practice: a theoretical rationale for regulating school choice'. *Educational Administration Quarterly*, **28**(4): 452–72.

Garms, W.I., Guthrie, J.W. and Pierce, L.C. (1978) *School Finance: The Economics and Politics of Public Education*. Englewood Cliffs, NJ: Prentice-Hall.

Glatter, R. (1994) 'Managing dilemmas in education: The tightrope walk of strategic choice in more autonomous insititutions'. Paper presented at the *8th International Intervisitation Program in Educational Administration: Persistent Dilemmas in Administrative Preparation and Practice*, Toronto, Canada and Buffalo, USA, May.

Glatter, R. and Woods, P. (1994) 'The impact of competition and choice on parents and school'. In Bartlett, W., Propper, C., Wilson, D. and Le Grand, J. (eds), *Quasi-markets in the Welfare State*. Bristol: SAUS.

Glatter, R., Johnson, D. and Woods, P. (1993) 'Marketing, choice and responses in education'. In Smith, M. and Busher, H. (eds), *Managing Schools in an Uncertain Environment: Resources, Marketing and Power*. Sheffield: Sheffield Hallam University/British Educational Management and Administration Society.

Glynn, J. (1987) *Public Sector Financial Control and Accounting*. Oxford: Blackwell.

Goldstein, H. (1987) *Multi-level Models in Educational and Social Research*. Oxford: Oxford University Press.

Golensky, M. (1993) 'The board–executive relationship in non-profit organisations: Partnership or power struggle?' *Non-profit Management and Leadership*, **4**(2): 177–91.

Good, T.L. (1989) 'Using classroom and school research to professionalise teaching'. In Creemers, B., Peters, T. and Reynolds, D. (eds), *School Effectiveness and School Improvement*. Amsterdam: Swets and Zeitlinger.

Greenfield, T.B. (1989) 'Organisations as social inventions: Rethinking assumptions about change'. In Bush, T. (ed.), *Managing Education: Theory and Practice*. Milton Keynes: Open University Press.

Greenfield, T. and Ribbins, P. (1993) *Greenfield on Educational Administration*. London: Routledge.

Halasz, G. (1993) 'The policy of school autonomy and the reform of educational administration: Hungarian changes in an East European perspective'. *International Review of Education*, **39**(6): 89–97.

Halsey, G. (1993) 'The impact of local management on school management style'. *Local Government Policy Making*, **19**(5): 49–56.

Hanushek, E. (1986) 'The economics of schooling: Production and efficiency in public schools'. *Journal of Economic Literature*, **24**: 1141–77.

Hardman, J. and Levačić, R. (1994a) 'A comparison of local education authorities per pupil funding of primary and secondary sectors'. In House of Commons Committee on Education, *Report of the Inquiry into the Disparity in Funding between Primary and Secondary Schools*, Vol. II, App. 20, pp. 197–208. London: HMSO.

Hardman, J. and Levačić, R. (1994b) 'The impact of competition on secondary schools: Factors associated with differential market success'. Paper presented at the *British Educational Research Association Annual Conference*, Oxford, September.

Hargreaves, D.H. and Hopkins, D. (1991) *The Empowered School: The Management and Practice of Development Planning*. London: Cassell.

Hargreaves, D.H., Hopkins, D., Leask, M., Connolly, M. and Robinson, P. (1989) *Planning for School Development*. London: DES.

Hartley, H. (1989) 'Zero-based budgeting for schools'. In Levačić, R. (ed.), *Financial Management in Education*. Milton Keynes: Open University Press.

Haviland, J. (1988) *Take Care Mr Baker!* London: Fourth Estate.

Hedger, K. (1992) 'The analysis of GCSE examination results in Shropshire'. *Management in Education*, 6(1): 29–33.

Henderson, I. (1993) 'School effectiveness studies using administrative data'. *Educational Research*, 35(1): 27–47.

Her Majesty's Inspectorate (1992a) *The Implementation of Local Management of Schools*. London: HMSO.

Her Majesty's Inspectorate (1992b) *Local Management of Schools and Pupils with Special Educational Needs*. London: HMSO.

Hill, D., Oakley Smith, B. and Spinks, J. (1990) *Local Management of Schools*. London: Paul Chapman.

Hill, N. (1994) *Value Added Analysis: Current Practice in Local Education Authorities*. Slough: National Foundation for Educational Research.

Hirschman, A.O. (1970) *Exit, Voice and Loyalty: Responses to Decline in Firms, Organisations and States*. Cambridge, MA: Harvard University Press.

Hodges, L. (1990) 'A clean slate'. *Education*, 3 August.

Hough, J.R. (1981) *A Study of School Costs*. Windsor: NFER-Nelson.

House of Commons Committee on Education (1994) *Report of the Inquiry into the Disparity in Funding between Primary and Secondary Schools*. London: HMSO.

Hoy, W.K. and Miskel, C.G. (1989) 'Schools and their external environments'. In Glatter, R. (ed.), *Educational Institutions and Their Environments: Managing the Boundaries*. Milton Keynes: Open University Press.

Hoy, W.K. and Tarter, C.J. (1993) 'A normative theory of participative decision-making in schools'. *Journal of Educational Administration*, 31(3): 4–19.

Hoyle, E. (1986) *The Politics of School Management*. Sevenoaks: Hodder and Stoughton.

Interim Advisory Committee on School Teachers' Pay and Conditions (1989) *Second Report* (The Chilver Report). London: HMSO.

Interim Advisory Committee on School Teachers' Pay and Conditions (1990) *Third Report*. London: HMSO.

Interim Advisory Committee on School Teachers' Pay and Conditions (1991) *Fourth Report*. London: HMSO.

Jesson, D. and Levačić, R. (1992) 'Survey of current resourcing practice'. In *Resourcing Sheffield Schools*. Sheffield: Sheffield City Council Education Department.

Jesson, D., Gray, J. and Tranmer, M. (1992) *GCSE Performance in Nottinghamshire 1991: Pupil and School Factors*. Nottingham: Nottingham City Council.

Keast, D. (1992a) 'A cluster of weakness'. *Times Educational Supplement*, 14 August.

Keast, D. (1992b) *Small Schools after ERA: 1991 Survey*. Exeter: Exeter Small Schools Network, University of Exeter.

Kelly, A. (1993) 'Like with like'. *Managing Schools Today*, 2(5): 19–21.

Kennedy, J. (1991) 'Interfacing finance'. *Managing Schools Today*, 1(3). Reproduced in Preedy, M. (ed.), *Managing the Effective School*. London: Paul Chapman.

Knight, B. (1989a) *Managing School Time*. Harlow: Longman.

Knight, B. (1989b) *Local Management of Schools*. London: Longman/Peat Marwick McClintock.

Knight, B. (1993) *Financial Management for Schools*. London: Heinemann.

Kogan, M. (1986) *Education Accountability*. London: Hutchinson.

Kogan, M., Johnson, D., Packwood, T. and Whitaker, T. (1984) *School Governing Bodies*. London: Heinemann.

Koppich, J.E. and Guthrie, J.W. (1993) 'Examining contemporary reform efforts in the USA'. In Beare, H. and Lowe Boyd, W. (eds), *Restructuring Schools*. Lewes: Falmer Press.

Laughlin, R., Broadbent, J., Shearn, D. and Willig-Atherton, H. (1992) 'Absorbing LMS, the coping mechanism of a small group'. Paper presented at the *British Educational Research Association Conference, Stirling University*, August.

Lawton, S.B. (1993) 'A decade of educational reform in Canada'. In Beare, H. and Lowe Boyd, W. (eds), *Restructuring Schools*. Lewes: Falmer Press.

Lee, T. (1992) 'Finding simple answers to complex questions: Funding special needs under LMS'. In Wallace, G. (ed.), *Local Management of Schools: Research and Experience*. Clevedon: Multilingual Matters.

Le Grand, J. and Bartlett, W. (1993) *Quasi-markets and Social Policy*. London: Macmillan.

Leibenstein, H. (1966) 'Allocative efficiency versus X-efficiency'. *American Economic Review*, **56**: 392–415.

Levačić, R. (1989) 'Financial management in education: An emerging function'. In Levačić, R. (ed.), *Financial Management in Education*. Milton Keynes: Open University Press.

Levačić, R. (1990a) 'Public choice: The economics of politics'. In Shackleton, L. (ed.), *New Thinking in Economics*. Aldershot: Edward Elgar.

Levačić, R. (1990b) 'Evaluating local management of schools: Methodology and practice'. *Financial Accountability and Management*, **6**(3): 209–227.

Levačić, R. (1992a) 'Local management of schools: Aims, scope and impact'. *Educational Management and Administration*, **20**(1): 16–29.

Levačić, R. (1992b) 'The LEA and its schools: The decentralised organisation and the internal market'. In Wallace, G. (ed.), *Local Management of Schools: Research and Experience*. Clevedon: Multilingual Matters.

Levačić, R. (1992c) 'An analysis of differences between historic and formula school budgets: Evidence from LEA submissions and from detailed study of two LEAs'. *Oxford Review of Education*, **18**(1): 75–100.

Levačić, R. (1993a) 'Assessing the impact of formula funding on schools'. *Oxford Review of Education*, **19**(4): 435–57.

Levačić, R. (1993b) 'Local management of schools as an organisational form: Theory and application'. *Journal of Education Policy*, **8**(2): 123–41.

Levačić, R. (1994) 'Improving student achievement by using value added of examination performance indicators'. In Crawford, M., Kydd, L. and Parker, S. (eds), *Educational Management in Action: A Collection of Case Studies*. London: Paul Chapman.

Levačić, R. and Glover, D. (1994a) 'The efficiency of the school: An examination of the application of the OFSTED inspection framework'. Paper presented at the *British Educational Management and Administration Society Annual Conference*, Manchester, September.

Levačić, R. and Glover, D. (1994b) *OFSTED Assessment of Schools' Efficiency: An Analysis of 66 Secondary School Inspection Reports*. Milton Keynes: Open University Press.

Levačić, R. and Woods, P. (1994) 'New forms of financial co-operation'. In Ranson, S. and Tomlinson. J. (eds), *School Co-operation: New Forms of Local Governance*. Harlow: Longman.

Levell, P. (1989) 'Anatomy of an LMS scheme'. *Education*, 10 November.

Levin, H. (1974) 'Measuring efficiency in educational production'. *Public Finance Quarterly*, **2**(1): 3–24.

Lindblom, C.E. (1959) 'The science of "muddling through"'. *Public Administration Review*, **19**: 79–99.

Lindblom, C.E. (1979) 'Still muddling, not yet through'. *Public Administration Review*, **39**: 517–26.

The LMS Initiative (1988) *Local Management of Schools: A Practical Guide*. London: LMS Initiative.

The LMS Initiative (1992) *Local Management in Schools: A Study into Formula Funding and Management Issues*. London: LMS Initiative.

Louis, K.S. and van Velzen, B.A.M. (1990/91) 'A look at choice in the Netherlands'. *Educational Leadership*, **48**(4): 66–72.

Lowe Boyd, W. (1992) 'The power of paradigms: Reconceptualising educational policy and management'. *Education Administration Quarterly*, **28**(4): 504–528.

MacPherson, A. (1992) *Measuring Added Value in Schools*. London: National Commission on Education.

MacPherson, R.J.S. (1993) 'The reconstruction of New Zealand education: A case of "high politics" reform?' In Beare, H. and Lowe Boyd, W. (eds), *Restructuring Schools*. Lewes: Falmer Press.

Malen, B., Ogawa, R.T. and Kranz, J. (1990) 'What do we know about school-based management? A case-study of the literature – a call for research'. In W. Clune and J. Witte (eds), *Choice and Control in American Education*, vol. 2. London: Falmer Press.

Margolis, S. (1991) 'Productivity and efficiency in education'. *Journal of Education*, **35**(2): 201–214.

Marr, A. (1992) 'Golden hellos and great expectations'. *Times Educational Supplement*, 10 January.

Marren, E. and Levačić, R. (1994) 'Senior management, classroom teacher and governor responses to local management of schools'. *Educational Management and Administration*, **22**(1): 39–53.

Matthews, R.C.O. (1991) 'The economics of professional ethics: Should the professions be more like business?' *The Economic Journal*, **101**: 737–50.

Maw, J. (1994) 'The deputy head's role under local management of schools'. Paper presented at the *British Educational Research Association Annual Conference*, Oxford, September.

Maychell, K. (1994) *Counting the Cost: The Impact of LMS on Schools' Patterns of Spending*. Slough: NFER.

McLean, I. (1987) *Public Choice: An Introduction*. Oxford: Blackwell.

Merrick, N. (1994) 'Evaluating voluntary extended review appraisal'. *Times Educational Supplement*, 29 January.

Ministry of Education of Western Australia (1987) *Better Schools in Western Australia: A Programme for Improvement*. Perth: Ministry of Education.

Minzberg, H. (1994) *The Rise and Fall of Strategic Planning*. London: Prentice-Hall.

Morgan, G. (1986) *Images of Organisation*. London: Sage.

Morris, R. (1994) *The Functions and Roles of Local Education Authorities*. Slough:

Education Management Information Unit, National Foundation for Educational Research.

Mortimore, P., Sammons, P., Stoll, L., Lewis, D. and Ecob, R. (1988) *School Matters: The Junior Years*. Wells: Open Books.

Mortimore, P., Mortimore, J., with Thomas, H., Cairns, R. and Taggart, B. (1992) *The Innovative Uses of Non-teaching Staff in Primary and Secondary Schools Project*. Final Report to the DFE. London: Institute of Education.

Mueller, D.C. (1989) *Public Choice II*. Cambridge: Cambridge University Press.

National Association of Head Teachers (1991) 'The management of finance 2: Basic budget management'. In *NAHT Guide to School Management*. Harlow: Longman.

National Audit Office (1994) *Value for Money in Grant Maintained Schools*. HMSO: London.

National Governors' Association (1986) *Time for Results: The Governors' 1991 Report on Education*. Washington, DC: NGA.

Nias, J., Southworth, G. and Campbell, P. (1992) *Whole School Curriculum Development in the Primary School*. London: Falmer Press.

O'Connor, M. (1993) 'The Balcarras experiment'. *Times Educational Supplement*, 14 May.

Office for Standards in Education (1993a) *Handbook for the Inspection of Schools*. London: HMSO.

Office for Standards in Education (1993b) *Standards and Quality in Education*. London: HMSO.

Office for Standards in Education (1994) *Handbook for the Inspection of Schools*. London: HMSO.

Office for Standards in Education/Audit Commission (1993) *Keeping Your Balance: Standards for Financial Administration in Schools*. London: OFSTED.

Organization for Economic and Cultural Development (1987) *Quality of Schooling: A Clarifying Report*. Paris: OECD.

Organization for Economic and Cultural Development (1992) *Education at a Glance: OECD Indicators*. Paris: OECD.

Owen, D. and Farrar, M. (1994) 'The resource implications of adopting flexible learning at Haggerston School'. In Crawford, M., Kydd, L. and Parker, S. (eds), *Educational Management in Action: A Selection of Case Studies*. London: Paul Chapman.

Picot, B. (1988) *Administering for Excellence: Effective Administration in Education*. Wellington: NZ Government Printer.

Pratt, J.W. and Zeckhauser, R.J. (1985) 'Principals and agents: An overview'. In Pratt, J.W. and Zeckhauser, R.J. (eds), *Principals and Agents: The Structure of Business*. Boston, MA: Harvard Business School Press.

Provenzo, E. (1989) 'School-based management and shared-decision making in Dade County public schools'. In Rosow, J.M. and Zager, R. (eds), *Allies in Educational Reform*. San Francisco, CA: Jossey-Bass.

Purkey, S.C. and Smith, M.S. (1983) 'Effective schools: A review'. *Elementary School Journal*, **83**(4): 427–52.

Rafferty, F. (1994) 'Many more heads leave jobs'. *Times Educational Supplement*, 2 September.

Ranson, S. (1992) *The Role of Local Government in Education*. Harlow: Longman.

Ranson, S. (1994) *The New System of Government for Education*. Swindon: ESRC.

Ranson, S. and Travers, T. (1994) 'Education'. In Jackson, P. and Lavender, M. (eds), *The Public Services Yearbook 1994*. London: CIPFA Public Finance Foundation/Chapman and Hall.

Reynolds, D. (1992) 'School effectiveness and school improvement: An updated review of the British literature'. In Reynolds, D. and Cuttance, P. (eds), *School Effectiveness: Research, Policy and Practice*. London: Cassell.

Riley, K. (1994) *Managing for Quality in an Uncertain Climate*. London: Local Government Management Board/Roehampton Institute.

Rutherford, J. (1985) 'School principals as effective leaders'. *Phi Delta Kappa*, **69**(1): 31–4.

Rutter, M., Maughan, B., Mortimore, P. and Ouston, J. (1979) *Fifteen Thousand Hours: Secondary Schools and their Effects on Children*. Shepton Mallet: Open Books.

Sallis, J. (1991) *School Governors: Your Questions Answered*. London: Hodder and Stoughton.

Scheerens, J. (1992) *Effective Schooling: Research, Theory and Practice*. London: Cassell.

School Teachers' Review Body (1992) *First Report*. Cm 1806. London: HMSO.

School Teachers' Review Body (1993) *Second Report*. London: HMSO

School Teachers' Review Body (1994) *Third Report*. London: HMSO.

Scott, P. (1989) 'Accountability, responsiveness and responsibility'. In Glatter, R. (ed.), *Educational Institutions and their Environments: Managing the Boundaries*. Milton Keynes: Open University Press.

Scottish Office Education Department (1992a) *Devolved School Management: Guidelines for Progress*. Edinburgh: SOED.

Scottish Office Education Department (1992b) *Using Ethos Indicators in Secondary School Self-evaluation*. Edinburgh: SOED.

Scottish Office Education Department (1992c) *Using Ethos Indicators in Primary School Self-evaluation*. Edinburgh: SOED.

Sheffield City Council Education Department (1992) *Resourcing Sheffield Schools*. Sheffield: Sheffield City Council.

Simkins, T. (1994) 'The consequences of school-based management in England and Wales: A review of some evidence from an economic perspective'. *Journal of Education Policy*, **9**(1): 15–34.

Simkins, T. and Lancaster, D. (1988) Block 5 *Managing School Resources*. In E325 *Managing Schools*. Milton Keynes: Open University.

Simon, H.A. (1947) *Administrative Behaviour*, 2nd edn. New York: Macmillan.

Smilanich, B. (1988) *Devolution in Edmonton Public Schools: Ten Years Later*. Edmonton, Canada (mimeo).

Smircich, L. (1983) 'Concepts of culture and organisational analysis'. *Administrative Science Quarterly*, **28**: 339–58.

Smyth, J. (ed.) (1993) *A Socially Critical View of the Self-managing School*. Lewes: Falmer Press.

South, L. (1987) 'Local financial management: An overview'. *International Journal of Educational Management*, **1**(1): 21–31.

Taylor Committee (1977) *A New Partnership for our Schools* (The Taylor Report). London: DES.

Thomas, G. (1990) *Setting up LMS: A Study of LEAs' Submissions to the DES*. Milton Keynes: Open University Learning Materials.

Thomas, G. (1991) *The Framework for LMS: A Study of LEAs' Approved Local Management of Schools Schemes*. Milton Keynes: Open University Learning Materials.

Thomas, G. and Levačić, R. (1991) 'Centralising in order to decentralise? Department of Education and Science scrutiny and approval of Local Management of Schools schemes'. *Journal of Education Policy*, 6(4): 401–416.

Thornton, M. (1994) 'A donation to clarity'. *Times Educational Supplement*, 29 April, p. 15.

Times Educational Supplement (1994) 'GM schools survey', 7 October, pp. 8–11.

Wallace, M. (1989) 'Towards a collegiate approach to curriculum management in primary and middle schools'. In Preedy, M. (ed.), *Approaches to Curriculum Management*. Milton Keynes: Open University Press.

Watkins, P. (1993) 'Pushing crisis and stress down the line: The self-managing school'. In Smyth, J. (ed.), *A Socially Critical View of the Self-managing School*. Lewes: Falmer Press.

Weick, K.E. (1976) 'Educational organisations as loosely coupled systems'. *Administrative Science Quarterly*, 21: 1–19.

Williamson, O.E. (1970) *Corporate Control and Business Behaviour*. Englewood Cliffs, NJ: Prentice-Hall.

Williamson, O.E. (1975) *Markets and Hierarchies: Analysis and Anti-trust Implications*. New York: Free Press/Collier Macmillan.

Willms, J.D. (1992) *Monitoring School Performance: A Guide for Educators*. Lewes: Falmer Press.

Woods, P. (1994) 'Parents and choice in local competitive arenas: First findings from the main phase of the PASCI study'. Paper presented at the *American Educational Research Association Annual Conference*, New Orleans, April.

Woods, P., Bagley, C. and Glatter, R. (1994) 'Dymanics of competition: The effects of local competitive arenas on schools'. Paper presented at the *CEDAR International Conference: Changing Educational Structures, Policy and Practice*, University of Warwick, March.

Index

TOTAL QUALITY MANAGEMENT AND THE SCHOOL

Stephen Murgatroyd and Colin Morgan

The management team within the school are currently faced with a great deal of pressure to achieve a range of 'performance' expectations in a climate of increasing uncertainty, financial stringency and competition. Total Quality Management is a framework and set of practical resources for managing organizations in the 1990s. Based on sound principles and a strong body of experience, Total Quality Management provides a school based management team with the tools they need to become highly effective in meeting the goals of their stakeholders, and in creating a place that teachers want to work in.

This book is the first to fully examine the practice of Total Quality Management in the context of schooling. It looks, for instance, at the nature of a school's strategic management in the context of growing competition and expectations for performance; and at the positioning of the school in terms of vision and mission. It considers the setting of 'outrageous' or exceptional goals to create momentum and alignment and explores the nature of high performing teams within the school. It discusses commitment-building as part of the new quality culture and involving stakeholders in the daily management of the school.

It is practical and well-illustrated with case vignettes and examples of Total Quality Management in action. It is based on the experience of two senior academic practitioners who have both carried out extensive work in school management and development.

Contents

240pp   0 335 15722 X (Paperback)